BAAC

W9-CHB-672

JAN – 2016

GET JIRO!
BLOOD & SUSHI

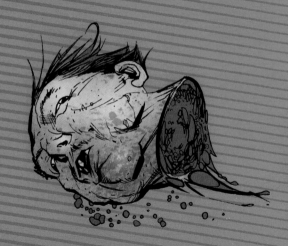

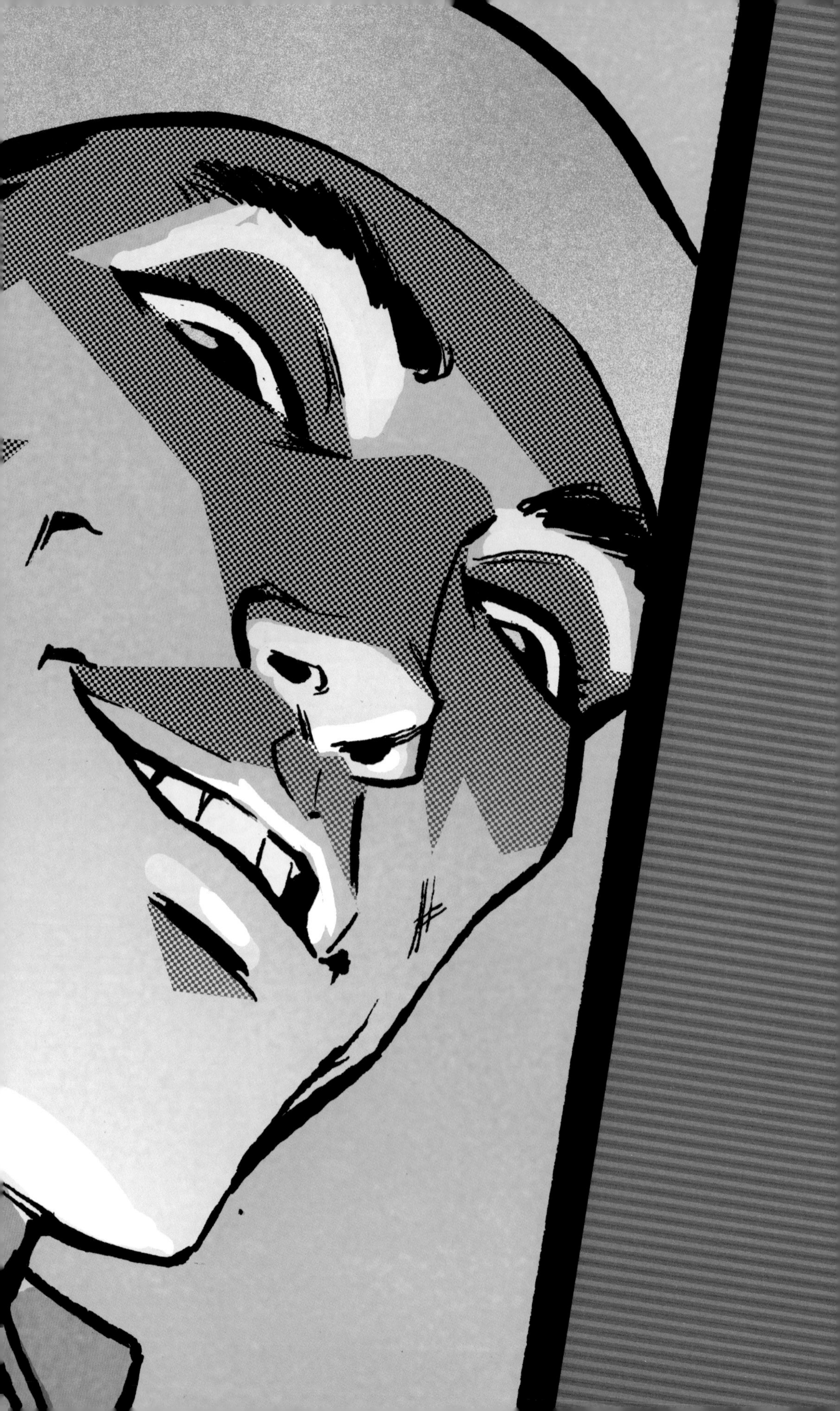

GET JIRO!
BLOOD & SUSHI

ANTHONY BOURDAIN
AND **JOEL ROSE** writers

ALÉ GARZA artist

JOSÉ VILLARRUBIA color

CLEM ROBINS letterer

DAVE JOHNSON cover

DAN GREEN — INKS ON PAGES 110-119, 127-131

GET JIRO! created by Anthony Bourdain and Joel Rose

Will Dennis & Jamie S. Rich Editors
Greg Lockard Associate Editor
Louis Prandi Publication Design

Shelly Bond VP & Executive Editor — Vertigo

Diane Nelson President
Dan DiDio and **Jim Lee** Co-Publishers
Geoff Johns Chief Creative Officer
Amit Desai Senior VP — Marketing & Global Franchise Management
Nairi Gardiner Senior VP — Finance
Sam Ades VP — Digital Marketing
Bobbie Chase VP — Talent Development
Mark Chiarello Senior VP — Art, Design & Collected Editions
John Cunningham VP — Content Strategy
Anne DePies VP — Strategy Planning & Reporting
Don Falletti VP — Manufacturing Operations
Lawrence Ganem VP — Editorial Administration & Talent Relations
Alison Gill Senior VP — Manufacturing & Operations
Hank Kanalz Senior VP — Editorial Strategy & Administration
Jay Kogan VP — Legal Affairs
Derek Maddalena Senior VP — Sales & Business Development
Jack Mahan VP — Business Affairs
Dan Miron VP — Sales Planning & Trade Development
Nick Napolitano VP — Manufacturing Administration
Carol Roeder VP — Marketing
Eddie Scannell VP — Mass Account & Digital Sales
Courtney Simmons Senior VP — Publicity & Communications
Jim (Ski) Sokolowski VP — Comic Book Specialty & Newsstand Sales
Sandy Yi Senior VP — Global Franchise Management

Special thanks to J.j. Kirby for art assists.

GET JIRO!: BLOOD & SUSHI Published by DC Comics. Copyright © 2015 Anthony
Bourdain, Joel Rose, and DC Comics. All Rights Reserved. All characters, their
distinctive likenesses and related elements featured in this publication are
trademarks of Anthony Bourdain and Joel Rose. VERTIGO is a trademark of
DC Comics. The stories, characters and incidents featured in this publication
are entirely fictional. DC Comics does not read or accept unsolicited
submissions of ideas, stories or artwork. DC COMICS 4000 WARNER BLVD,
BURBANK, CA 91522. A WARNER BROS. ENTERTAINMENT COMPANY. PRINTED IN
CANADA. FIRST PRINTING. ISBN: 978-1-4012-5226-7.

PEFC Certified
Printed on paper from
sustainably managed
forests and controlled
sources
PEFC/01-31-106   www.pefc.org

LIBRARY OF CONGRESS CATALOGING-IN-PUBLICATION DATA

BOURDAIN, ANTHONY.
 GET JIRO : BLOOD AND SUSHI / ANTHONY BOURDAIN, JOEL ROSE, WRITERS ;
ALÉ GARZA, ARTIST.
   PAGES CM
  ISBN 978-1-4012-5226-7 (HARDBACK)
 1. COOKS—COMIC BOOKS, STRIPS, ETC. 2. YAKUZA—COMIC BOOKS, STRIPS,
ETC. 3. GRAPHIC NOVELS. I. ROSE, JOEL, AUTHOR. II. GARZA, ALÉ, ILLUSTRATOR.
III. TITLE. IV. TITLE: BLOOD AND SUSHI.
 PN6727.B679G53 2015
 741.5'973—DC23
                          2015019798

KAISEKI

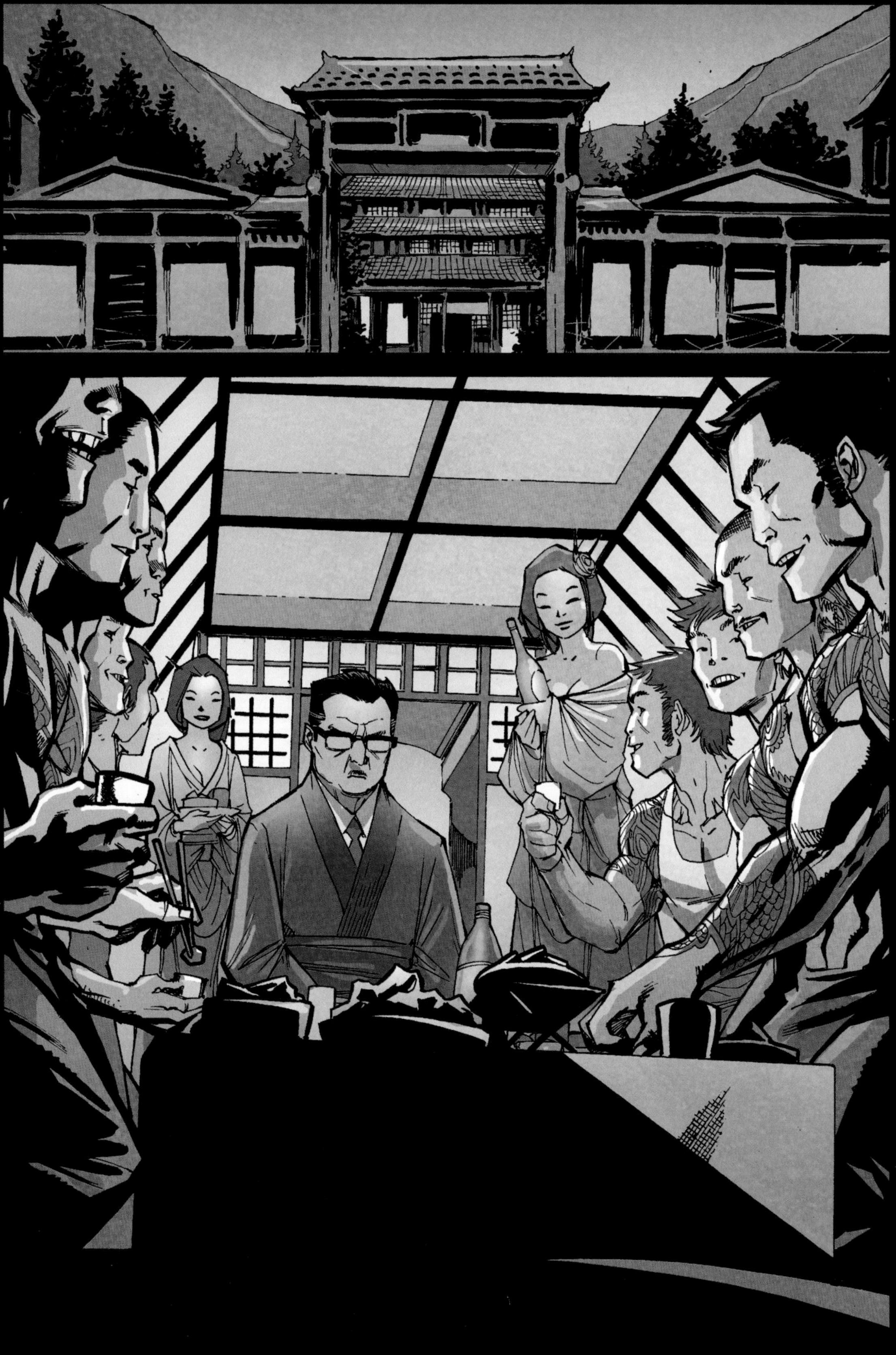

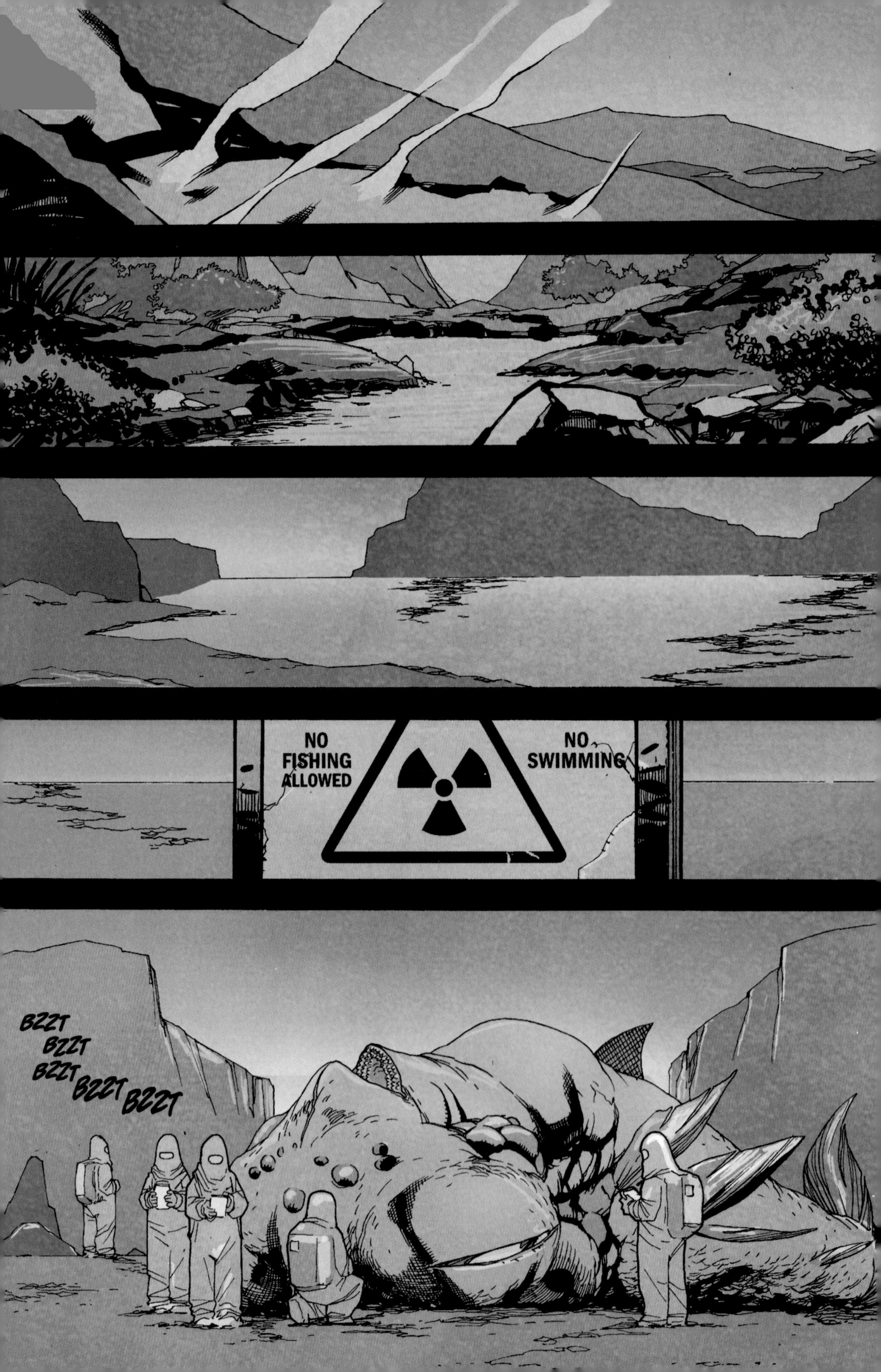
NO FISHING ALLOWED
NO SWIMMING
BZZT BZZT BZZT BZZT BZZT

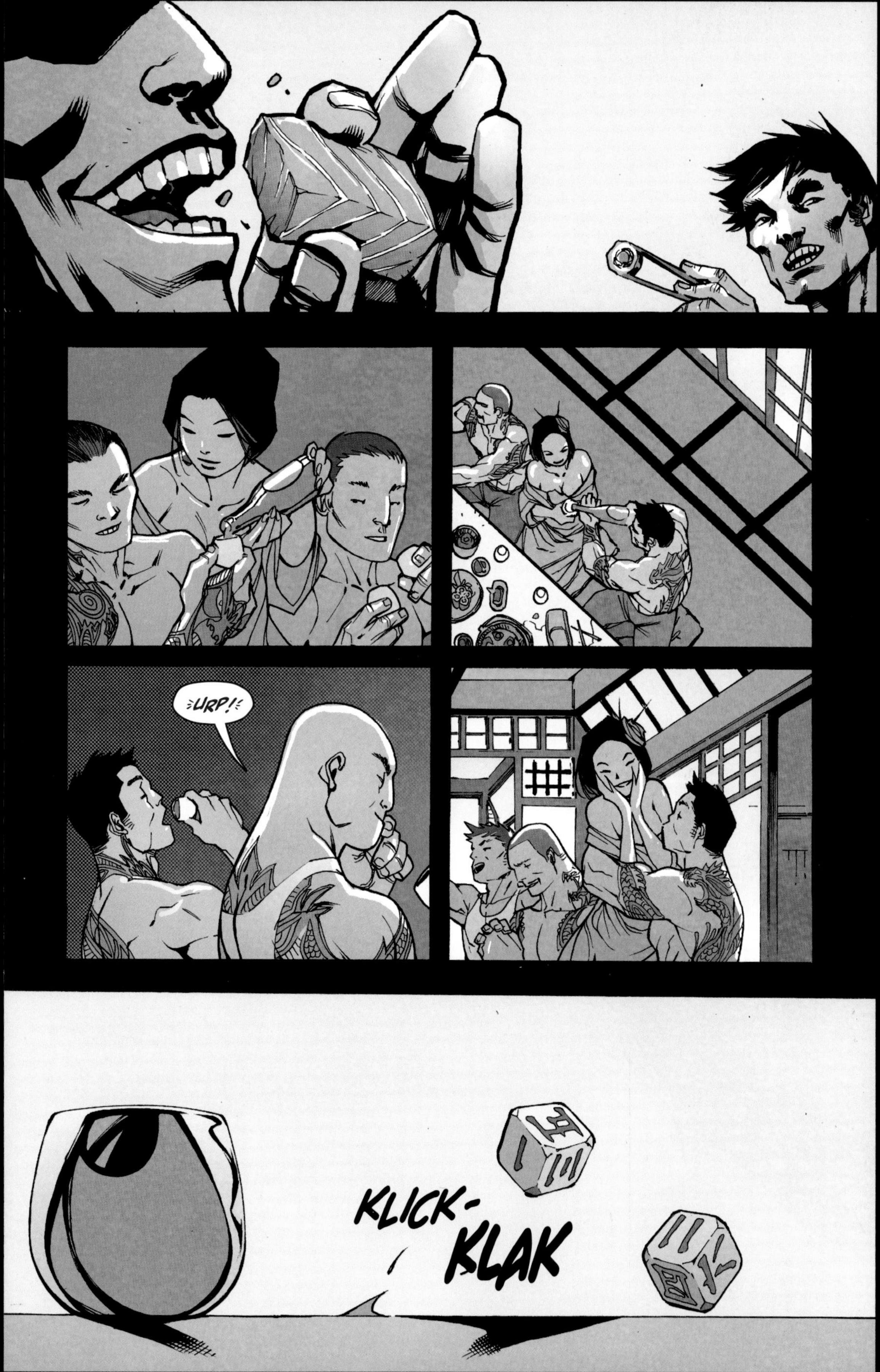
URP!
KLICK-
KLAK

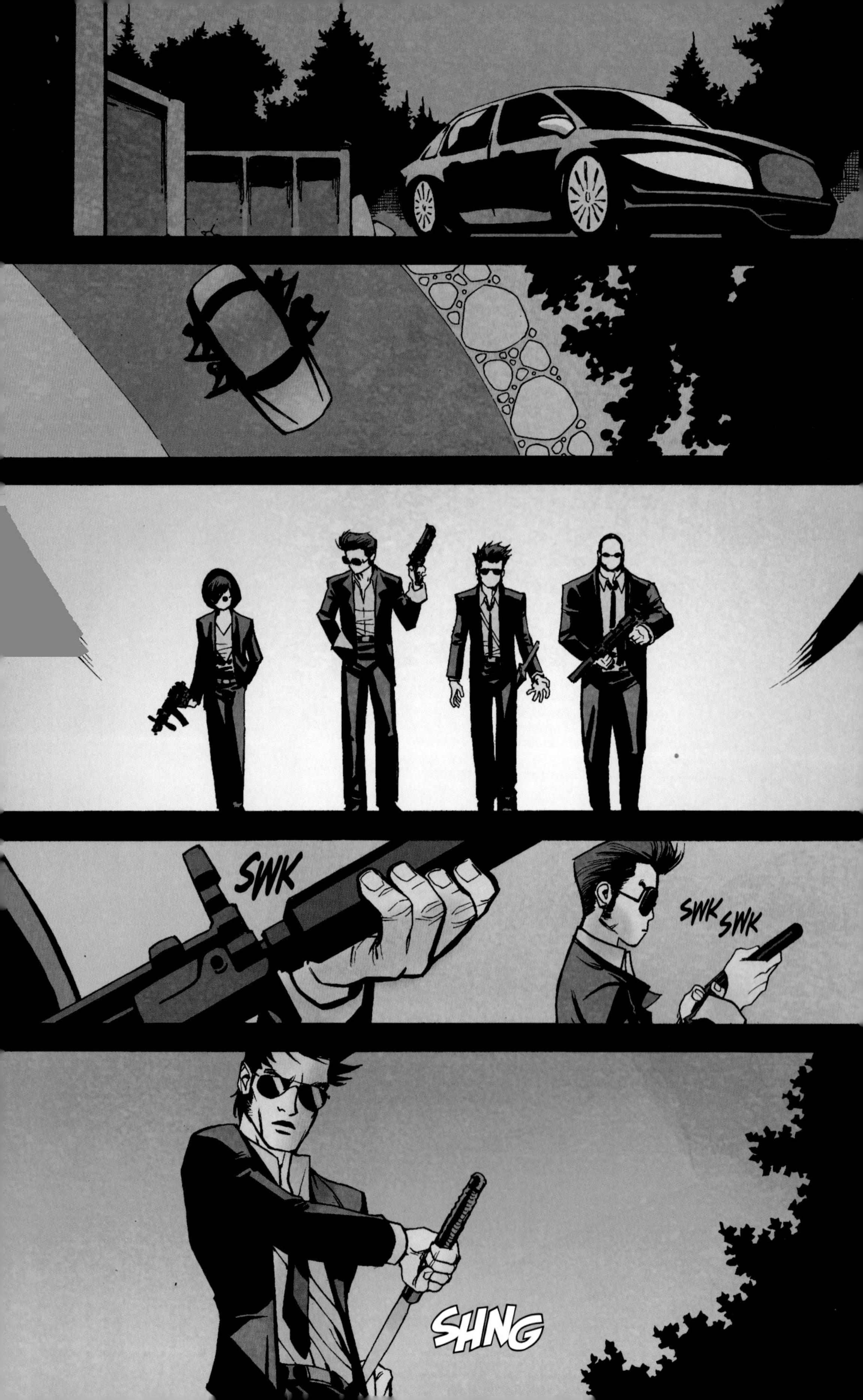
SWK
SWK
SWK
SHNG

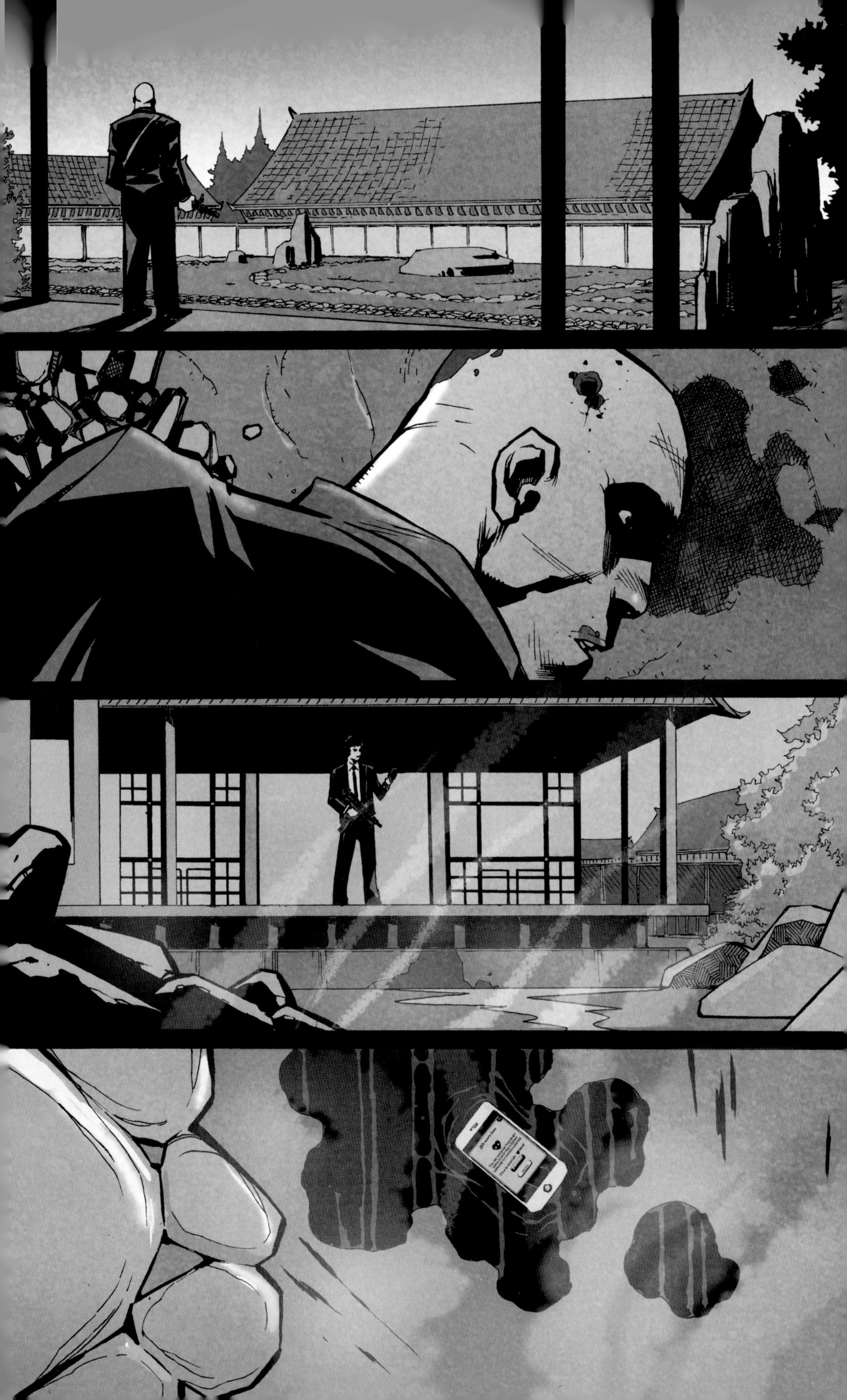

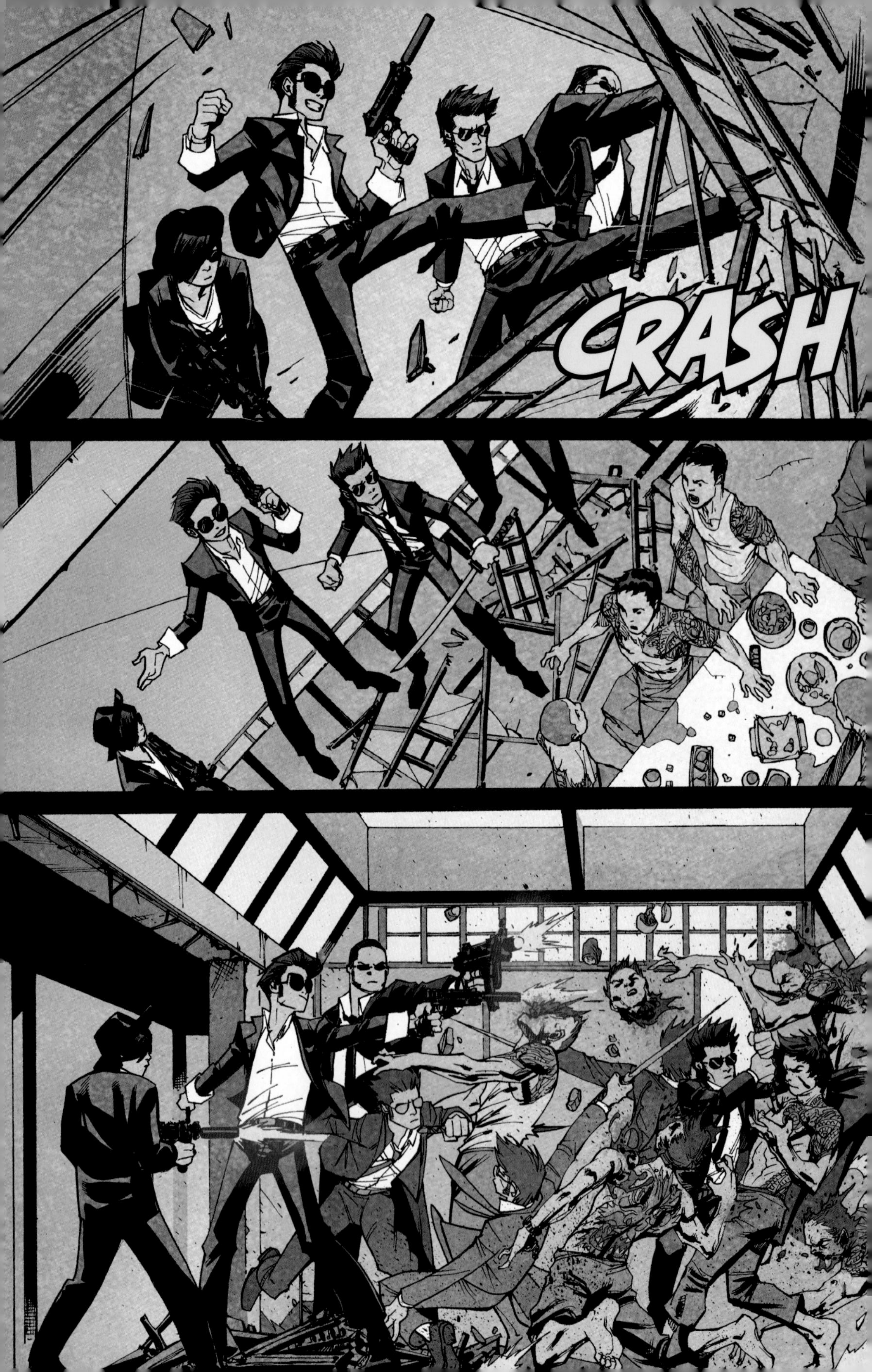
CRASH

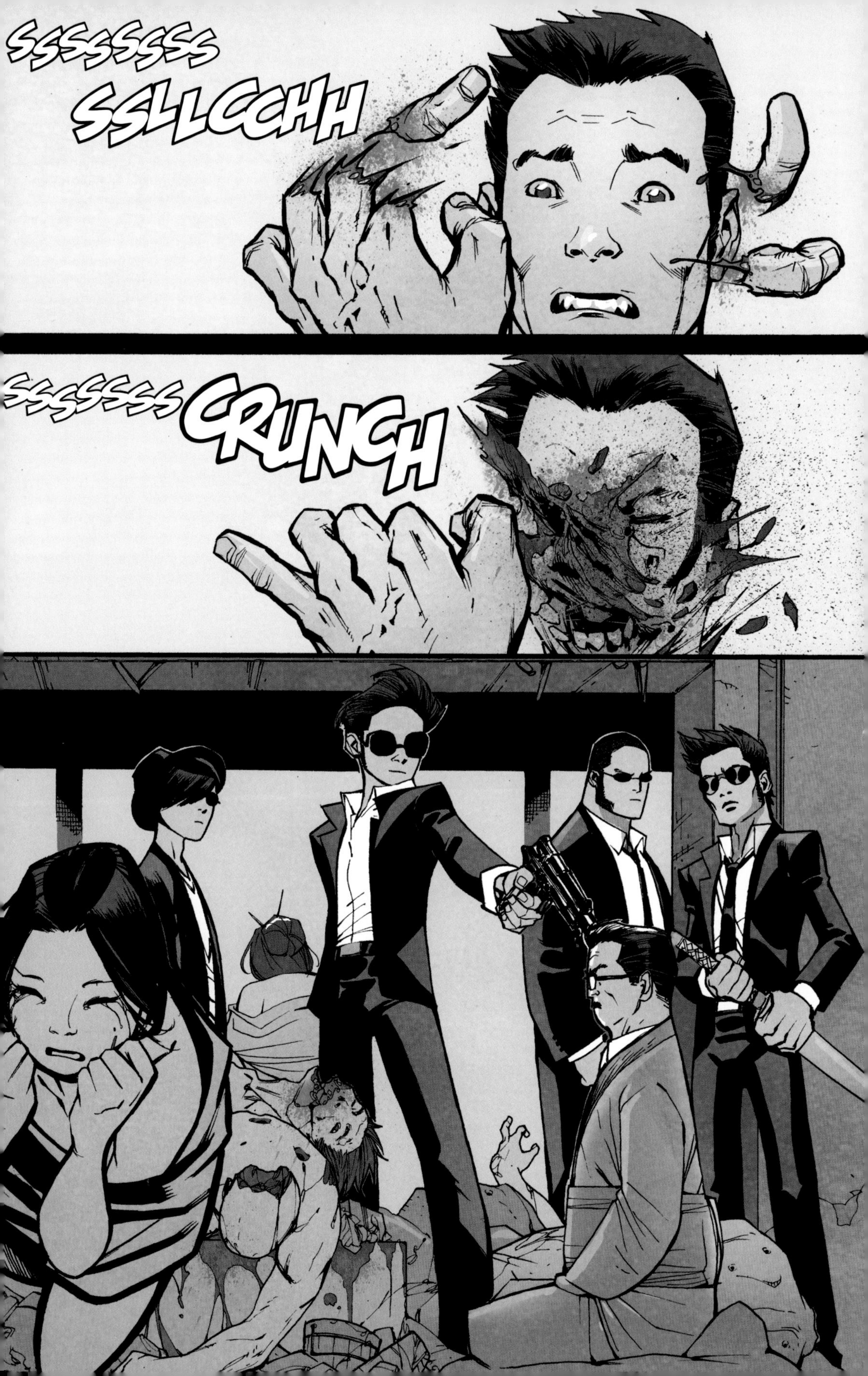
SSSSSSSS
SSLLCCHH
SSSSSSS CRUNCH

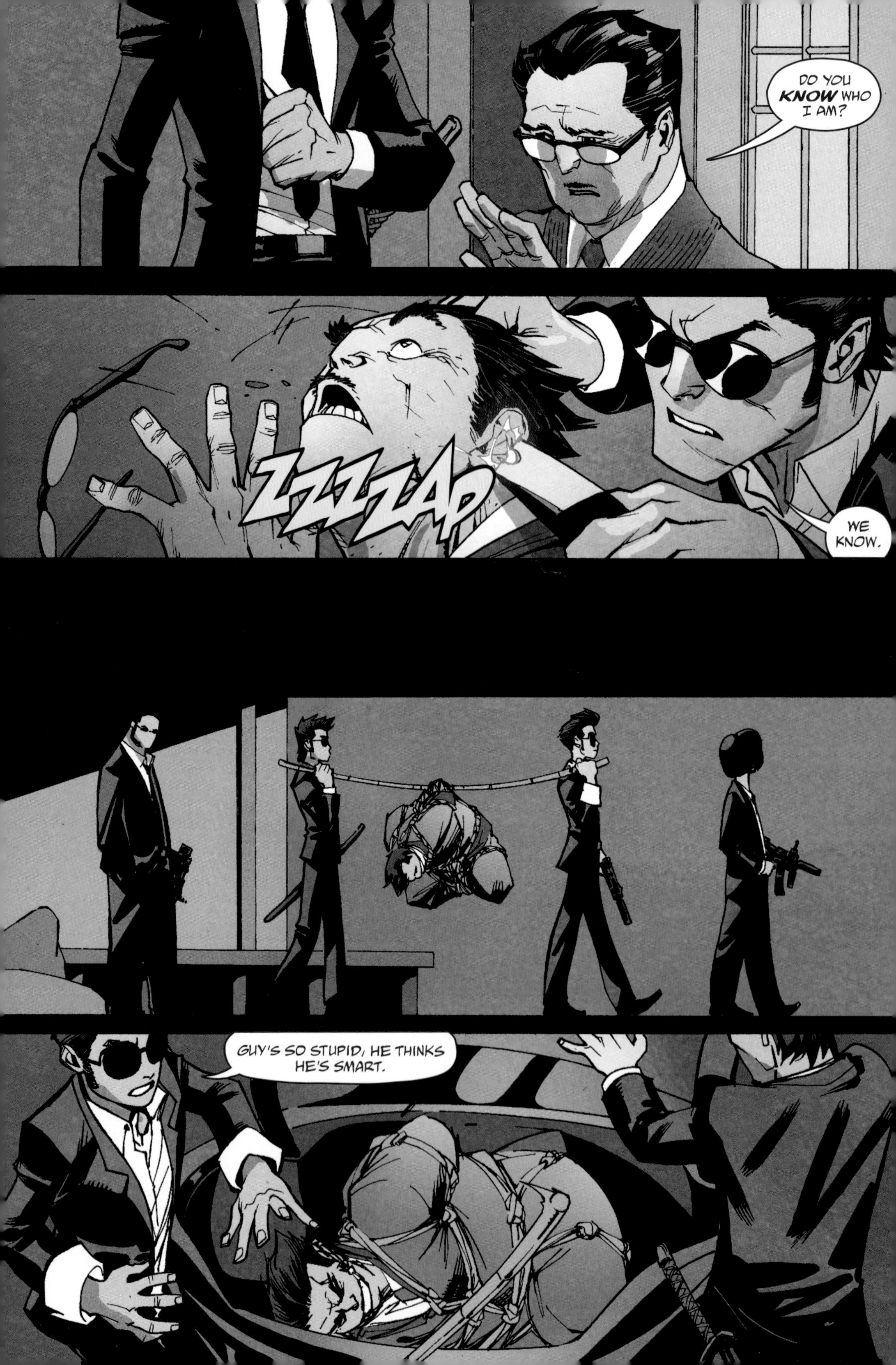
DO YOU KNOW WHO I AM?
ZZZZAP
WE KNOW.
GUY'S SO STUPID, HE THINKS HE'S SMART.

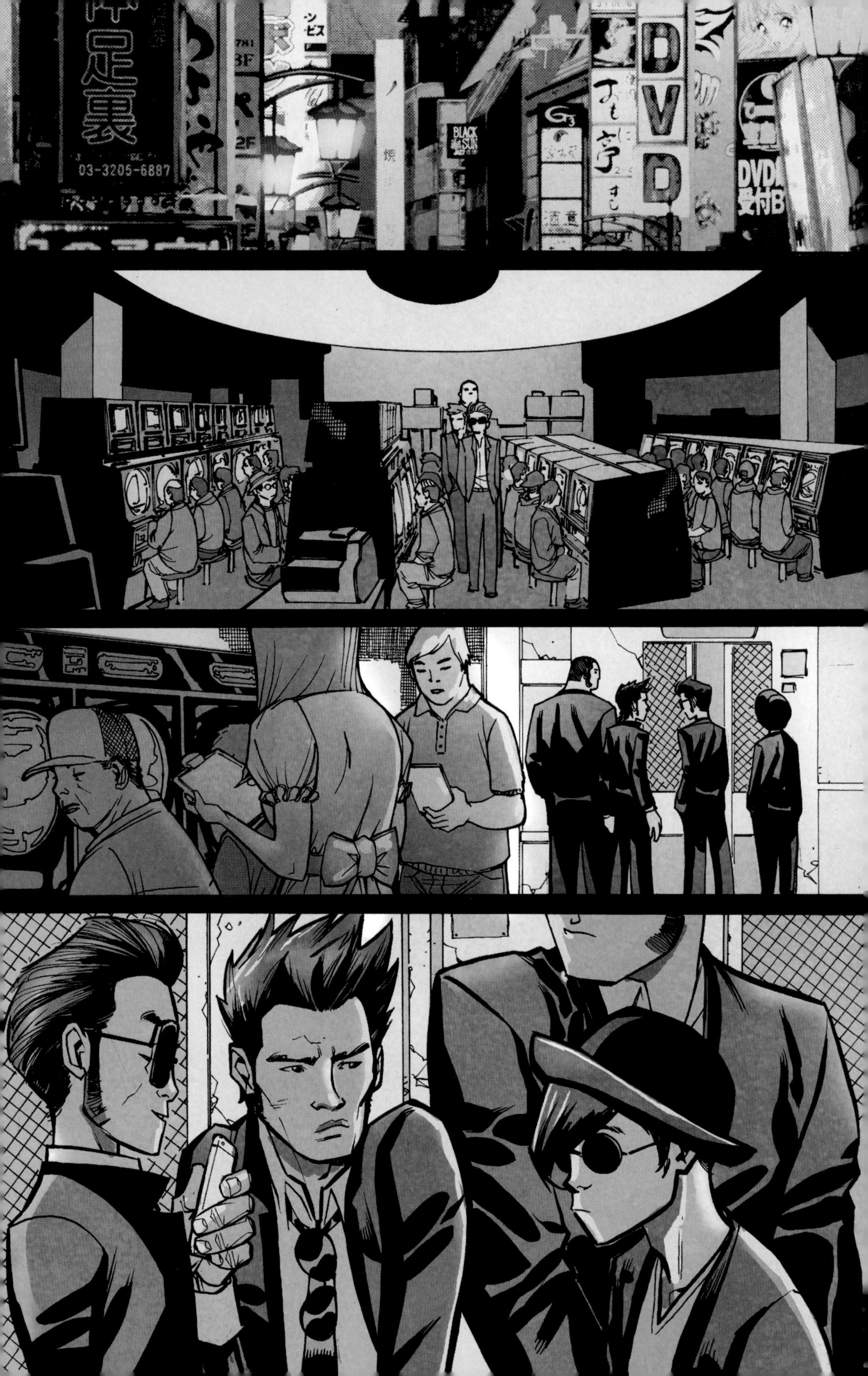
足裏
03-3205-6887
3F
2F
BLACK SUN
DVD
DVD

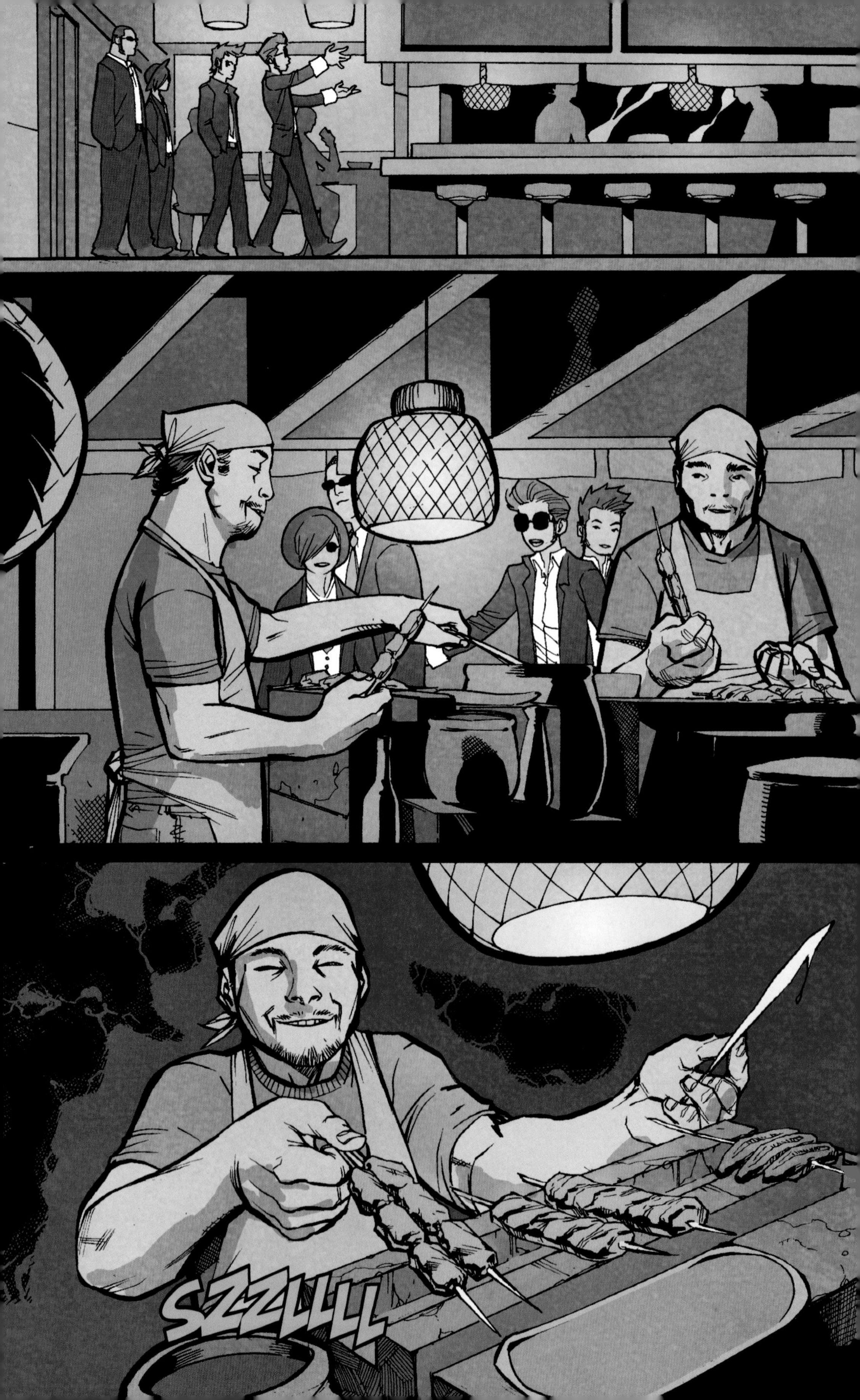
SZZLLLL

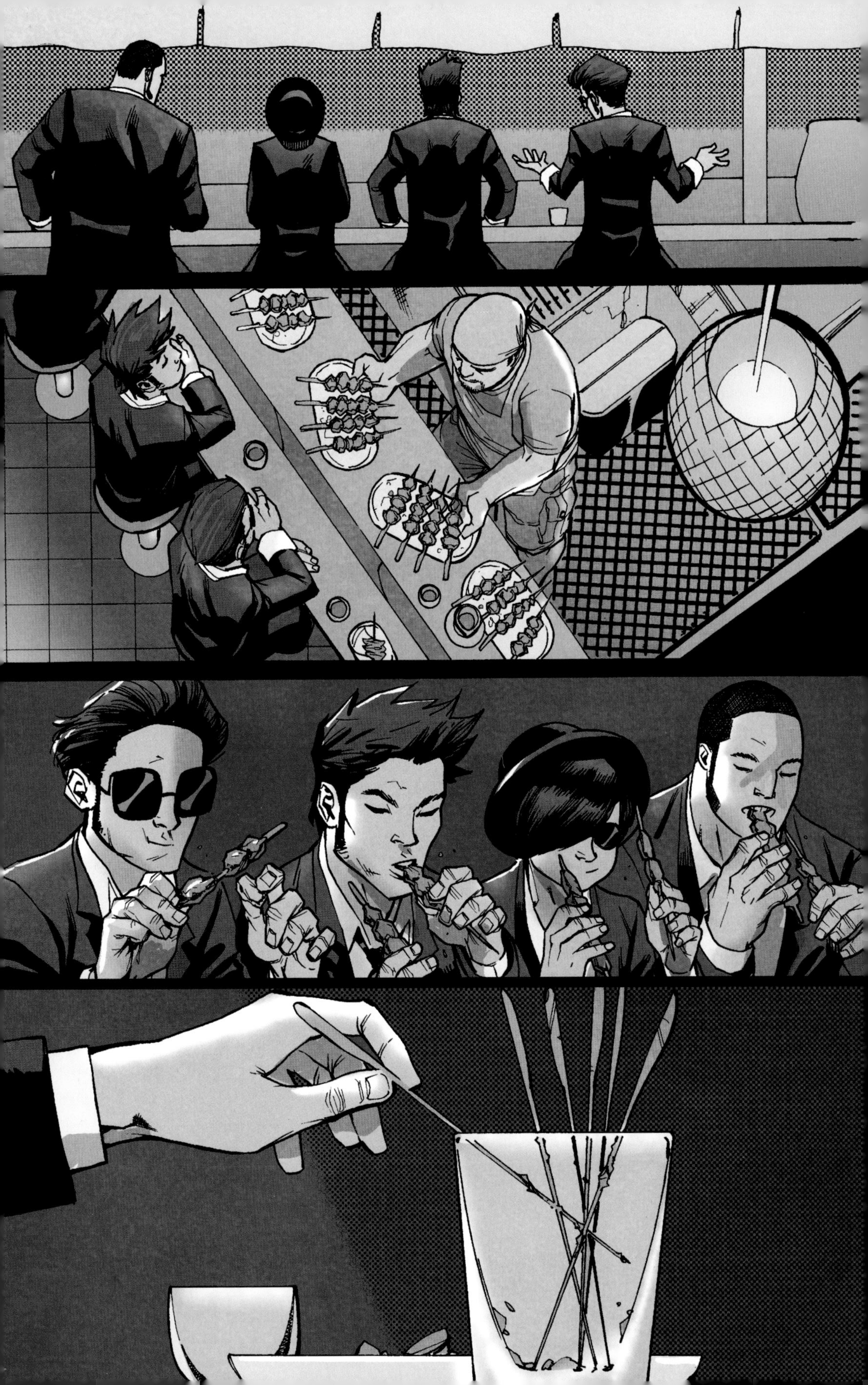

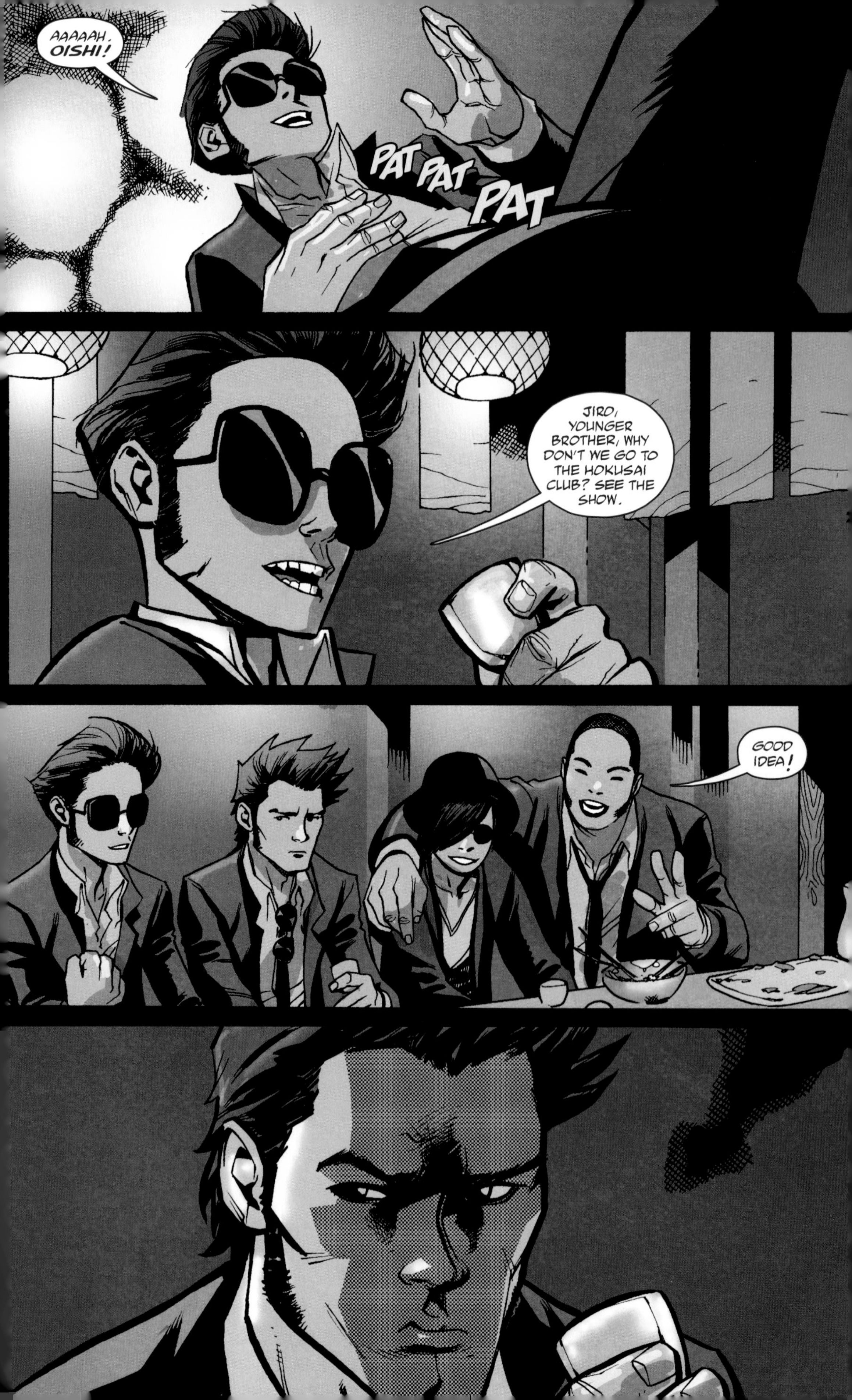
AAAAAH. OISHI!
PAT PAT PAT
JIRO, YOUNGER BROTHER, WHY DON'T WE GO TO THE HOKUSAI CLUB? SEE THE SHOW.
GOOD IDEA!

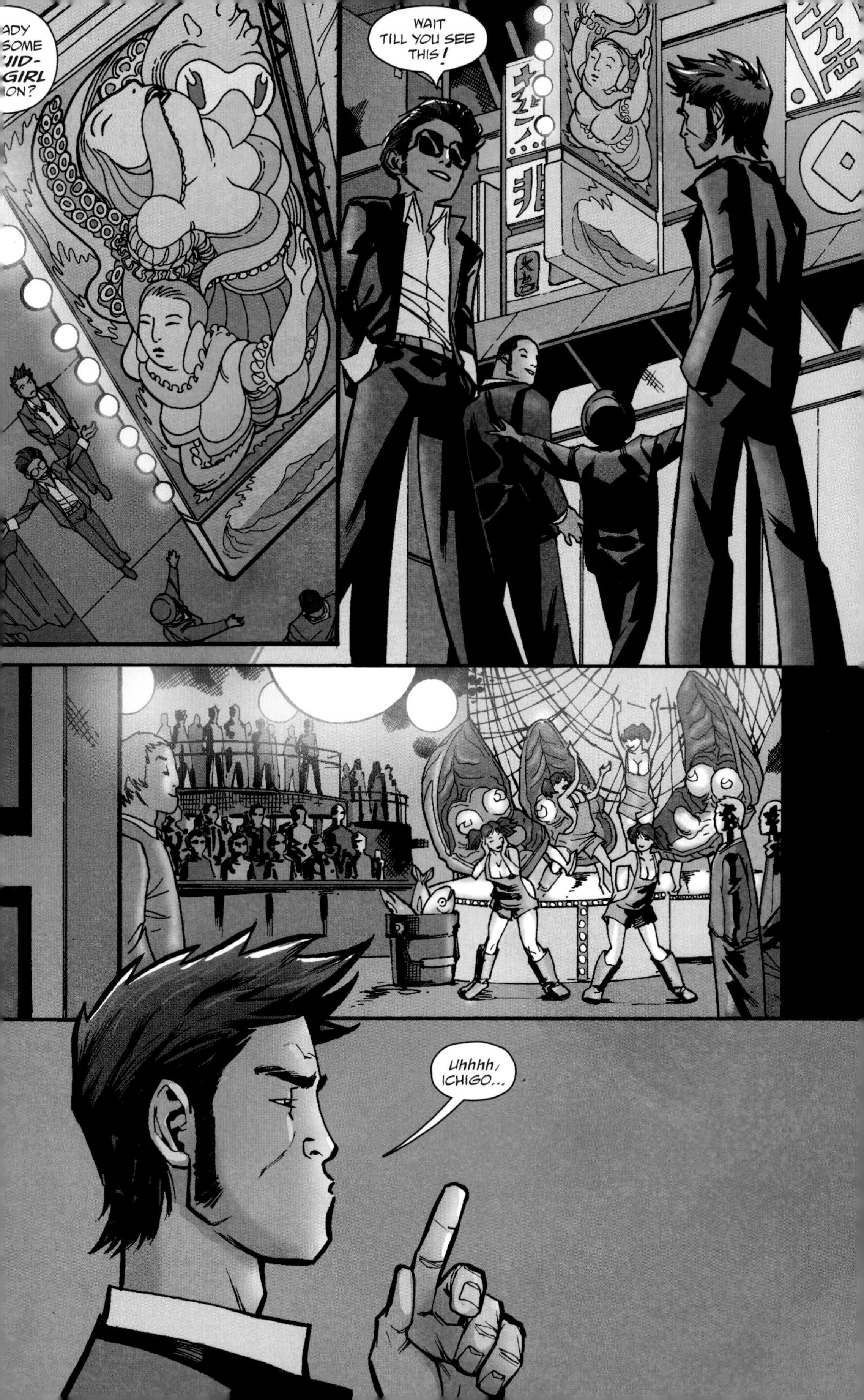
ADY
SOME
UID-
GIRL
ON?
WAIT TILL YOU SEE THIS!
Uhhhh, ICHIGO...

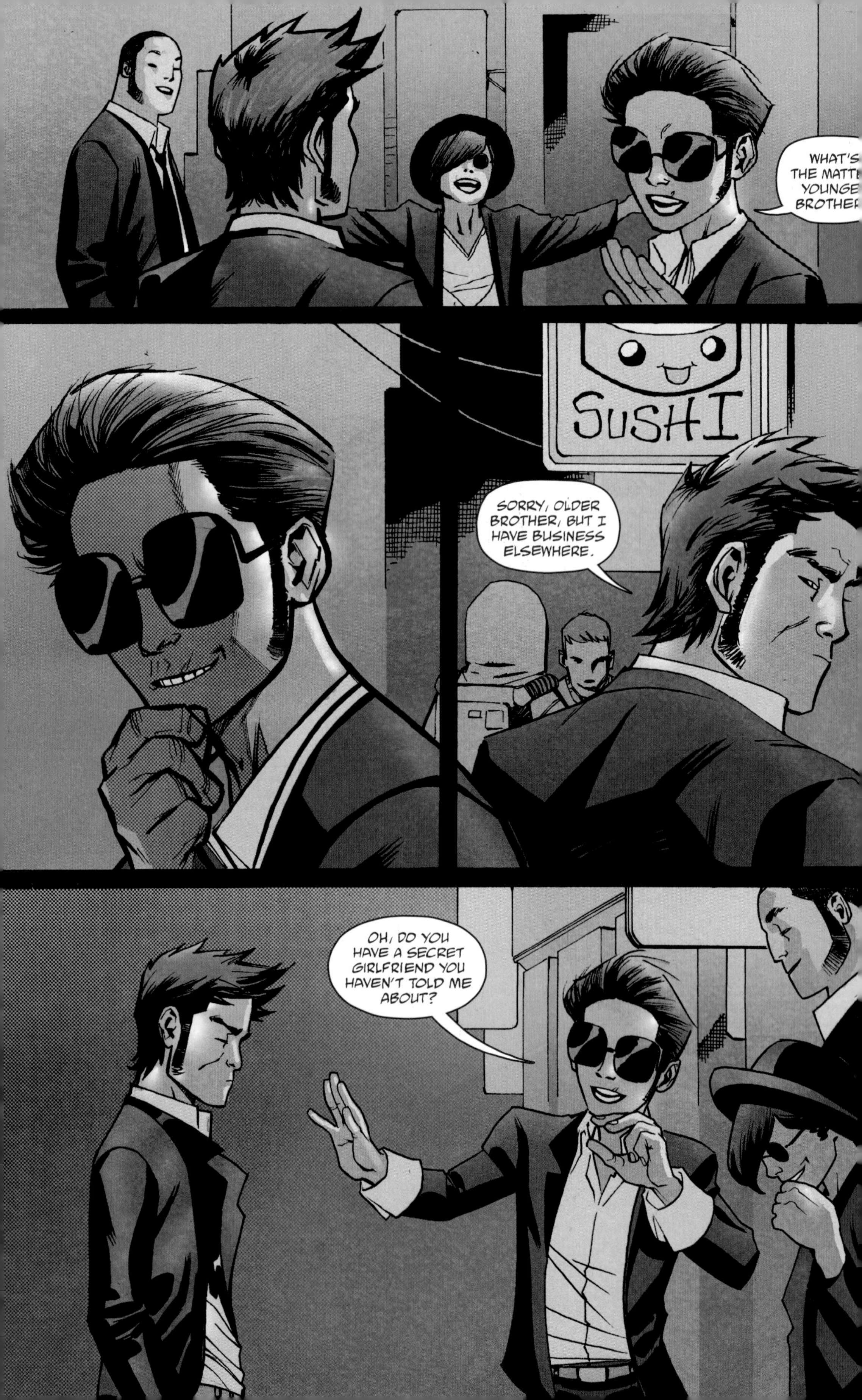

WHAT'S THE MATT YOUNGE BROTHE
SUSHI
SORRY, OLDER BROTHER, BUT I HAVE BUSINESS ELSEWHERE.
OH, DO YOU HAVE A SECRET GIRLFRIEND YOU HAVEN'T TOLD ME ABOUT?

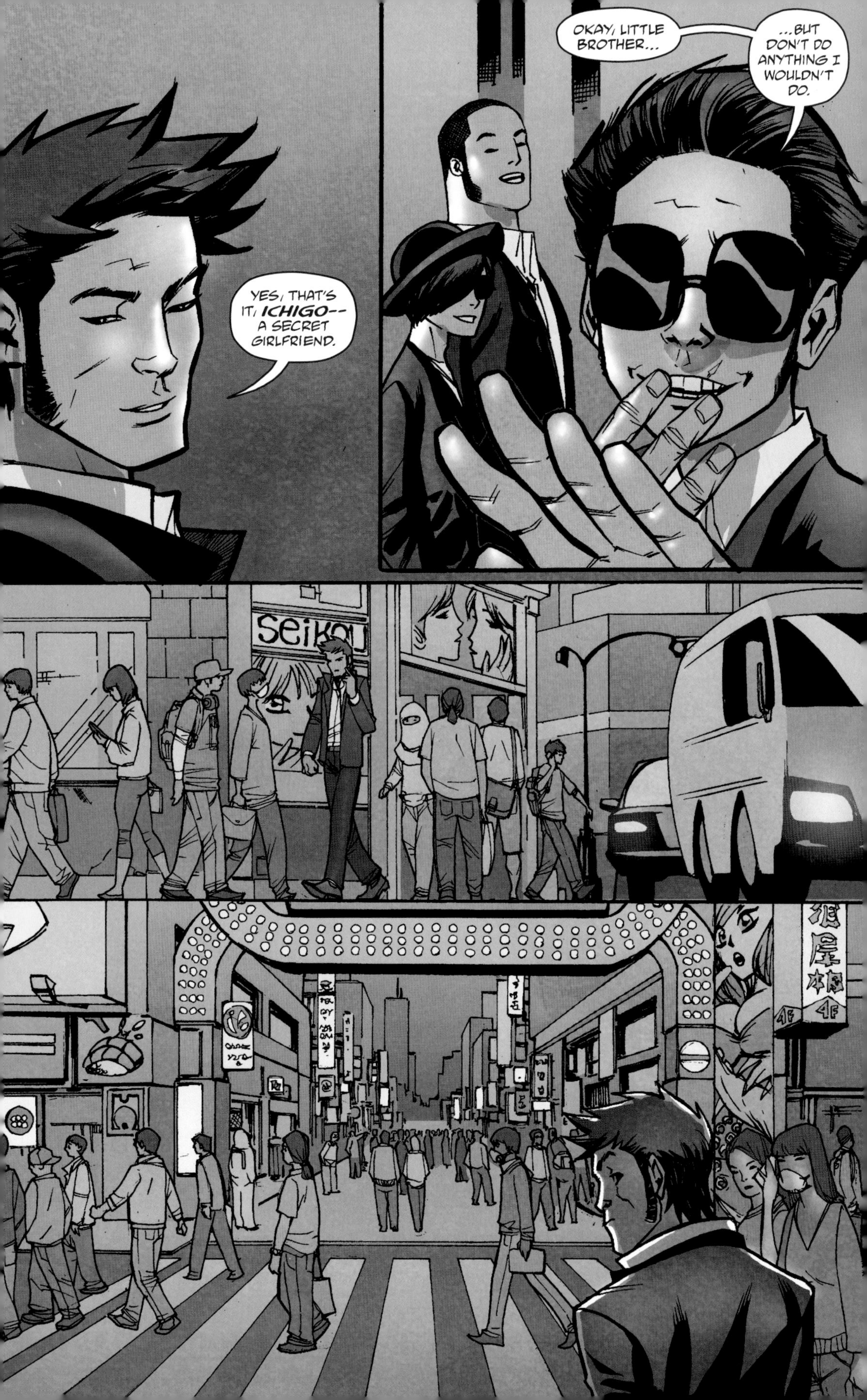
YES, THAT'S IT, ICHIGO-- A SECRET GIRLFRIEND.
OKAY, LITTLE BROTHER...
...BUT DON'T DO ANYTHING I WOULDN'T DO.
seikou

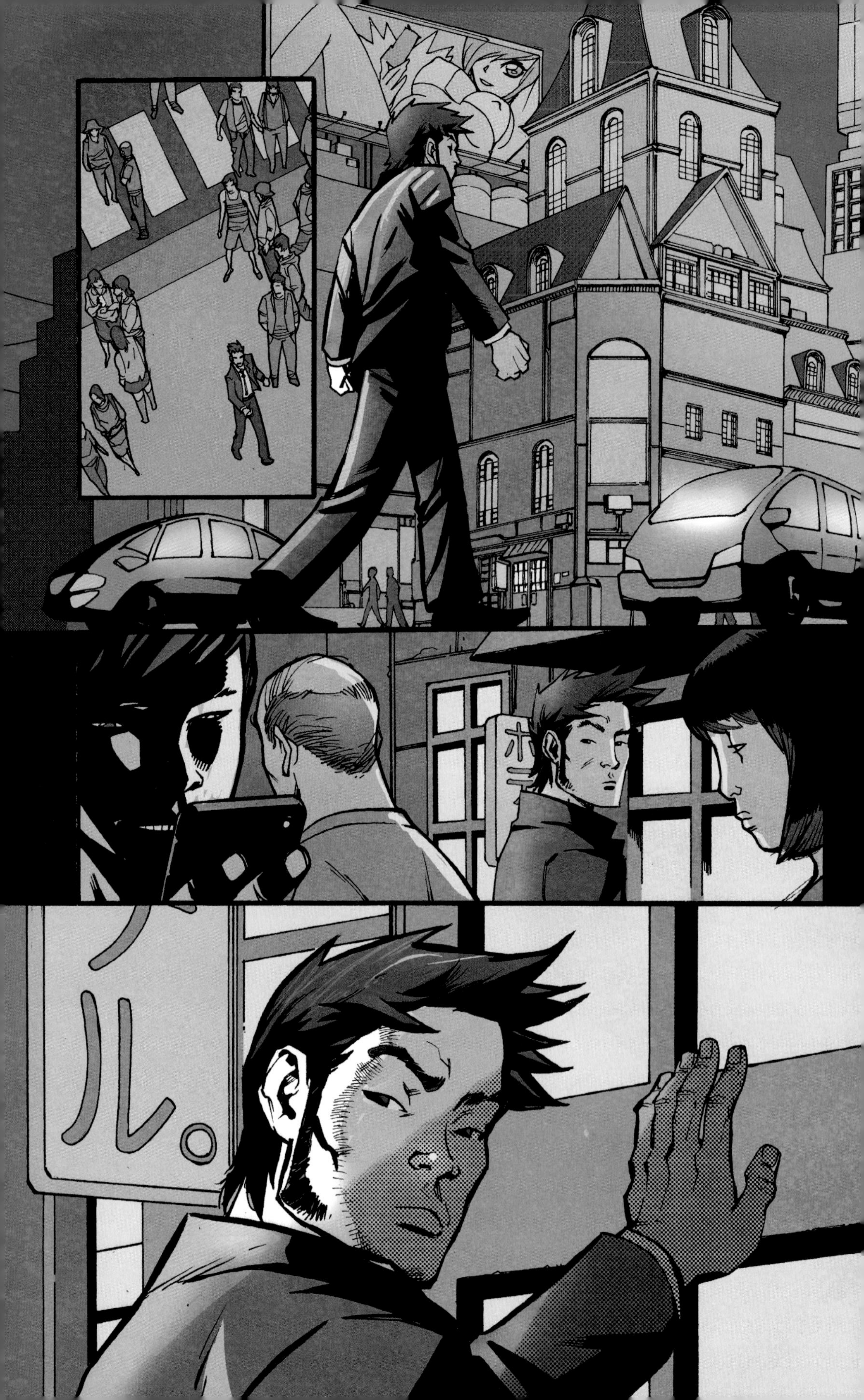

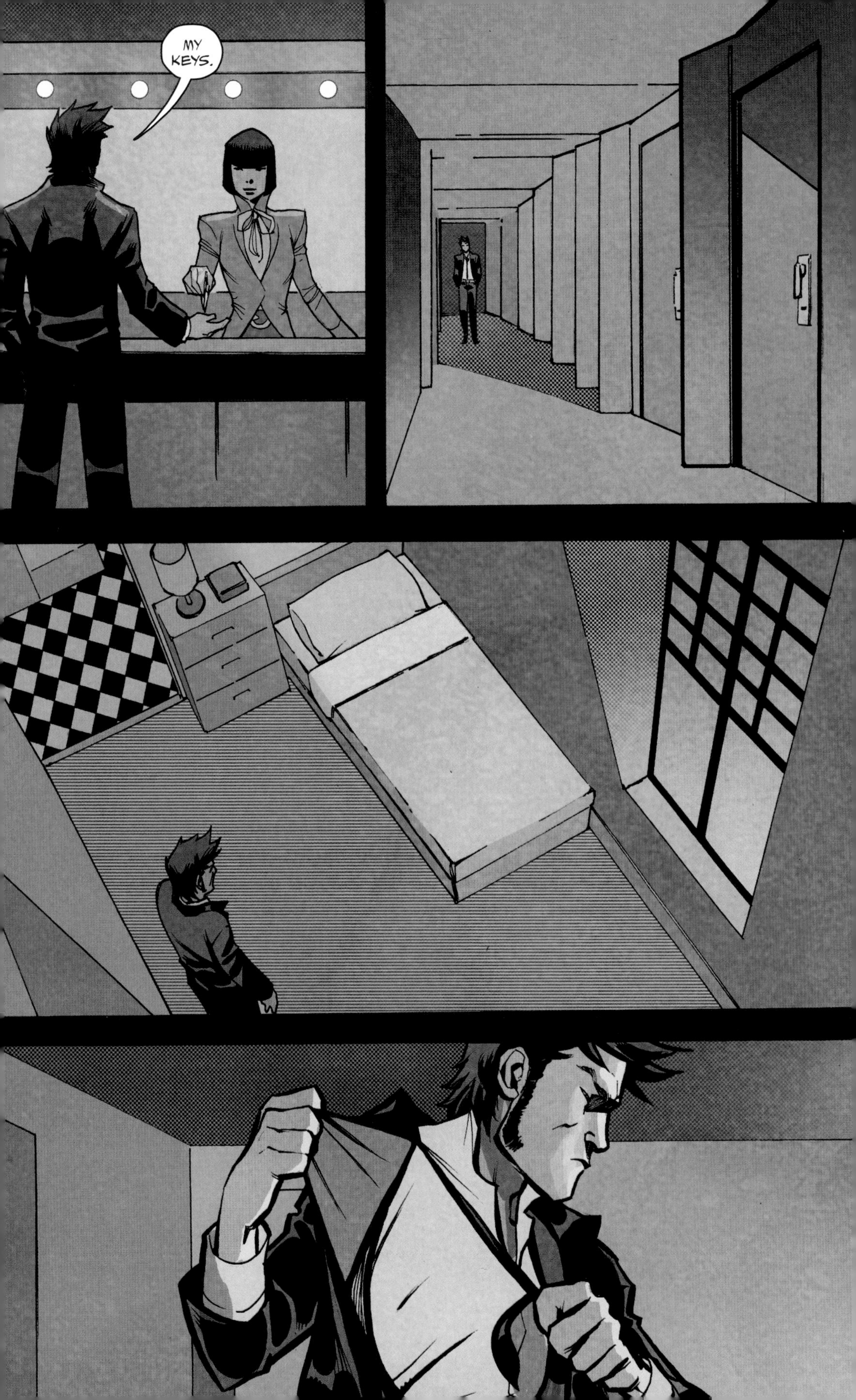
MY KEYS.

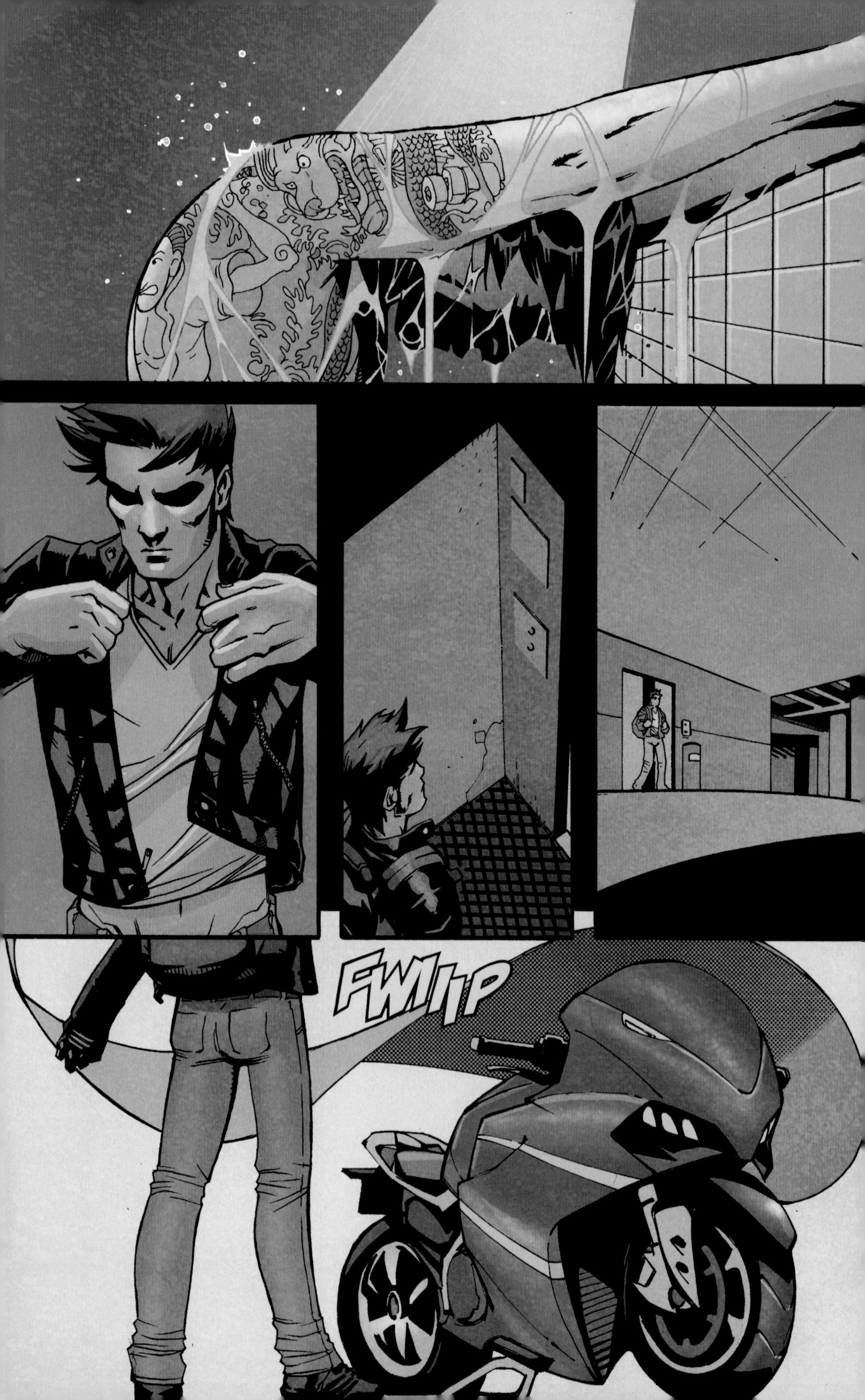
FWIIP

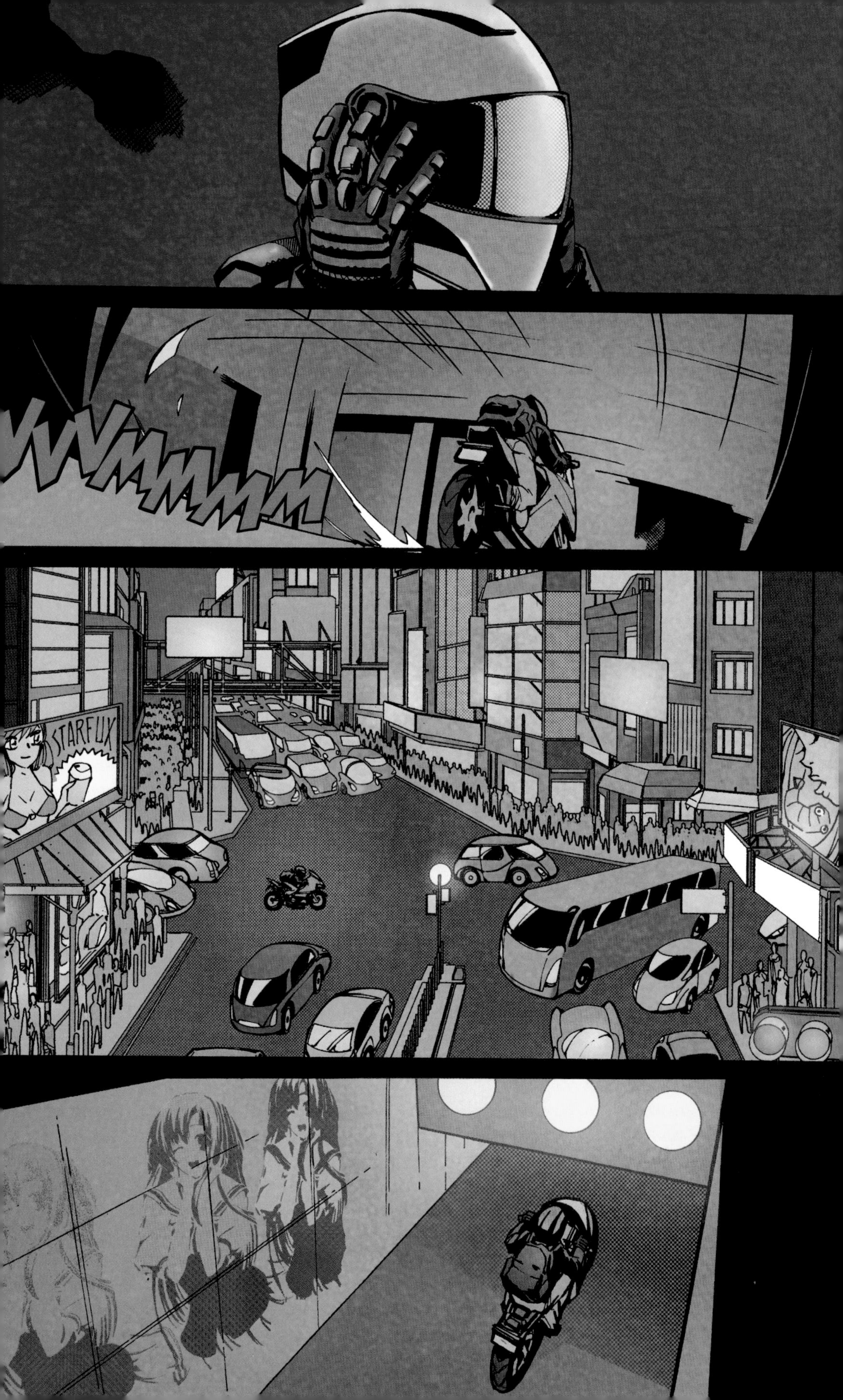
VVNMMMMM
STARFUX

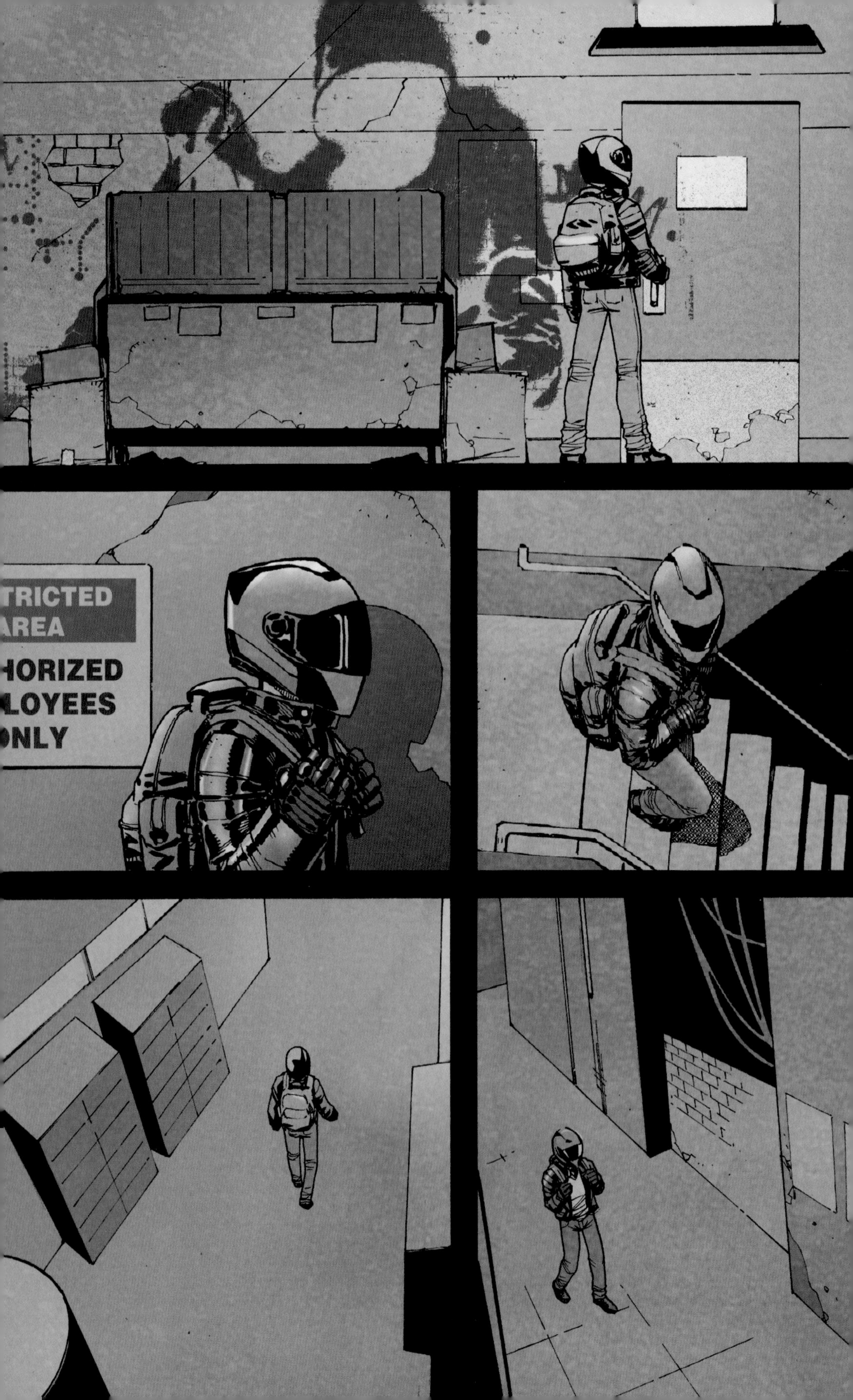
TRICTED
AREA
HORIZED
LOYEES
ONLY

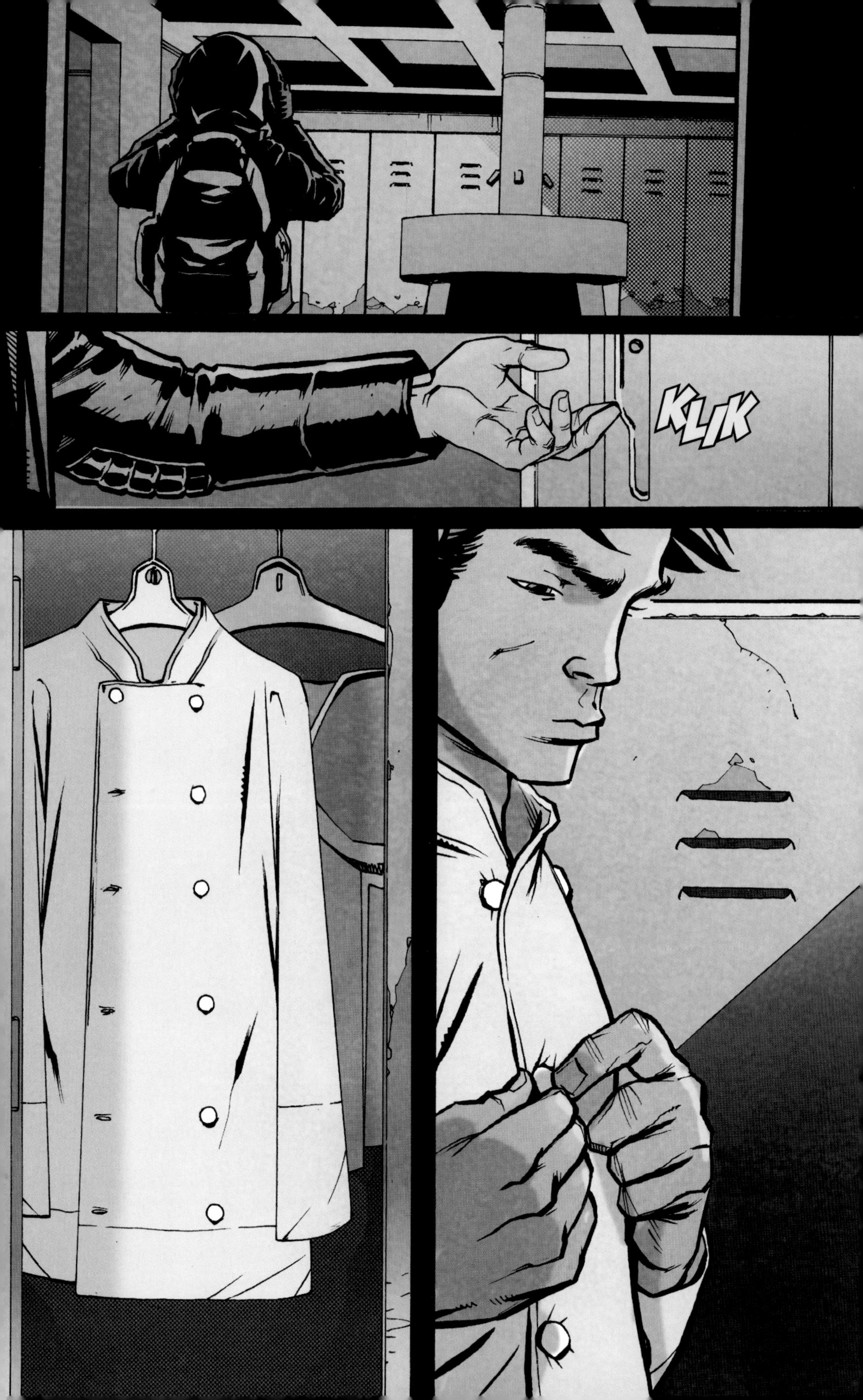
KLIK

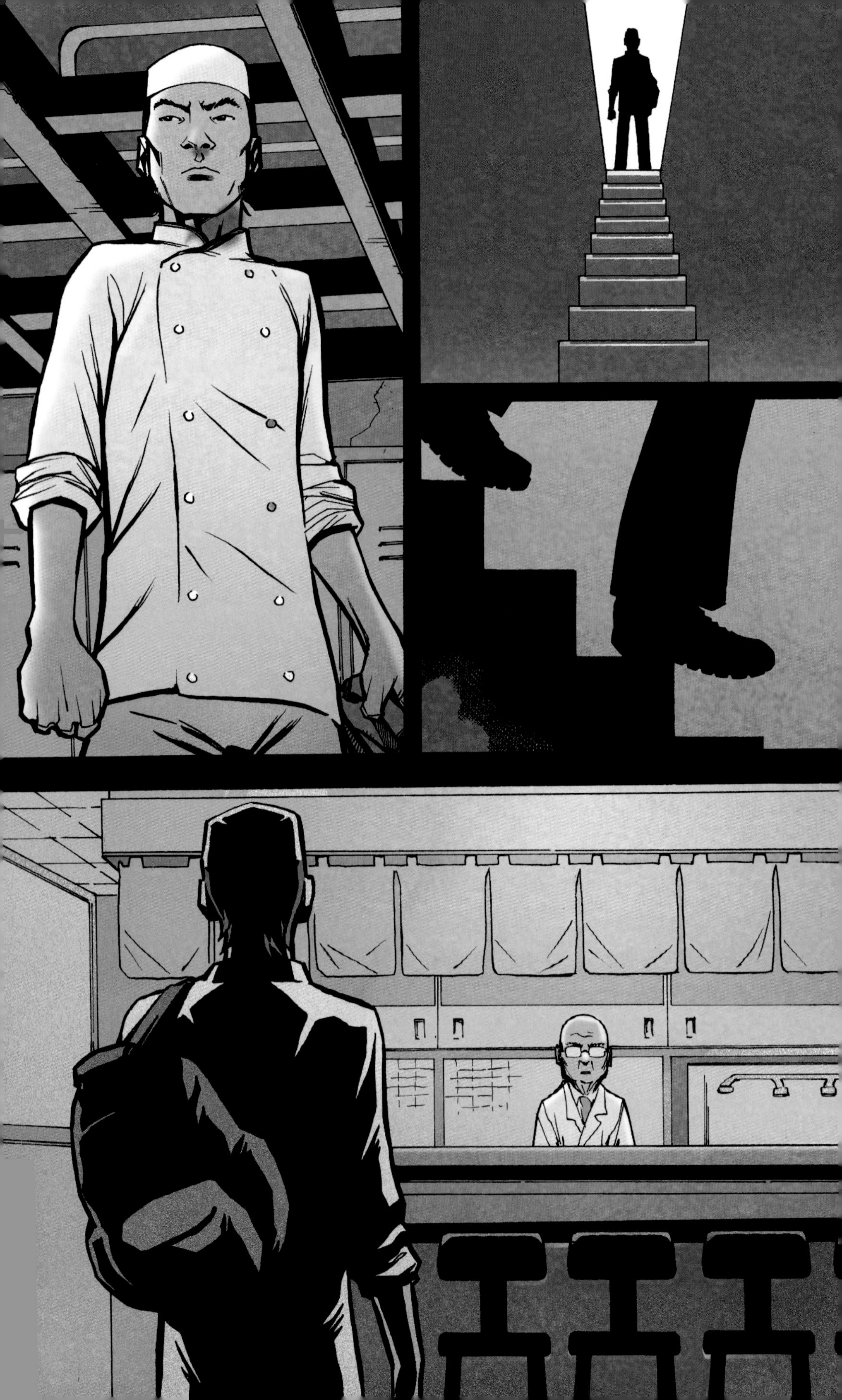

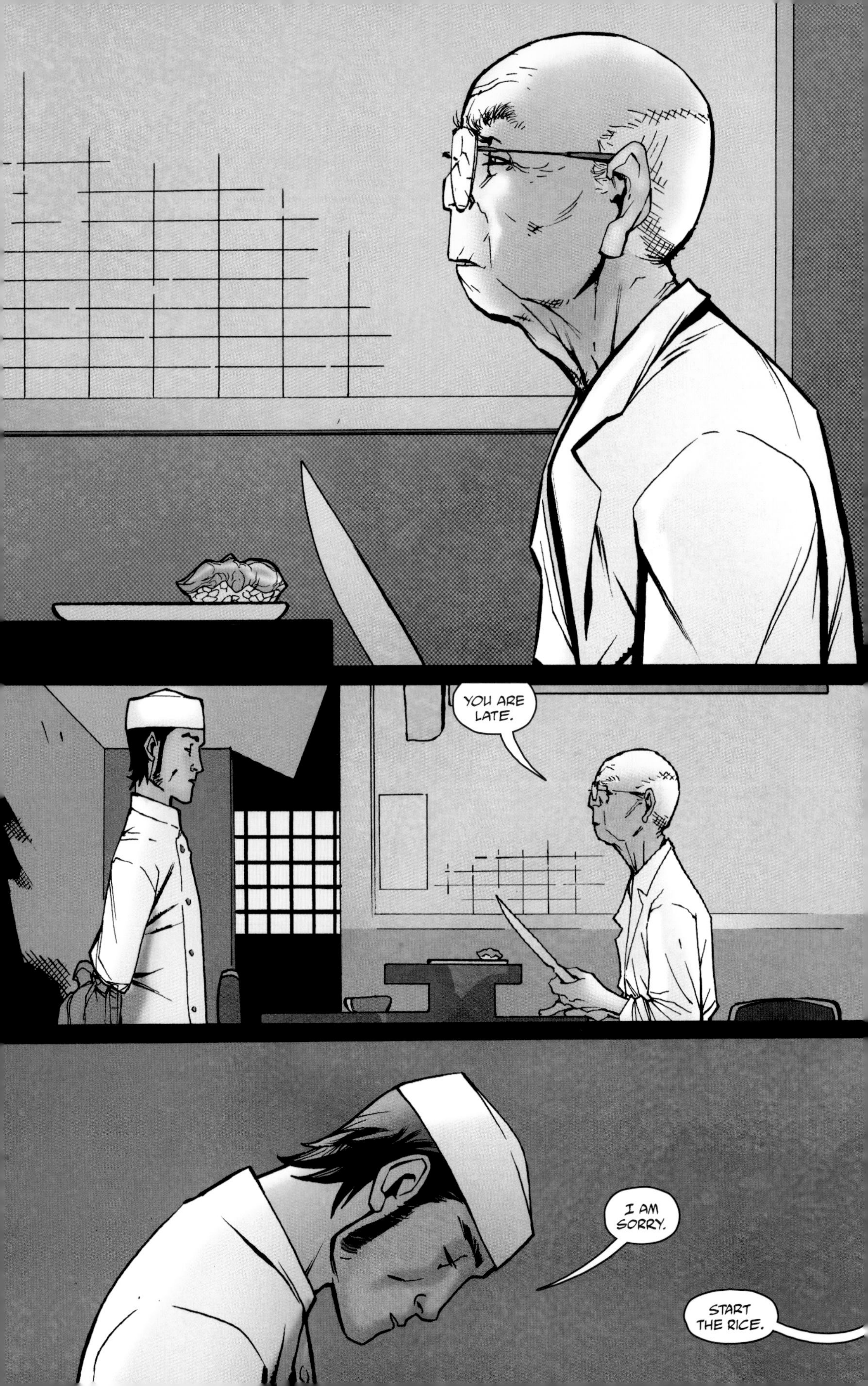
YOU ARE LATE.
I AM SORRY.
START THE RICE.

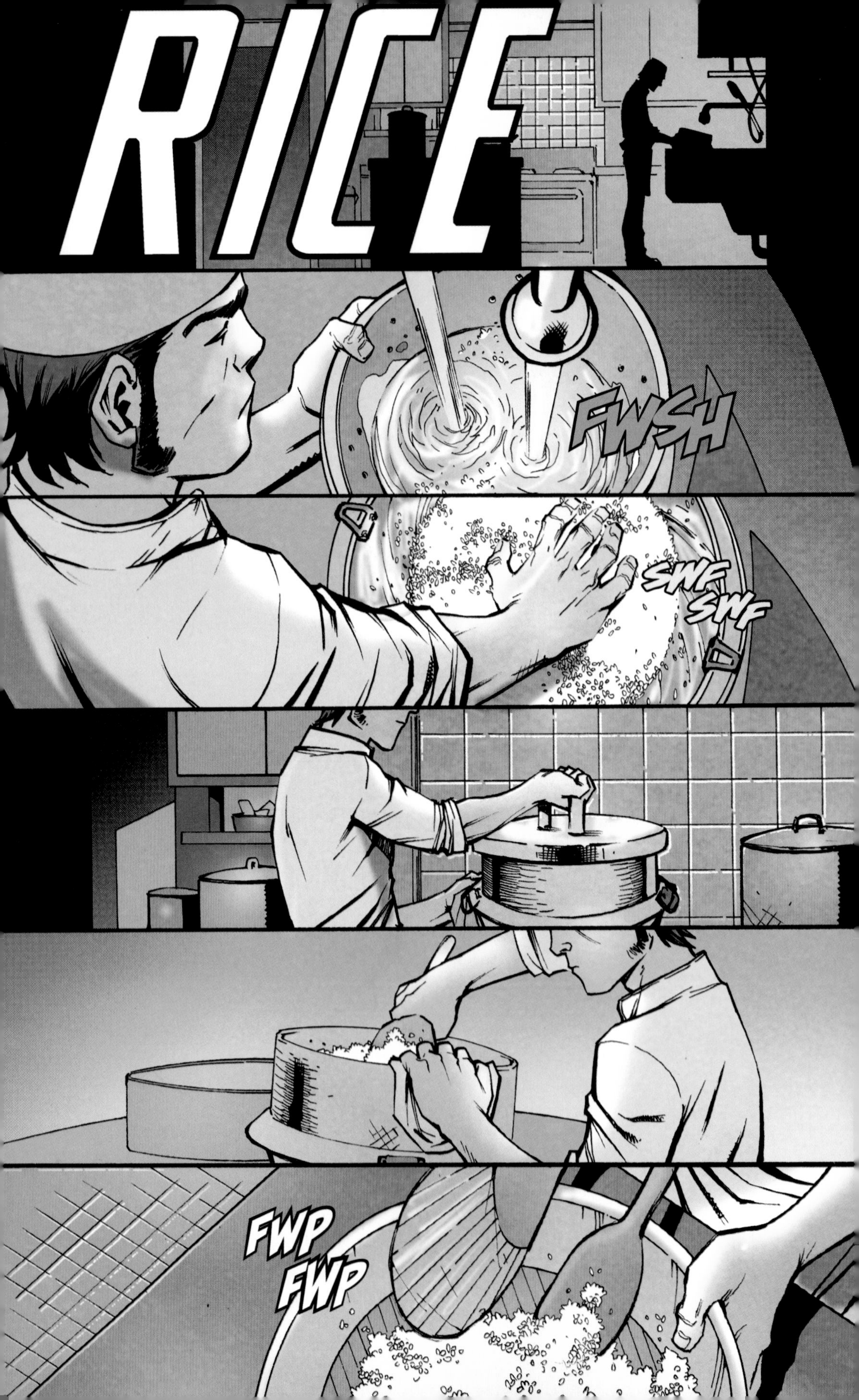
RICE
FWSH
SWF
SWF
FWP
FWP

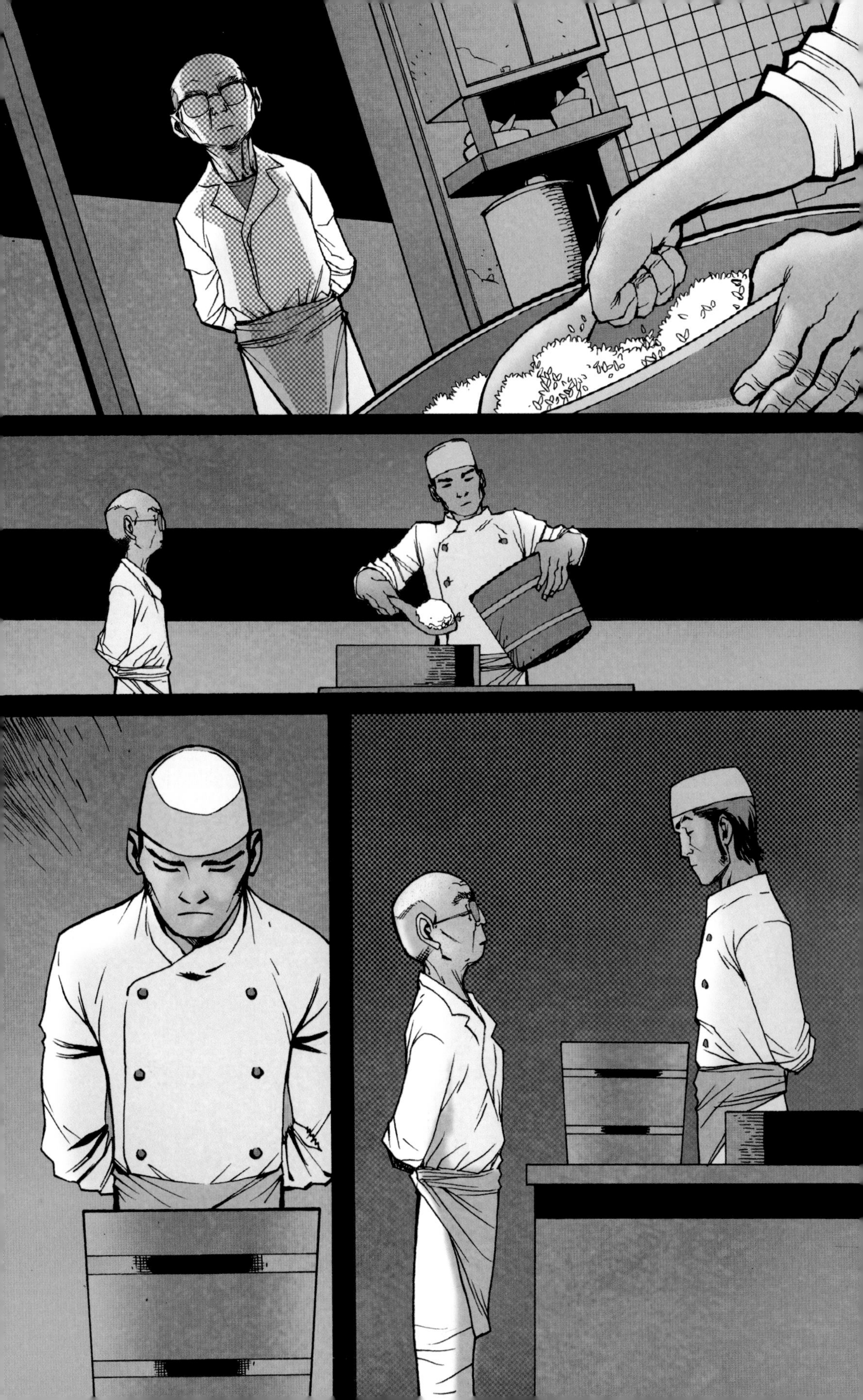

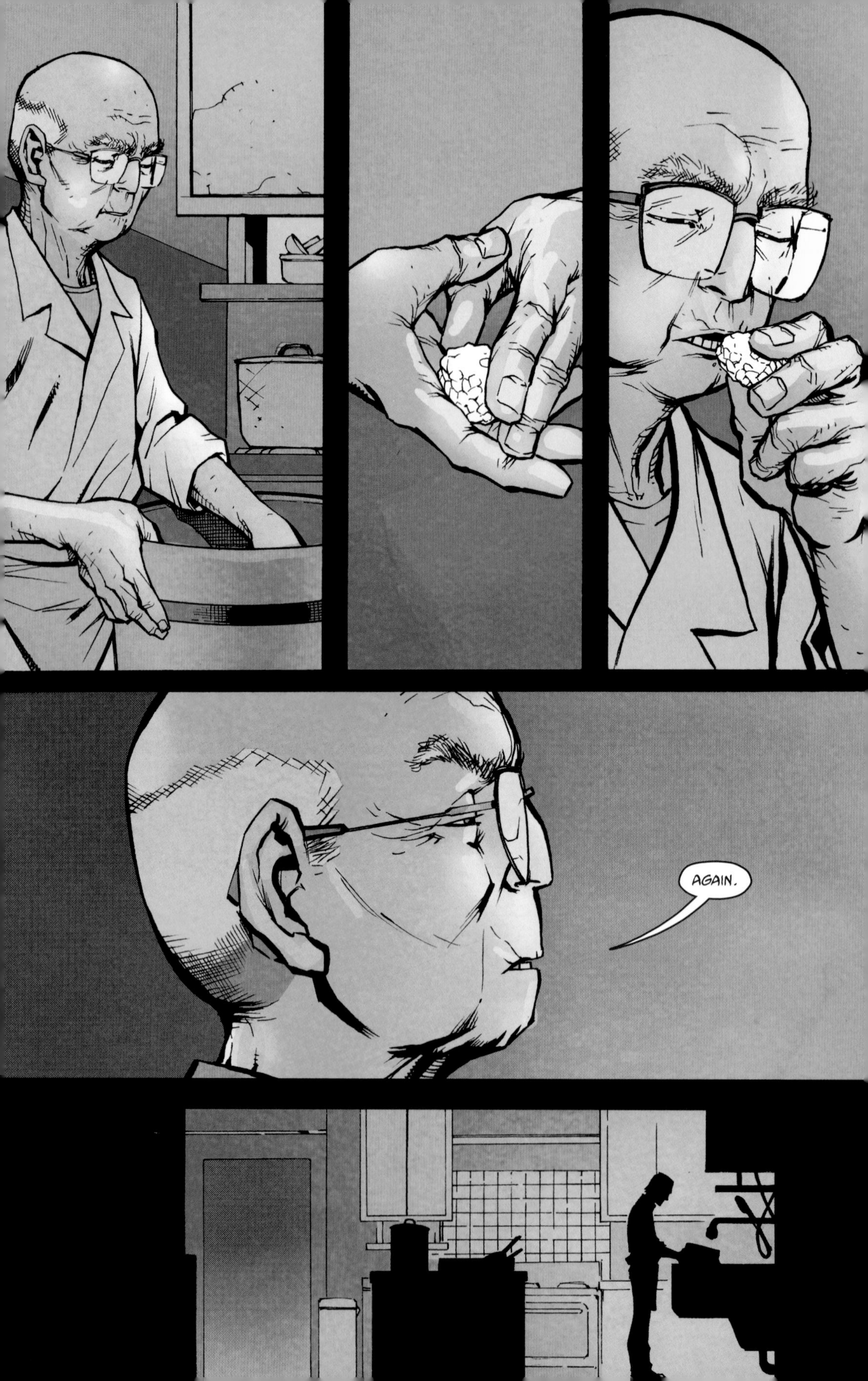
AGAIN.

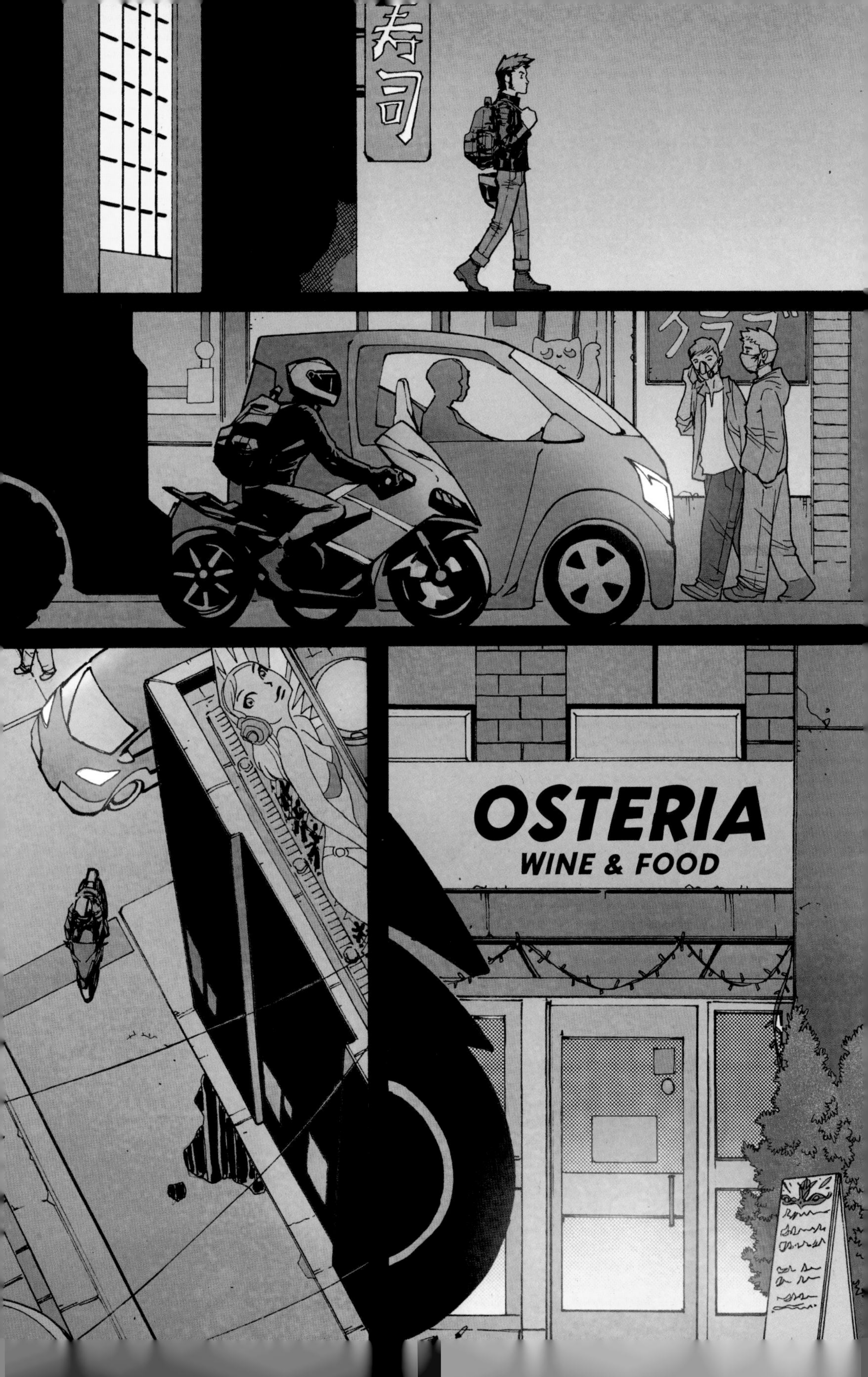
寿司
OSTERIA
WINE & FOOD

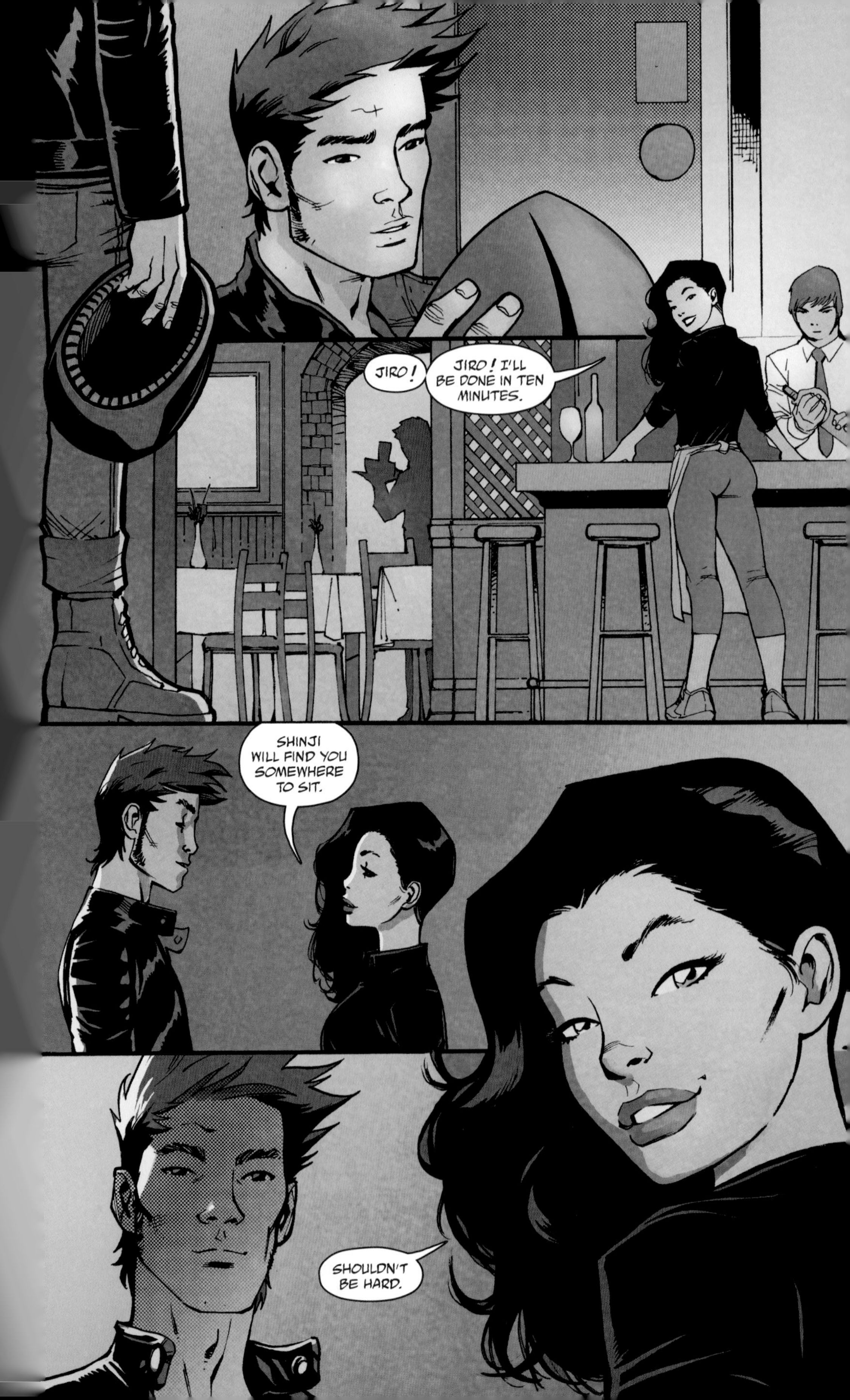
JIRO!
JIRO! I'LL BE DONE IN TEN MINUTES.
SHINJI WILL FIND YOU SOMEWHERE TO SIT.
SHOULDN'T BE HARD.

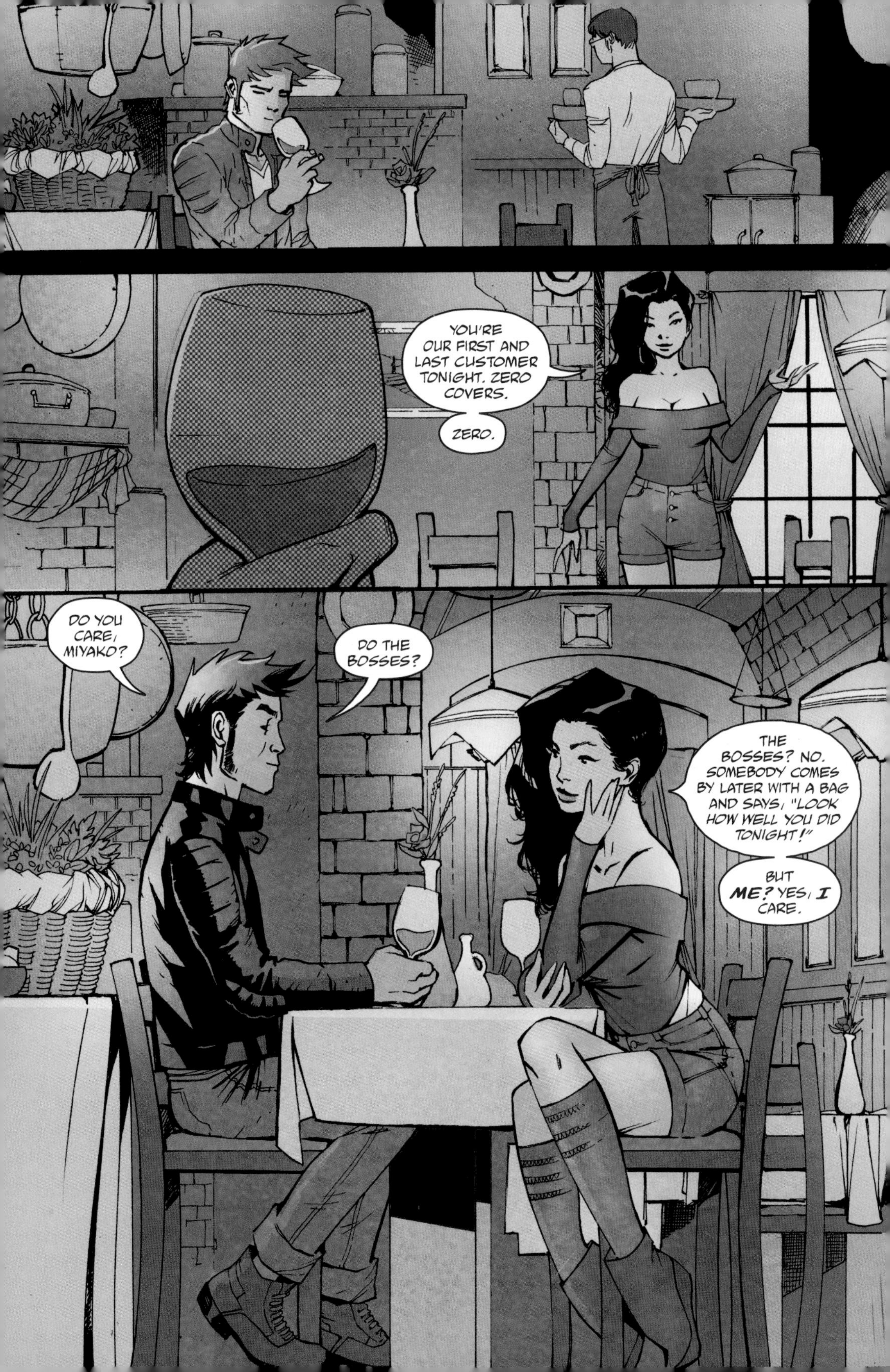
YOU'RE OUR FIRST AND LAST CUSTOMER TONIGHT. ZERO COVERS.
ZERO.
DO YOU CARE, MIYAKO?
DO THE BOSSES?
THE BOSSES? NO. SOMEBODY COMES BY LATER WITH A BAG AND SAYS, "LOOK HOW WELL YOU DID TONIGHT!"
BUT ME? YES, I CARE.

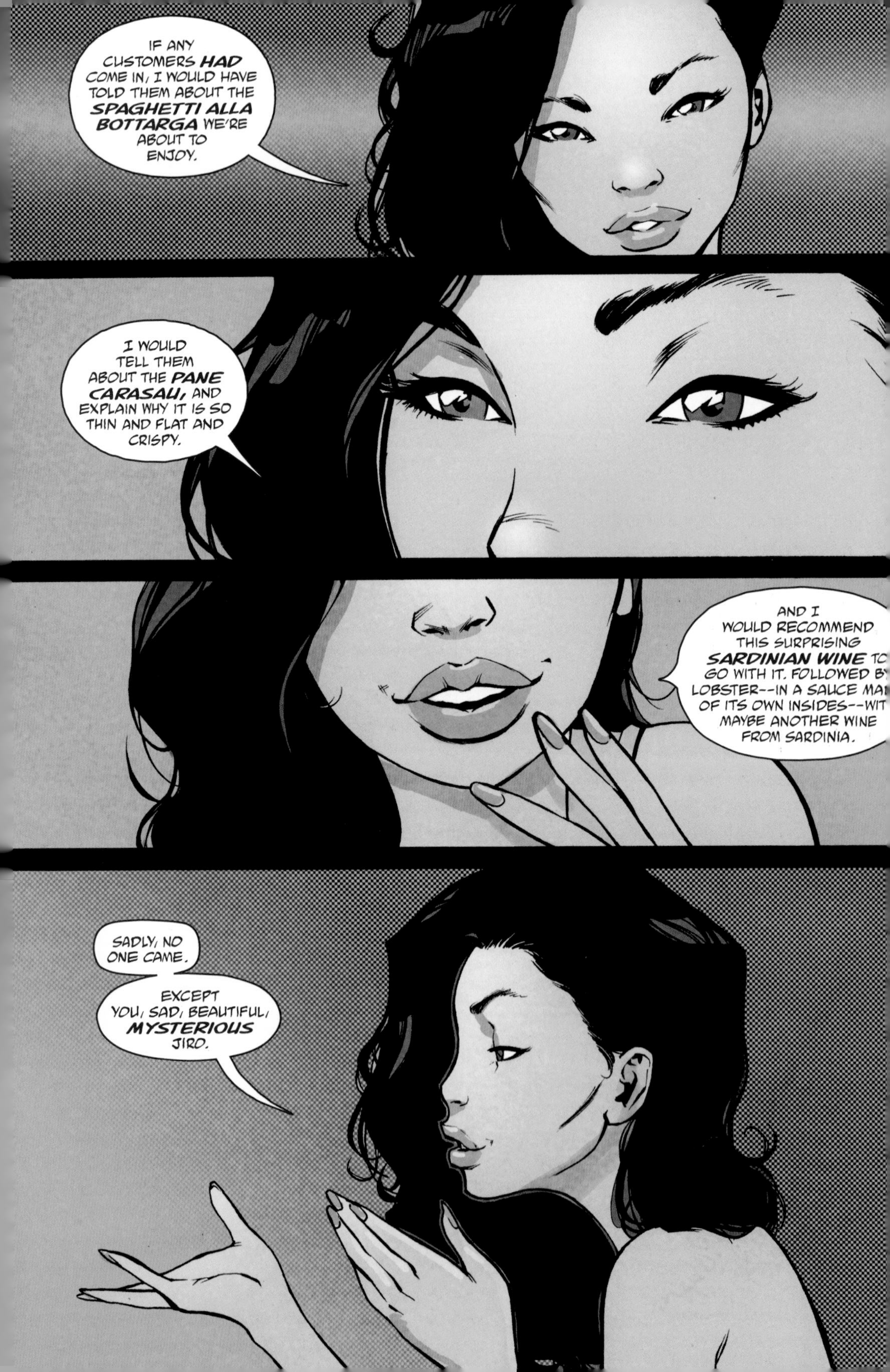
IF ANY CUSTOMERS HAD COME IN, I WOULD HAVE TOLD THEM ABOUT THE SPAGHETTI ALLA BOTTARGA WE'RE ABOUT TO ENJOY.
I WOULD TELL THEM ABOUT THE PANE CARASAU, AND EXPLAIN WHY IT IS SO THIN AND FLAT AND CRISPY.
AND I WOULD RECOMMEND THIS SURPRISING SARDINIAN WINE TO GO WITH IT. FOLLOWED BY LOBSTER--IN A SAUCE MA OF ITS OWN INSIDES--WIT MAYBE ANOTHER WINE FROM SARDINIA.
SADLY, NO ONE CAME.
EXCEPT YOU, SAD, BEAUTIFUL, MYSTERIOUS JIRO.

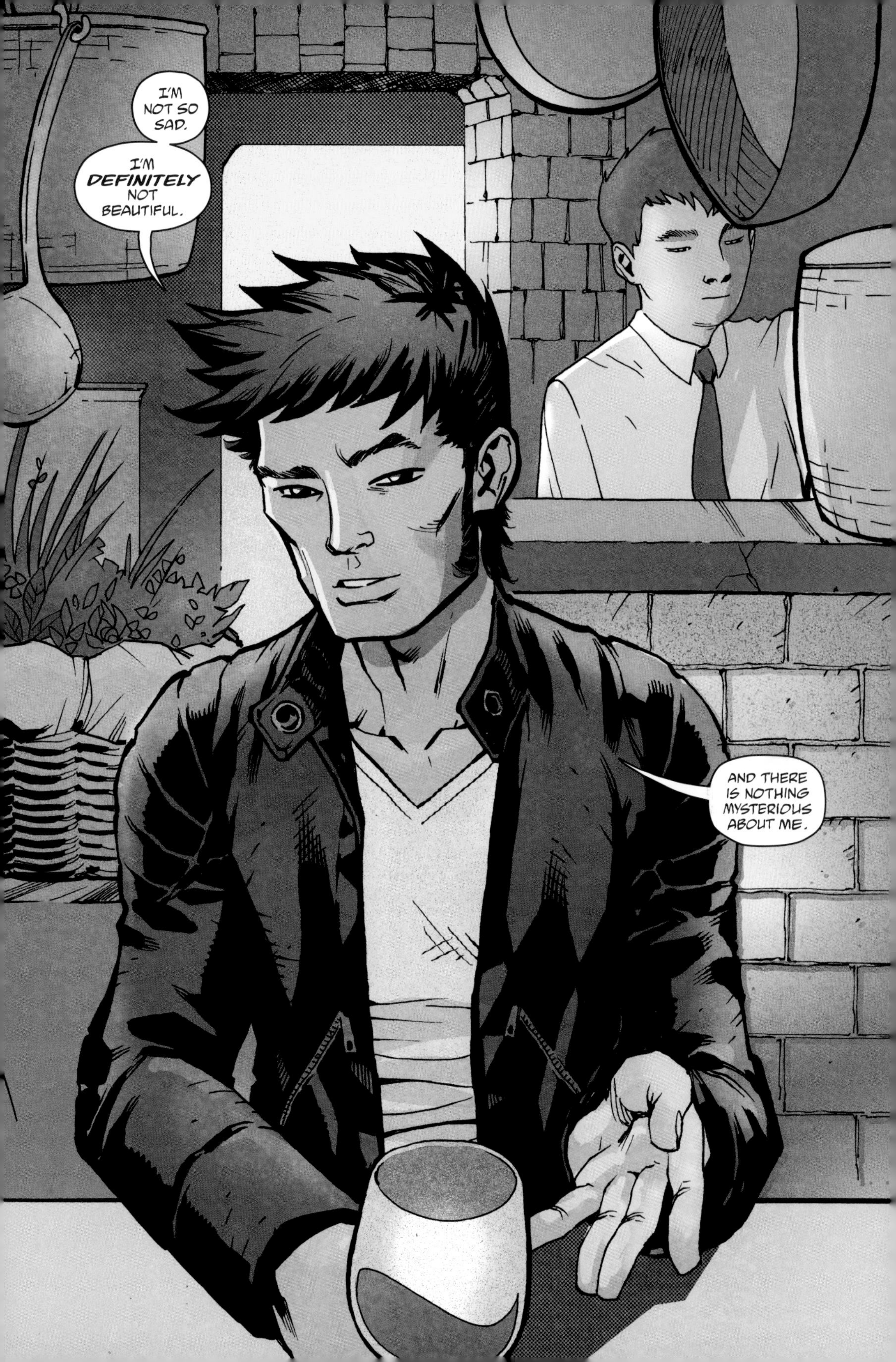
I'M NOT SO SAD.
I'M *DEFINITELY* NOT BEAUTIFUL.
AND THERE IS NOTHING MYSTERIOUS ABOUT ME.

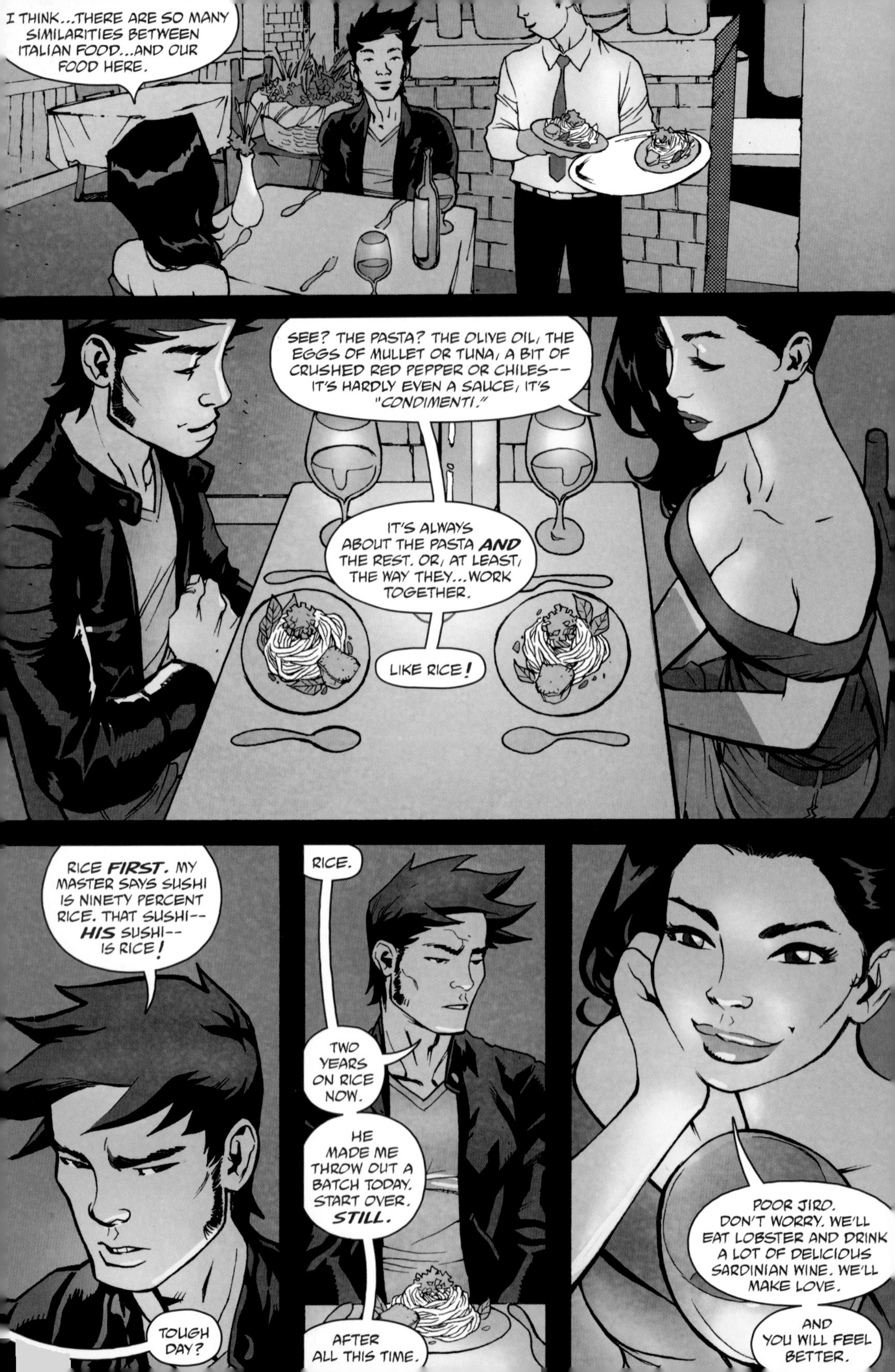
I THINK...THERE ARE SO MANY SIMILARITIES BETWEEN ITALIAN FOOD...AND OUR FOOD HERE.
SEE? THE PASTA? THE OLIVE OIL, THE EGGS OF MULLET OR TUNA, A BIT OF CRUSHED RED PEPPER OR CHILES-- IT'S HARDLY EVEN A SAUCE, IT'S "CONDIMENTI."
IT'S ALWAYS ABOUT THE PASTA AND THE REST. OR, AT LEAST, THE WAY THEY...WORK TOGETHER.
LIKE RICE!
RICE FIRST. MY MASTER SAYS SUSHI IS NINETY PERCENT RICE. THAT SUSHI-- HIS SUSHI-- IS RICE!
TOUGH DAY?
RICE.
TWO YEARS ON RICE NOW.
HE MADE ME THROW OUT A BATCH TODAY. START OVER. STILL.
AFTER ALL THIS TIME.
POOR JIRO. DON'T WORRY. WE'LL EAT LOBSTER AND DRINK A LOT OF DELICIOUS SARDINIAN WINE. WE'LL MAKE LOVE.
AND YOU WILL FEEL BETTER.

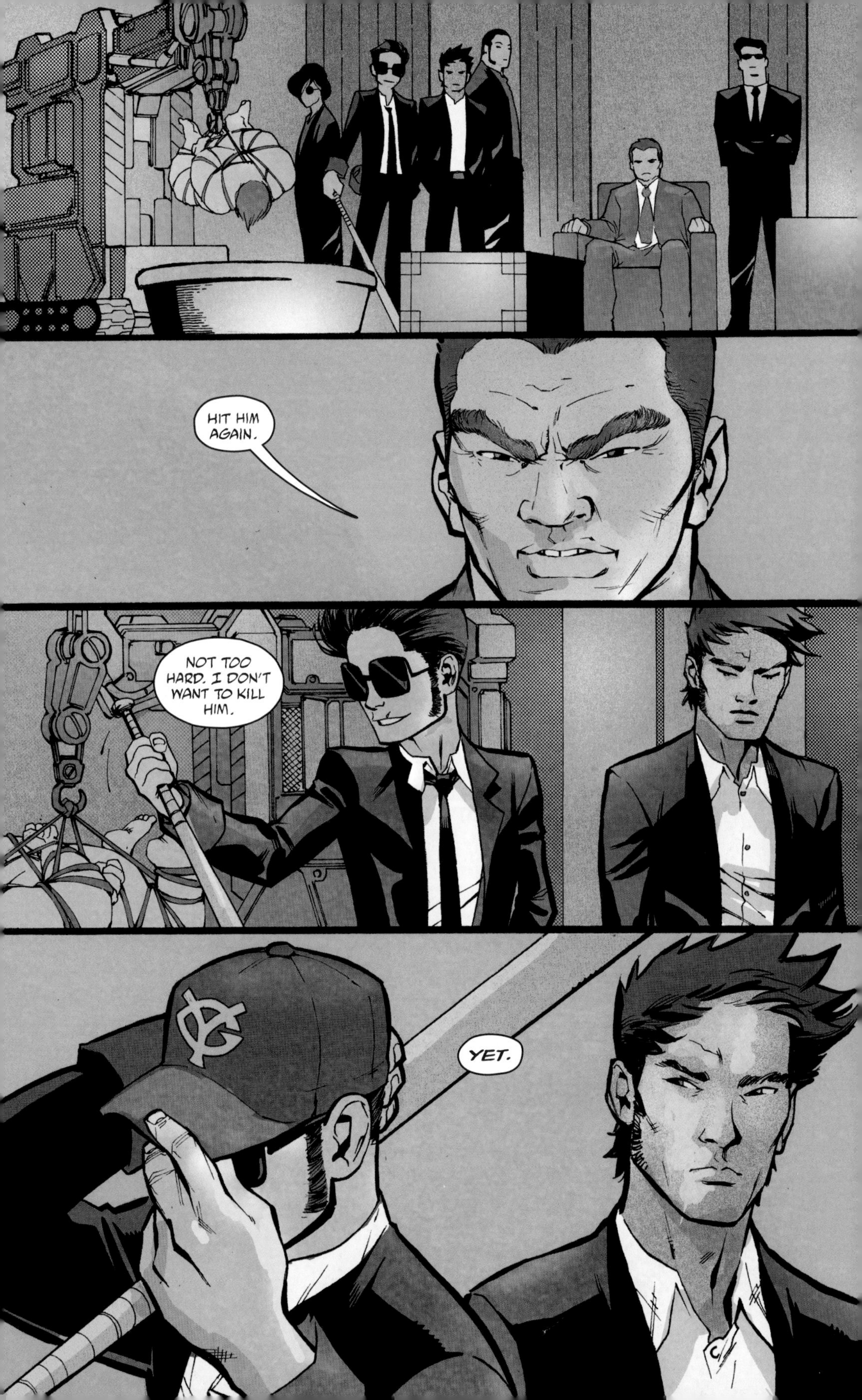
HIT HIM AGAIN.
NOT TOO HARD. I DON'T WANT TO KILL HIM.
YET.

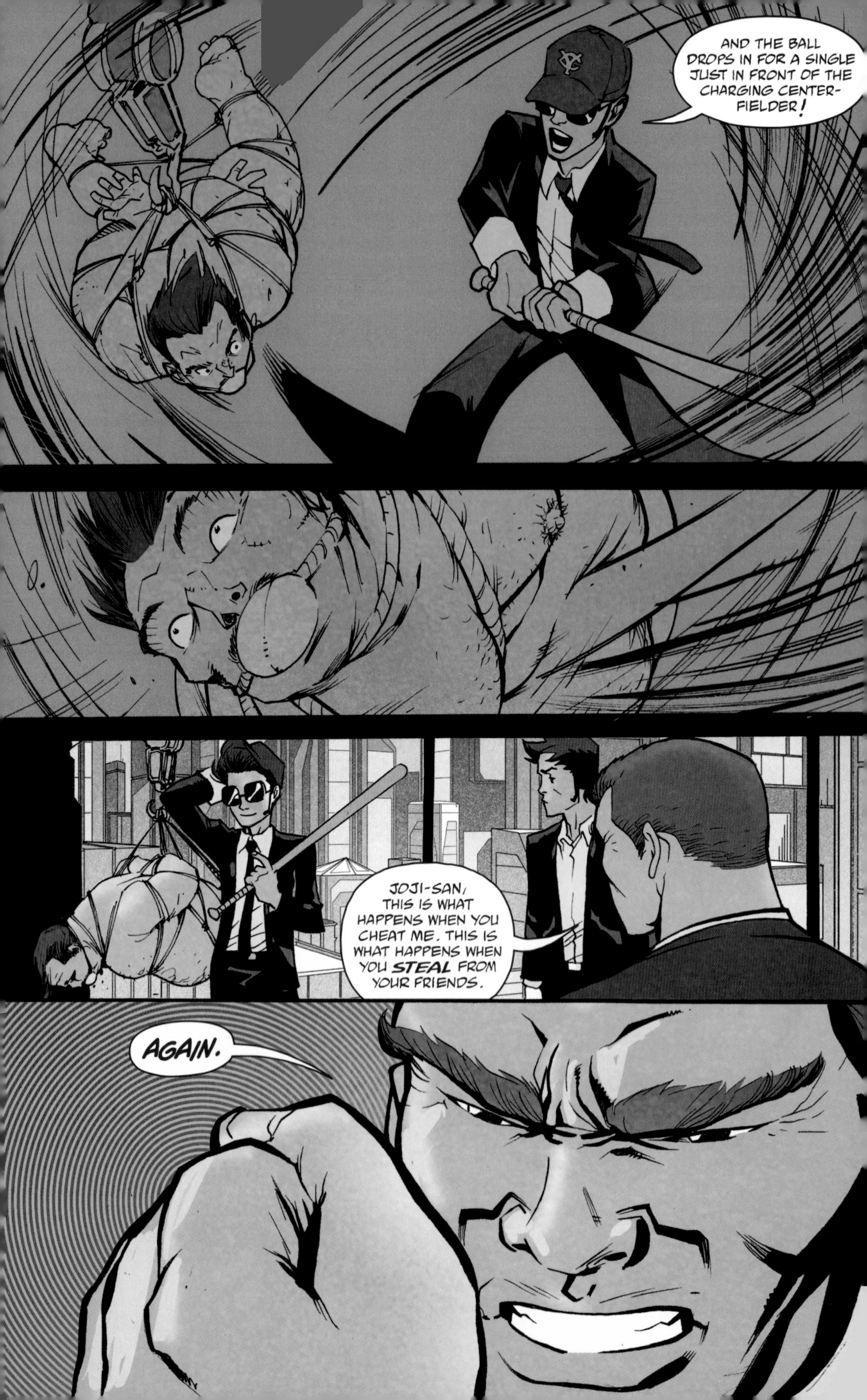
AND THE BALL DROPS IN FOR A SINGLE JUST IN FRONT OF THE CHARGING CENTER-FIELDER!
JOJI-SAN, THIS IS WHAT HAPPENS WHEN YOU CHEAT ME. THIS IS WHAT HAPPENS WHEN YOU STEAL FROM YOUR FRIENDS.
AGAIN.

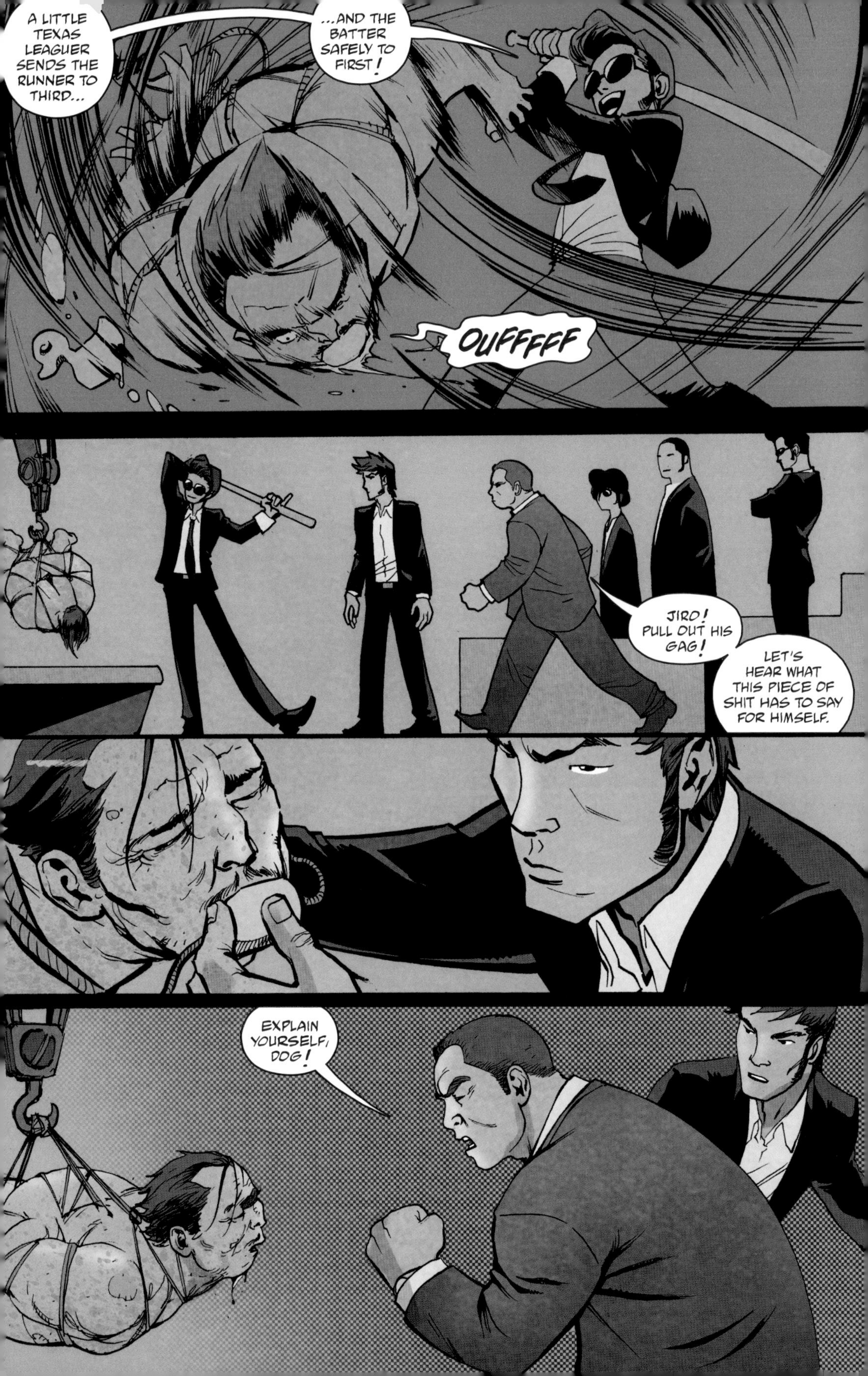
A LITTLE TEXAS LEAGUER SENDS THE RUNNER TO THIRD...
...AND THE BATTER SAFELY TO FIRST!
OUFFFFF
JIRO! PULL OUT HIS GAG!
LET'S HEAR WHAT THIS PIECE OF SHIT HAS TO SAY FOR HIMSELF.
EXPLAIN YOURSELF, DOG!

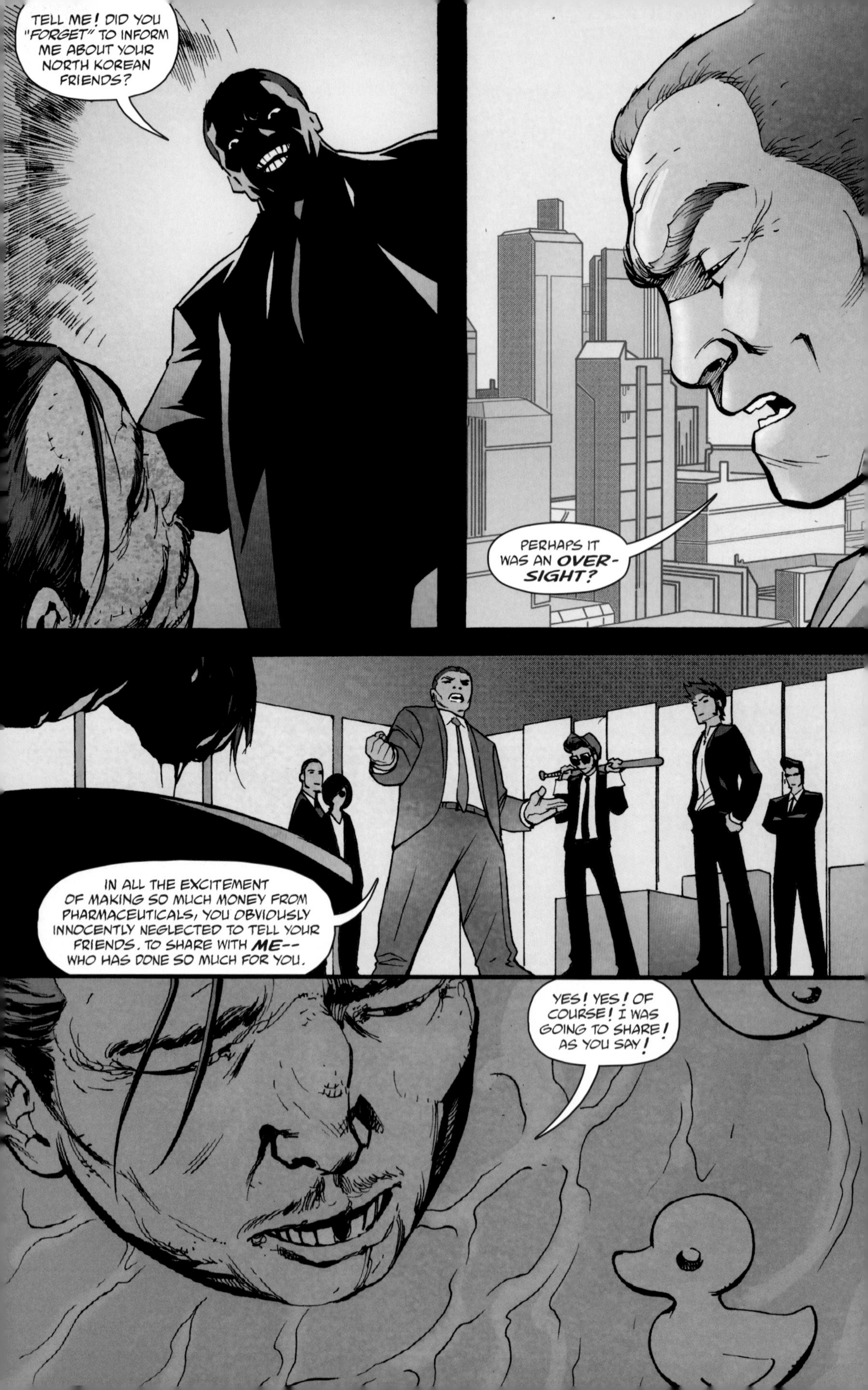
TELL ME! DID YOU "FORGET" TO INFORM ME ABOUT YOUR NORTH KOREAN FRIENDS?
PERHAPS IT WAS AN OVER-SIGHT?
IN ALL THE EXCITEMENT OF MAKING SO MUCH MONEY FROM PHARMACEUTICALS, YOU OBVIOUSLY INNOCENTLY NEGLECTED TO TELL YOUR FRIENDS. TO SHARE WITH ME-- WHO HAS DONE SO MUCH FOR YOU.
YES! YES! OF COURSE! I WAS GOING TO SHARE! AS YOU SAY!

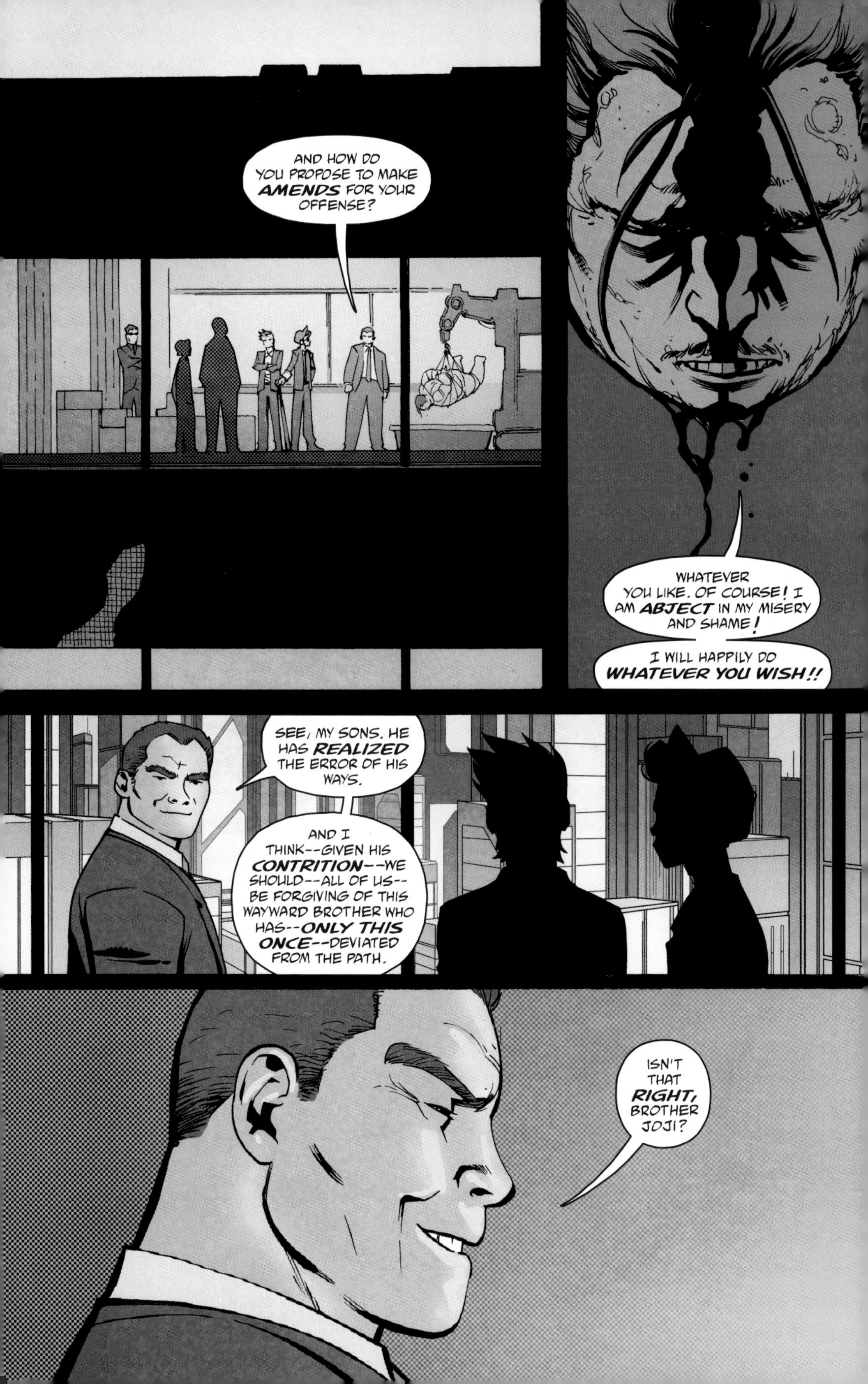
AND HOW DO YOU PROPOSE TO MAKE **AMENDS** FOR YOUR OFFENSE?
WHATEVER YOU LIKE. OF COURSE! I AM **ABJECT** IN MY MISERY AND SHAME!
I WILL HAPPILY DO **WHATEVER YOU WISH!!**
SEE, MY SONS. HE HAS **REALIZED** THE ERROR OF HIS WAYS.
AND I THINK--GIVEN HIS **CONTRITION**--WE SHOULD--ALL OF US--BE FORGIVING OF THIS WAYWARD BROTHER WHO HAS--**ONLY THIS ONCE**--DEVIATED FROM THE PATH.
ISN'T THAT **RIGHT,** BROTHER JOJI?

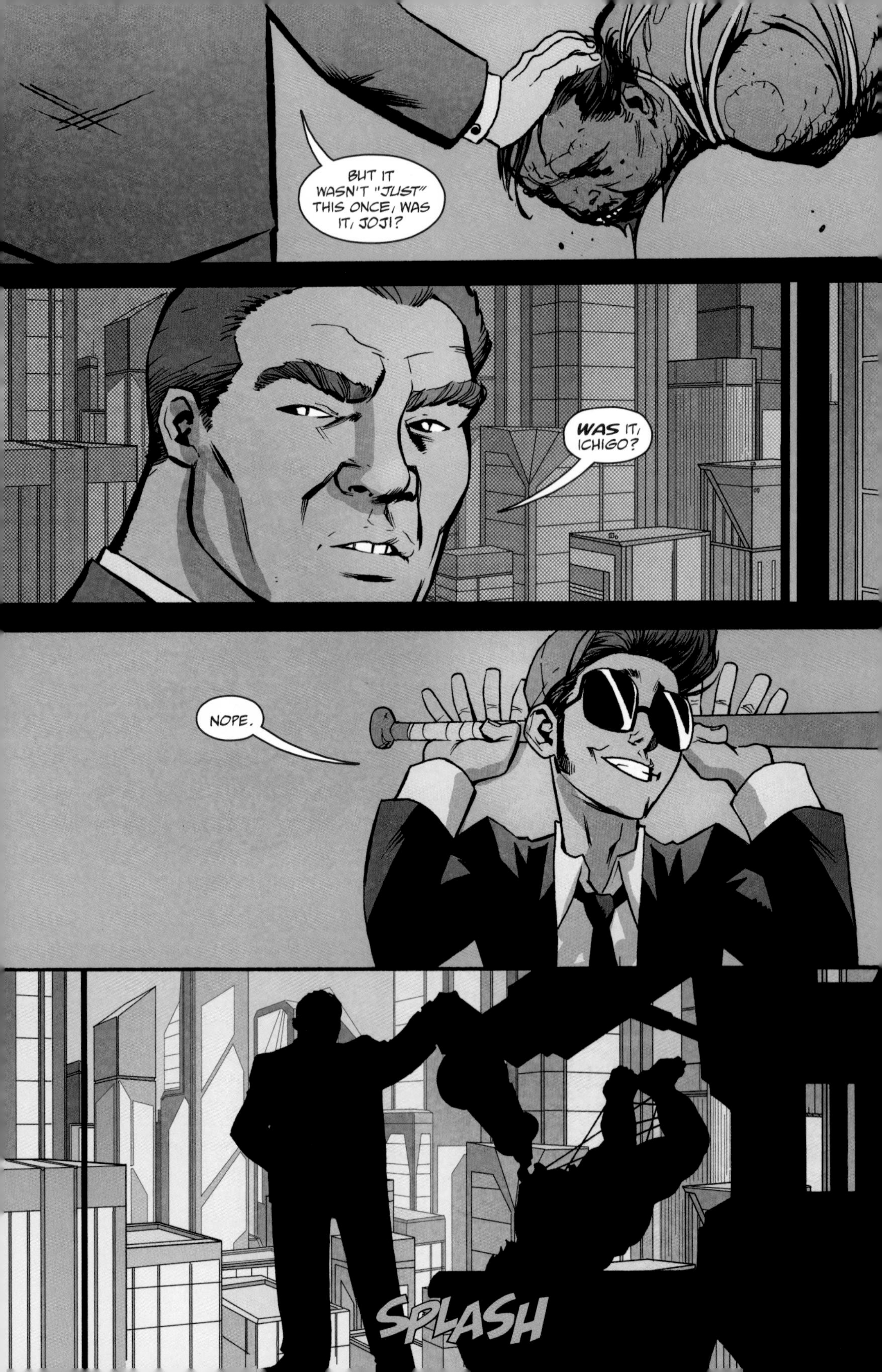
BUT IT WASN'T "JUST" THIS ONCE, WAS IT, JOJI?
WAS IT, ICHIGO?
NOPE.
SPLASH

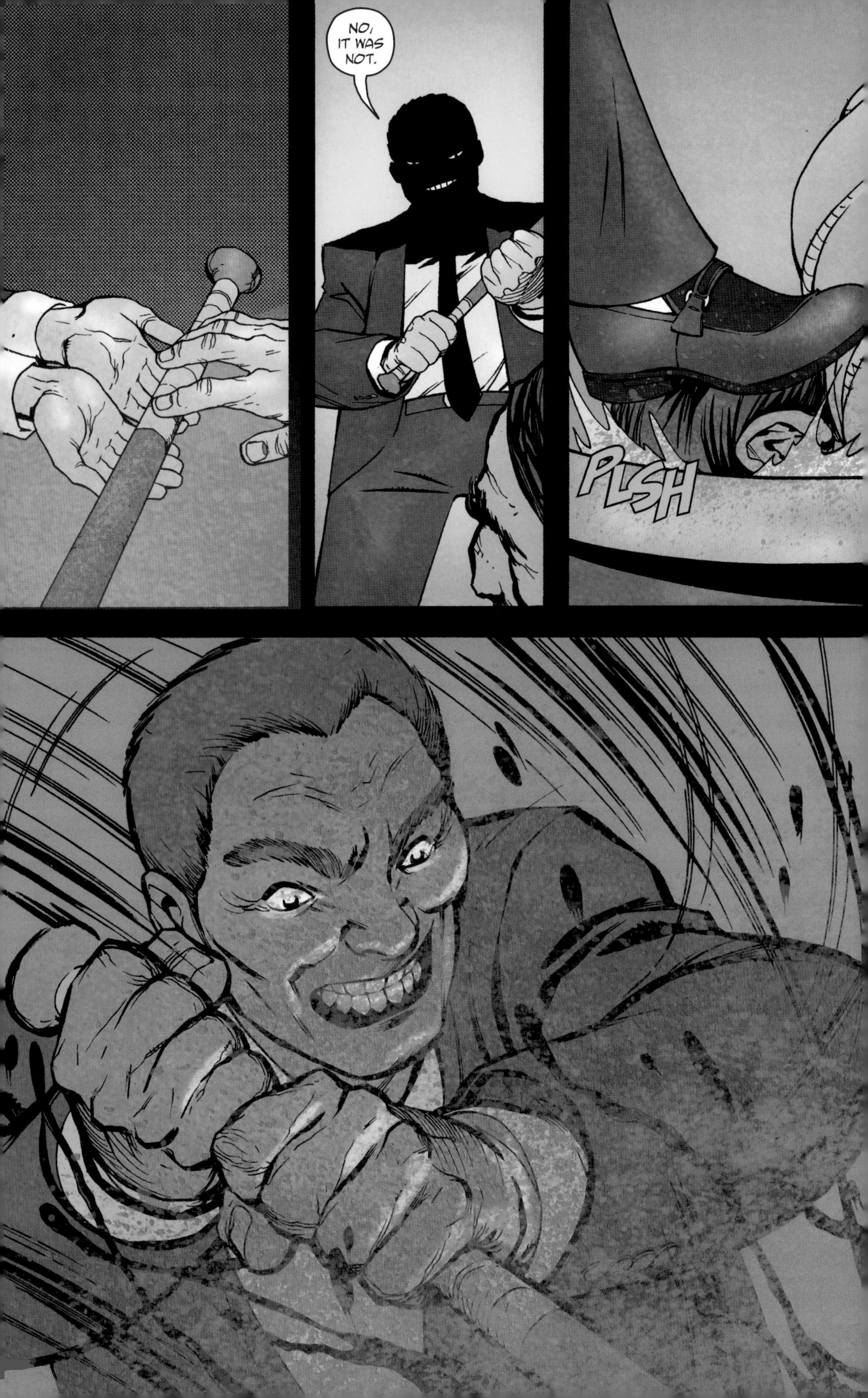
NO, IT WAS NOT.
PLSH

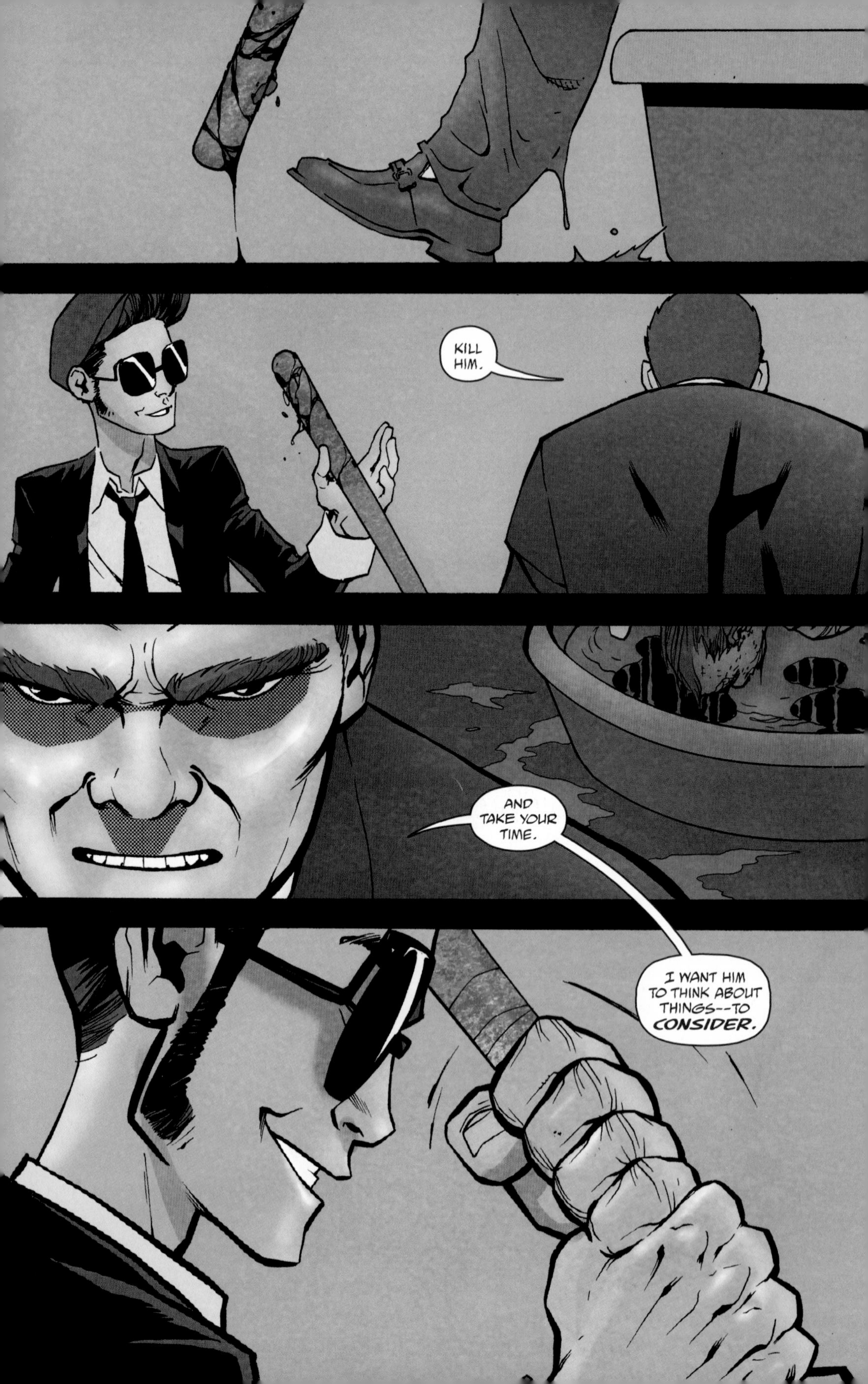
KILL HIM.
AND TAKE YOUR TIME.
I WANT HIM TO THINK ABOUT THINGS--TO CONSIDER.

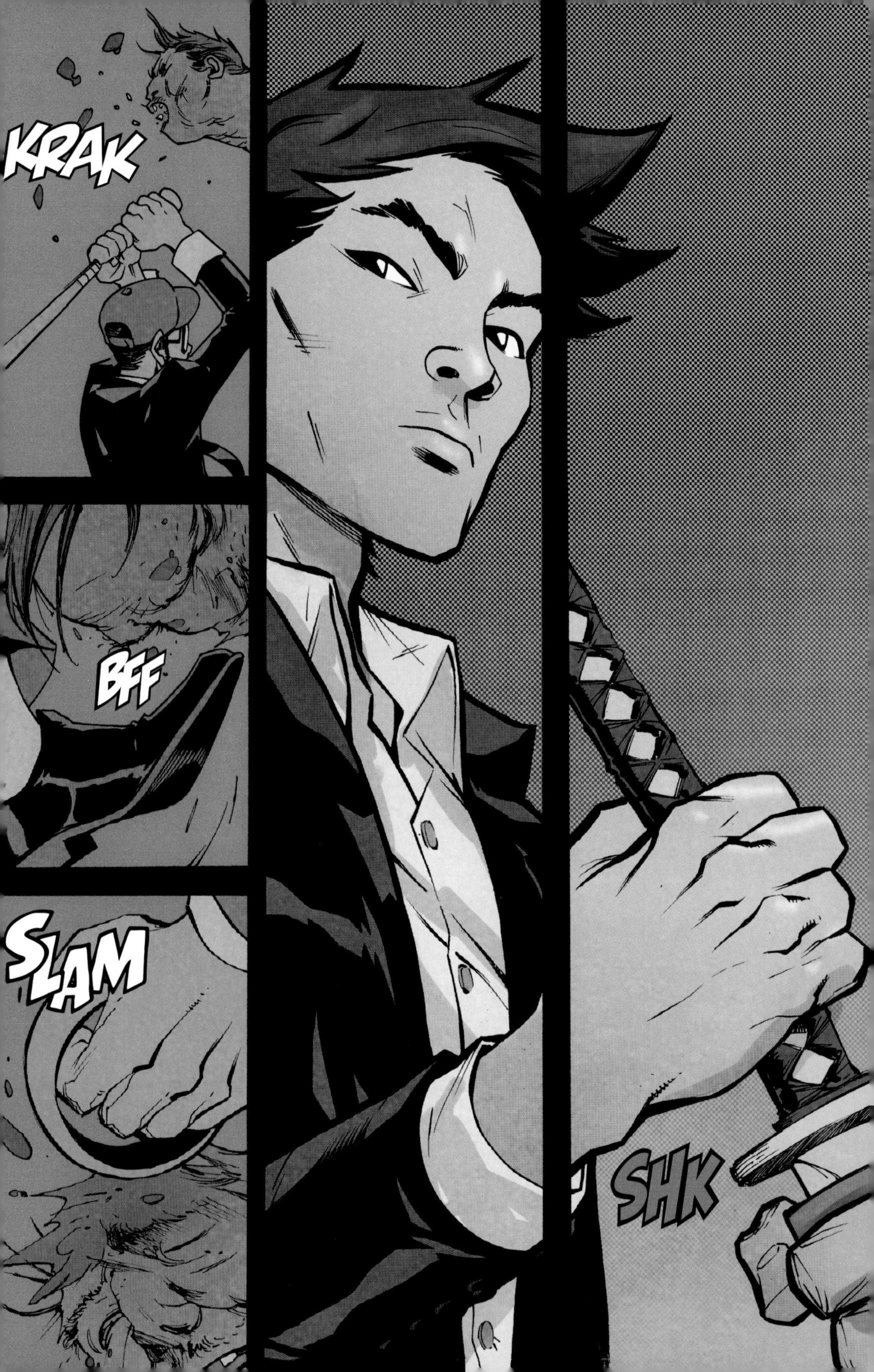
KRAK
BFF
SLAM
SHK

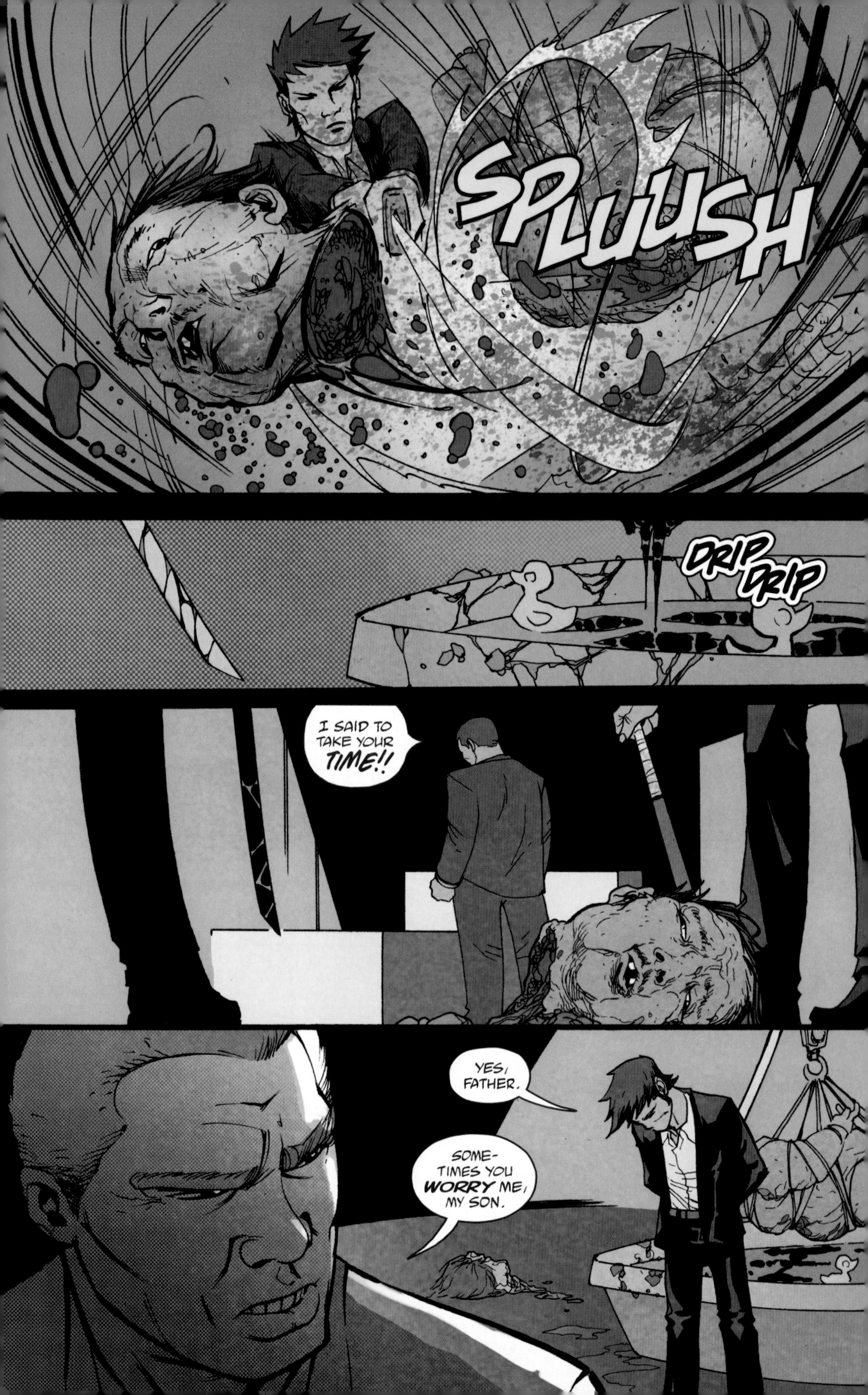
SPLUUSH
DRIP DRIP
I SAID TO TAKE YOUR TIME!!
YES, FATHER.
SOME-TIMES YOU WORRY ME, MY SON.

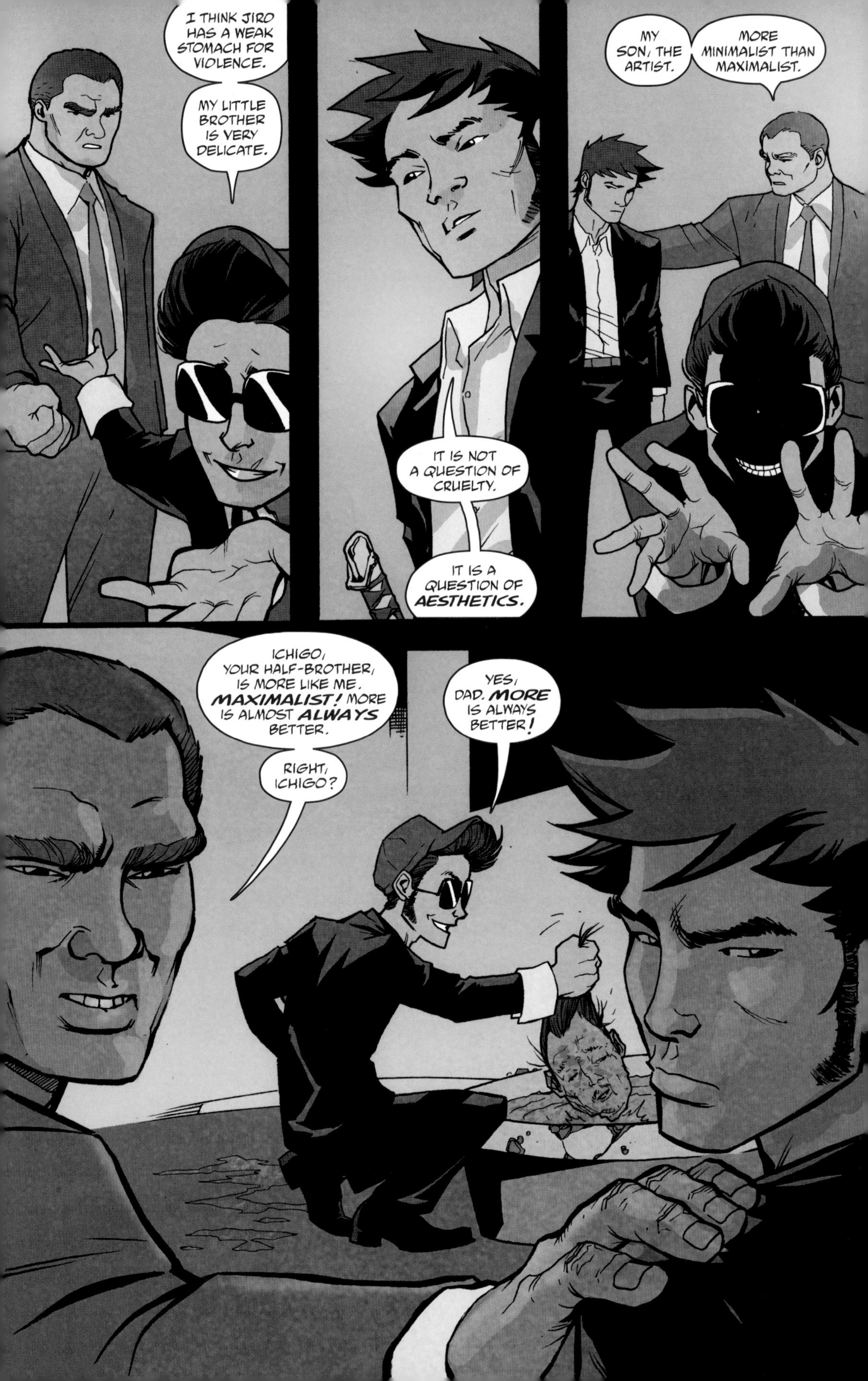

I THINK JIRO HAS A WEAK STOMACH FOR VIOLENCE.
MY LITTLE BROTHER IS VERY DELICATE.
IT IS NOT A QUESTION OF CRUELTY.
IT IS A QUESTION OF AESTHETICS.
MY SON, THE ARTIST.
MORE MINIMALIST THAN MAXIMALIST.
ICHIGO, YOUR HALF-BROTHER, IS MORE LIKE ME. MAXIMALIST! MORE IS ALMOST ALWAYS BETTER.
RIGHT, ICHIGO?
YES, DAD. MORE IS ALWAYS BETTER!

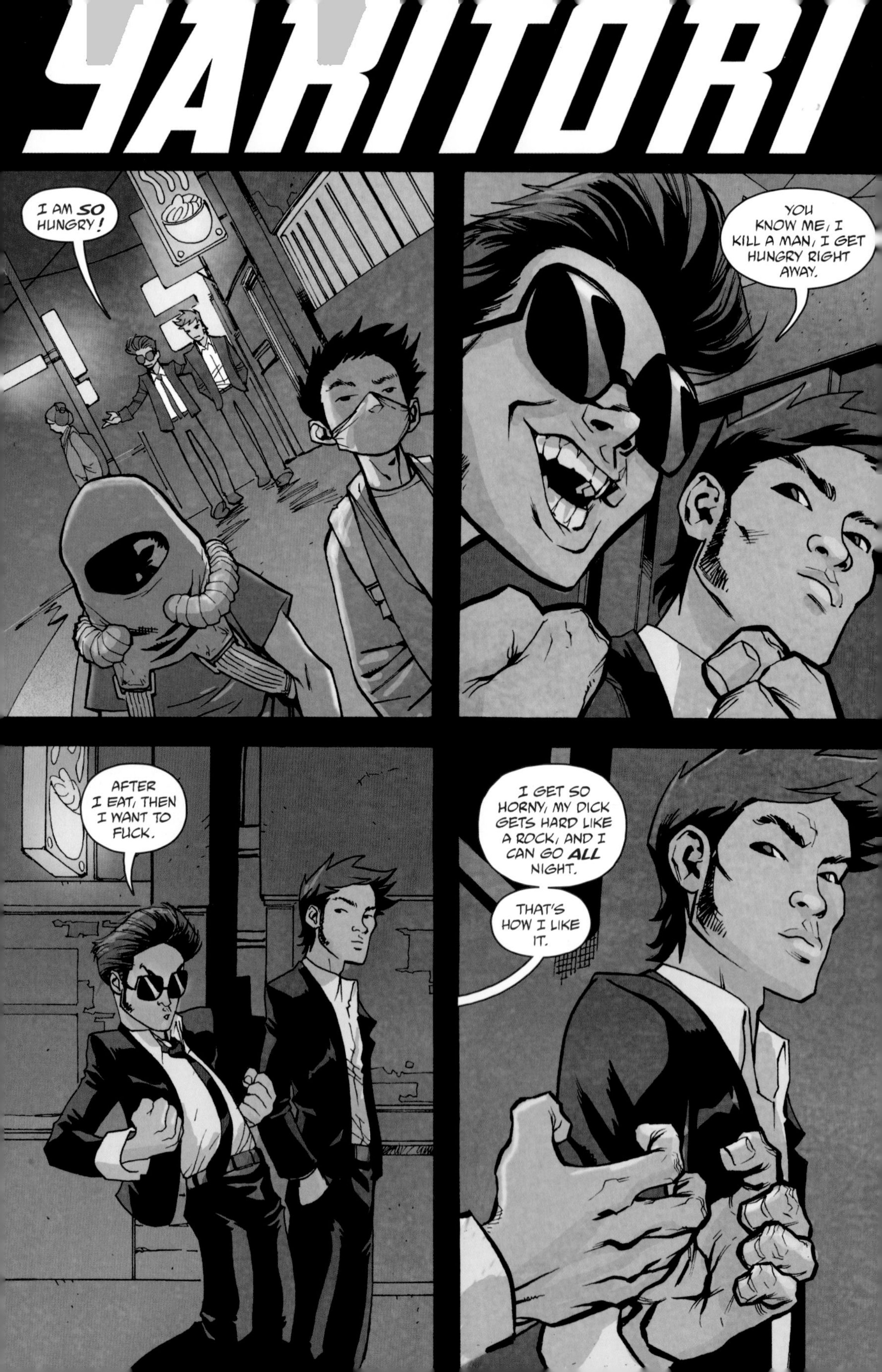
YAKITORI
I AM SO HUNGRY!
YOU KNOW ME, I KILL A MAN, I GET HUNGRY RIGHT AWAY.
AFTER I EAT, THEN I WANT TO FUCK.
I GET SO HORNY, MY DICK GETS HARD LIKE A ROCK, AND I CAN GO ALL NIGHT.
THAT'S HOW I LIKE IT.

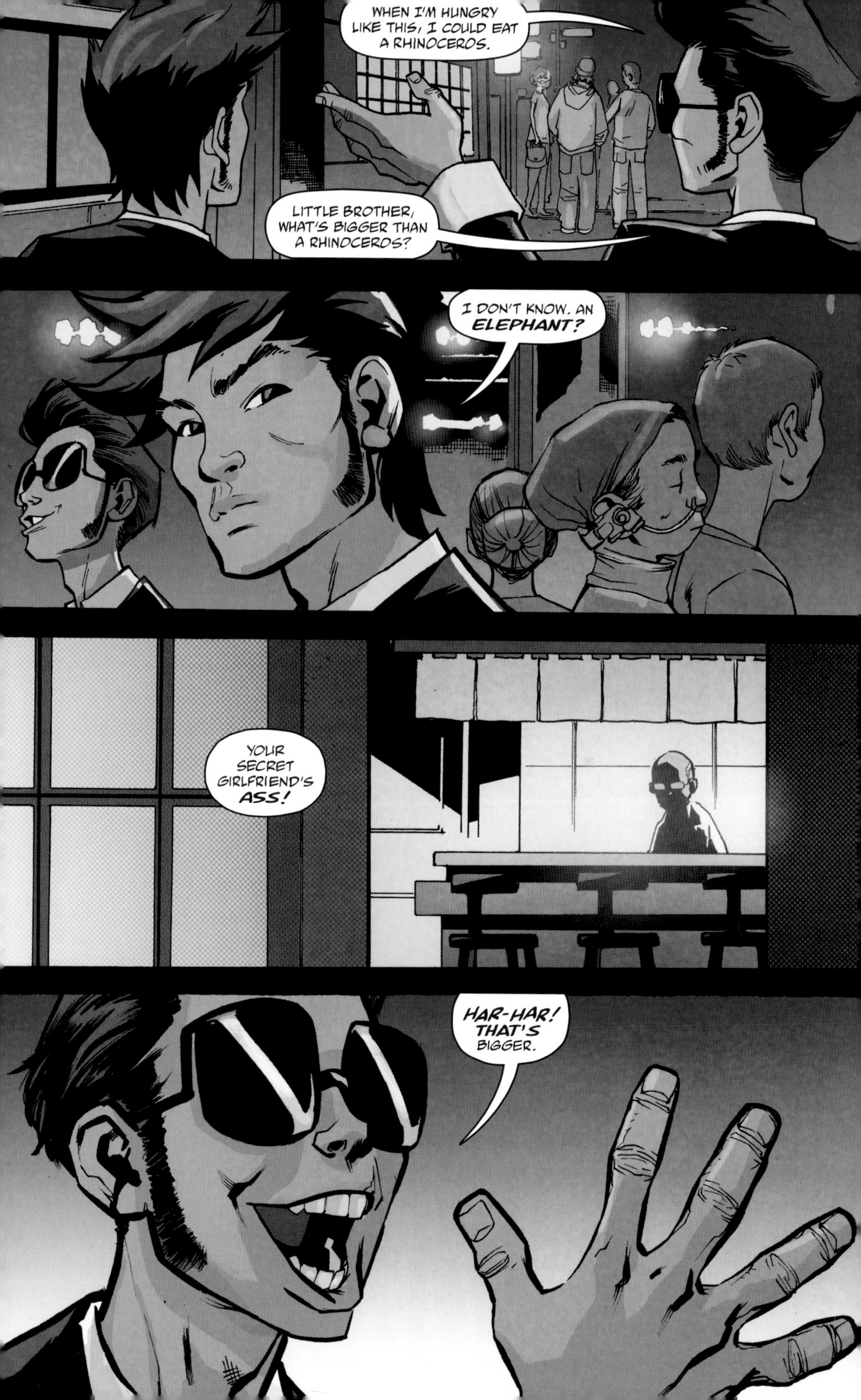
WHEN I'M HUNGRY LIKE THIS, I COULD EAT A RHINOCEROS.
LITTLE BROTHER, WHAT'S BIGGER THAN A RHINOCEROS?
I DON'T KNOW. AN ELEPHANT?
YOUR SECRET GIRLFRIEND'S ASS!
HAR-HAR! THAT'S BIGGER.

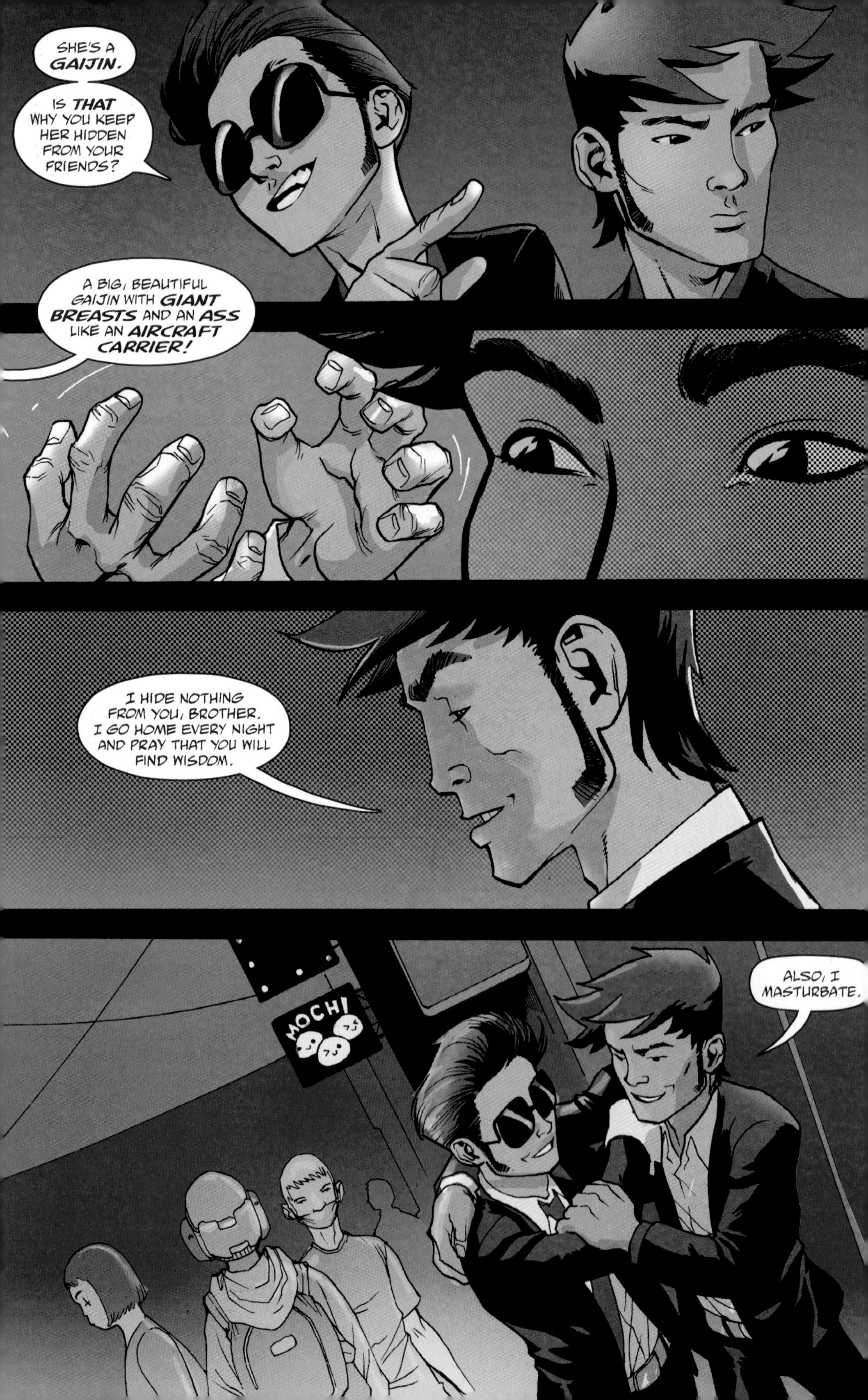
SHE'S A GAIJIN.
IS THAT WHY YOU KEEP HER HIDDEN FROM YOUR FRIENDS?
A BIG, BEAUTIFUL GAIJIN WITH GIANT BREASTS AND AN ASS LIKE AN AIRCRAFT CARRIER!
I HIDE NOTHING FROM YOU, BROTHER. I GO HOME EVERY NIGHT AND PRAY THAT YOU WILL FIND WISDOM.
MOCHI
ALSO, I MASTURBATE.

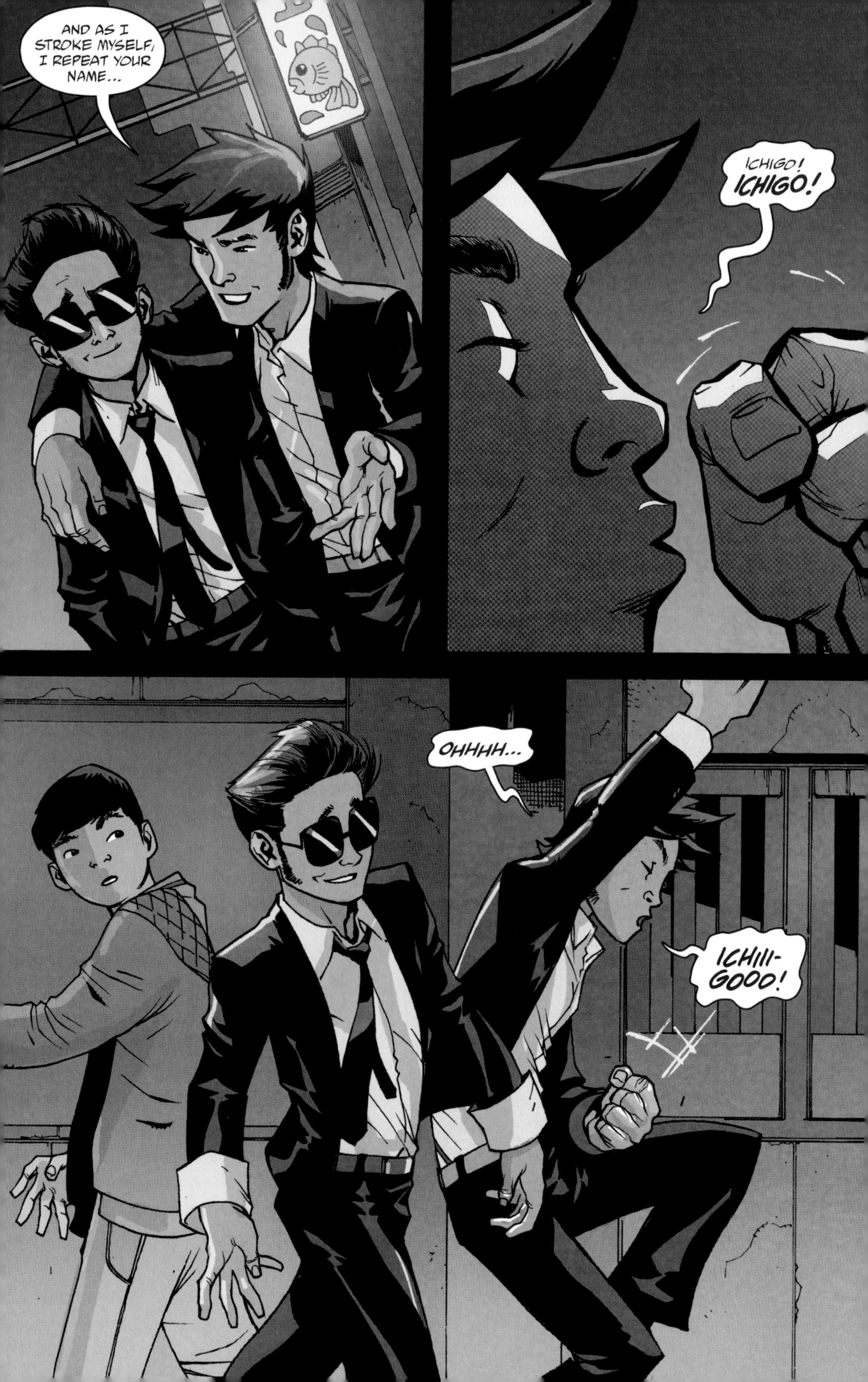
AND AS I STROKE MYSELF, I REPEAT YOUR NAME...
ICHIGO! ICHIGO!
OHHHH...
ICHIII-GOOO!

I WANT TO **MEET** THIS BIG AMERICAN!

IS SHE BLONDE?

I CONFESS, ICHIGO-SAN. SHE **IS** BLONDE. SHE IS A **GIANT**. WHEN SHE SQUATS ON MY TINY PENIS, THE HOUSE SHAKES. THE PEARS IN MY GARDEN FALL FROM THE TREE. CHILDREN CRY.

YOU MOCK ME, JIRO. DON'T THINK I DON'T KNOW. YOU THINK YOU'RE SMARTER THAN ICHIGO. YOU THINK YOU'RE TOO **GOOD** FOR THIS BUSINESS.

I AM S ONLY WH CHOC WHER **EAT**, BROT

BUT LOOK AT YOU, YOU'RE A YOUNG CHICKEN, AND YOU KNOW WHAT WE DO WITH YOUNG CHICKENS? WE **EAT** YOUNG CHICKENS!

SOOO SMART! SMARTER THAN EVERYONE.

TH WHE SHO EAT

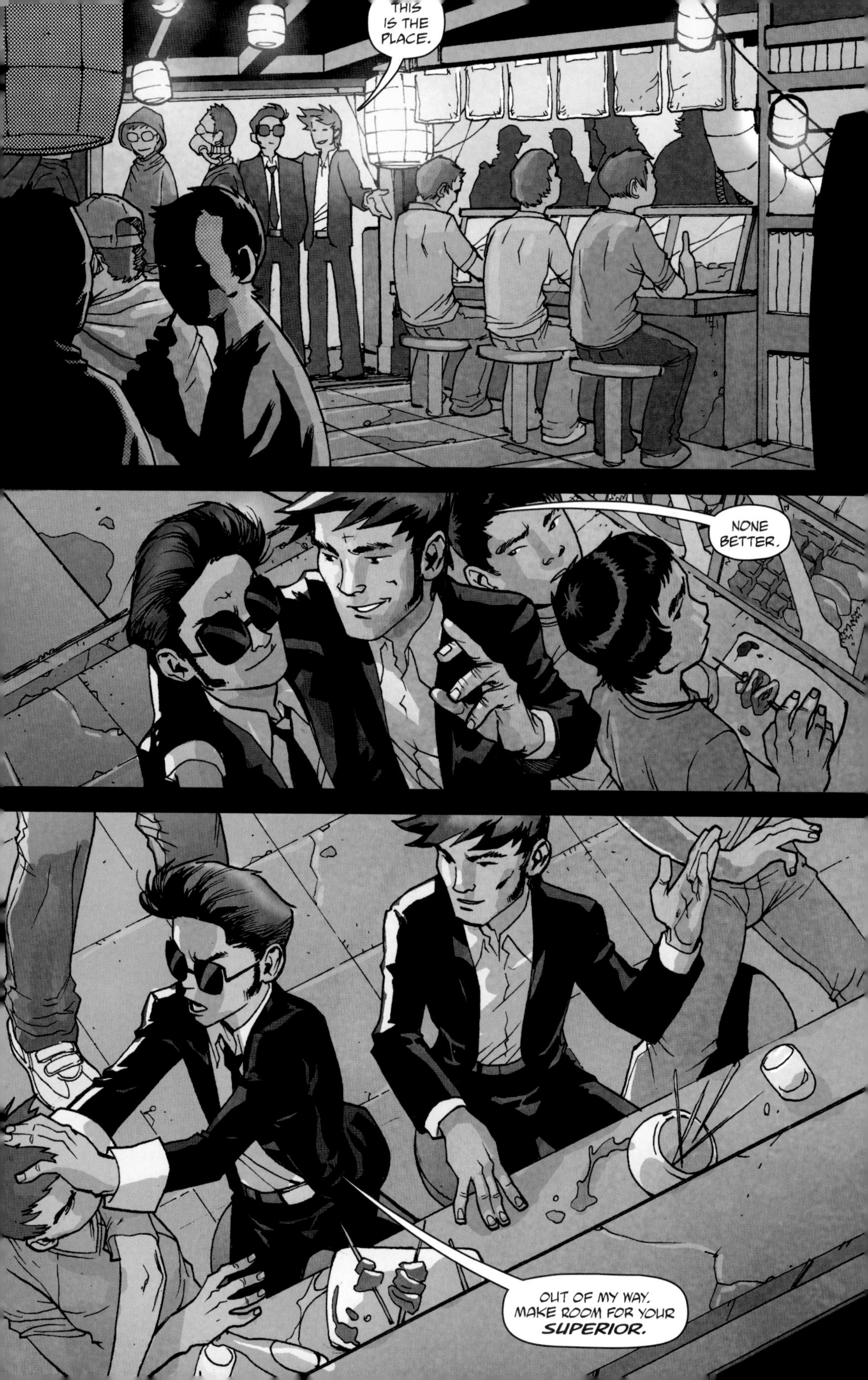
THIS IS THE PLACE.
NONE BETTER.
OUT OF MY WAY. MAKE ROOM FOR YOUR SUPERIOR.

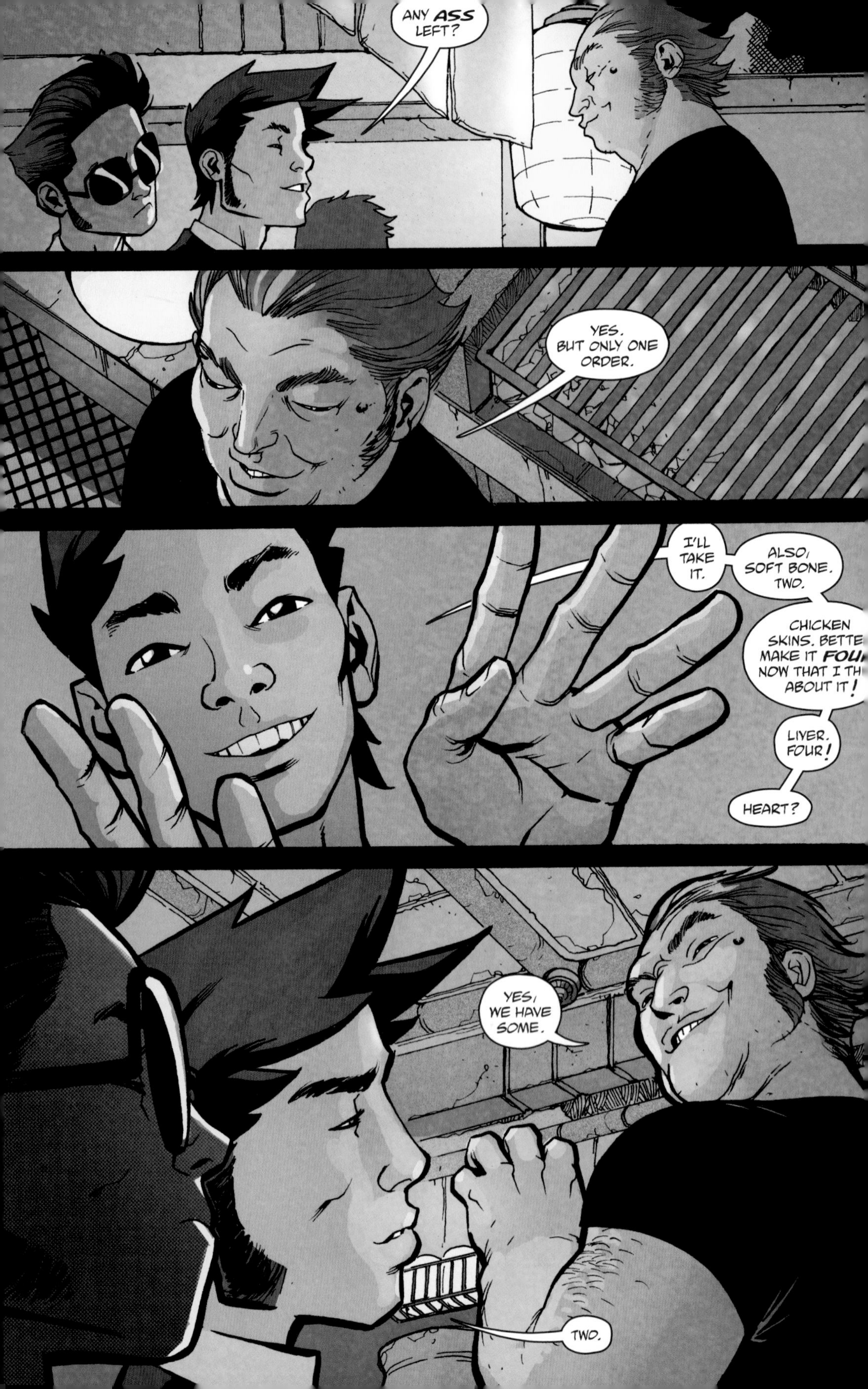
ANY ASS LEFT?
YES. BUT ONLY ONE ORDER.
I'LL TAKE IT.
ALSO, SOFT BONE. TWO.
CHICKEN SKINS. BETTE MAKE IT FOU NOW THAT I TH ABOUT IT!
LIVER. FOUR!
HEART?
YES, WE HAVE SOME.
TWO.

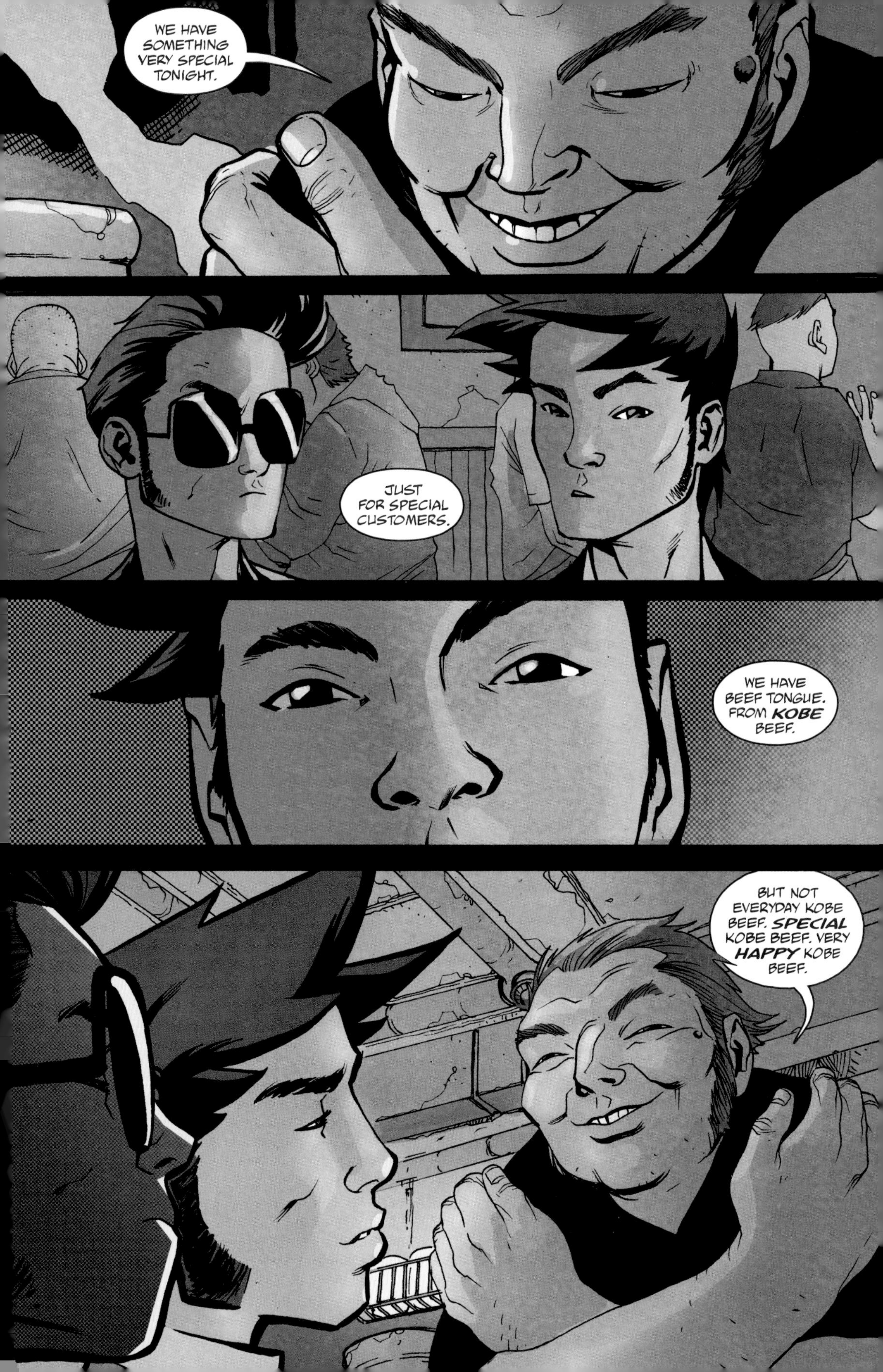
WE HAVE SOMETHING VERY SPECIAL TONIGHT.
JUST FOR SPECIAL CUSTOMERS.
WE HAVE BEEF TONGUE. FROM KOBE BEEF.
BUT NOT EVERYDAY KOBE BEEF. SPECIAL KOBE BEEF. VERY HAPPY KOBE BEEF.

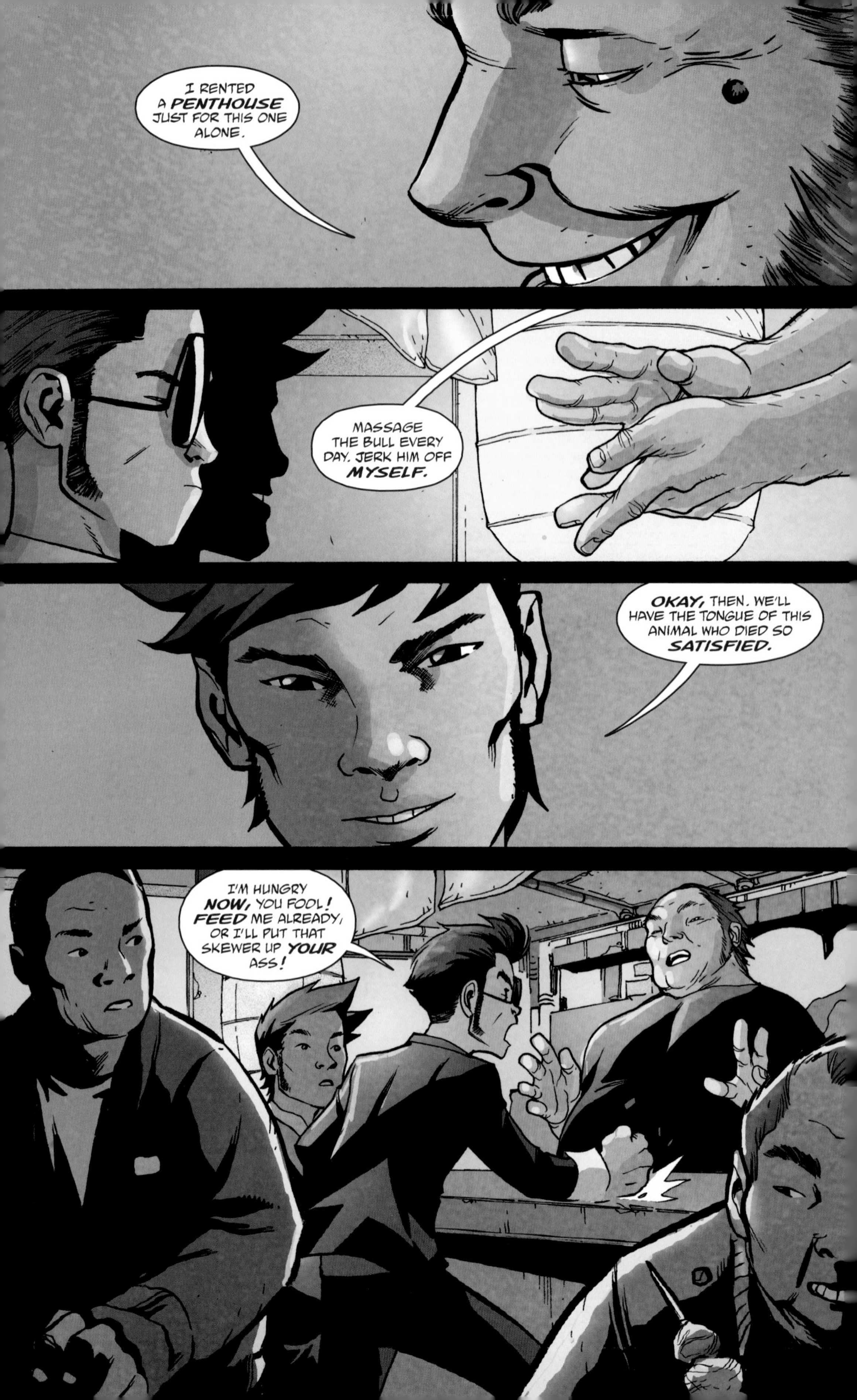
I RENTED A PENTHOUSE JUST FOR THIS ONE ALONE.
MASSAGE THE BULL EVERY DAY. JERK HIM OFF MYSELF.
OKAY, THEN. WE'LL HAVE THE TONGUE OF THIS ANIMAL WHO DIED SO SATISFIED.
I'M HUNGRY NOW, YOU FOOL! FEED ME ALREADY, OR I'LL PUT THAT SKEWER UP YOUR ASS!

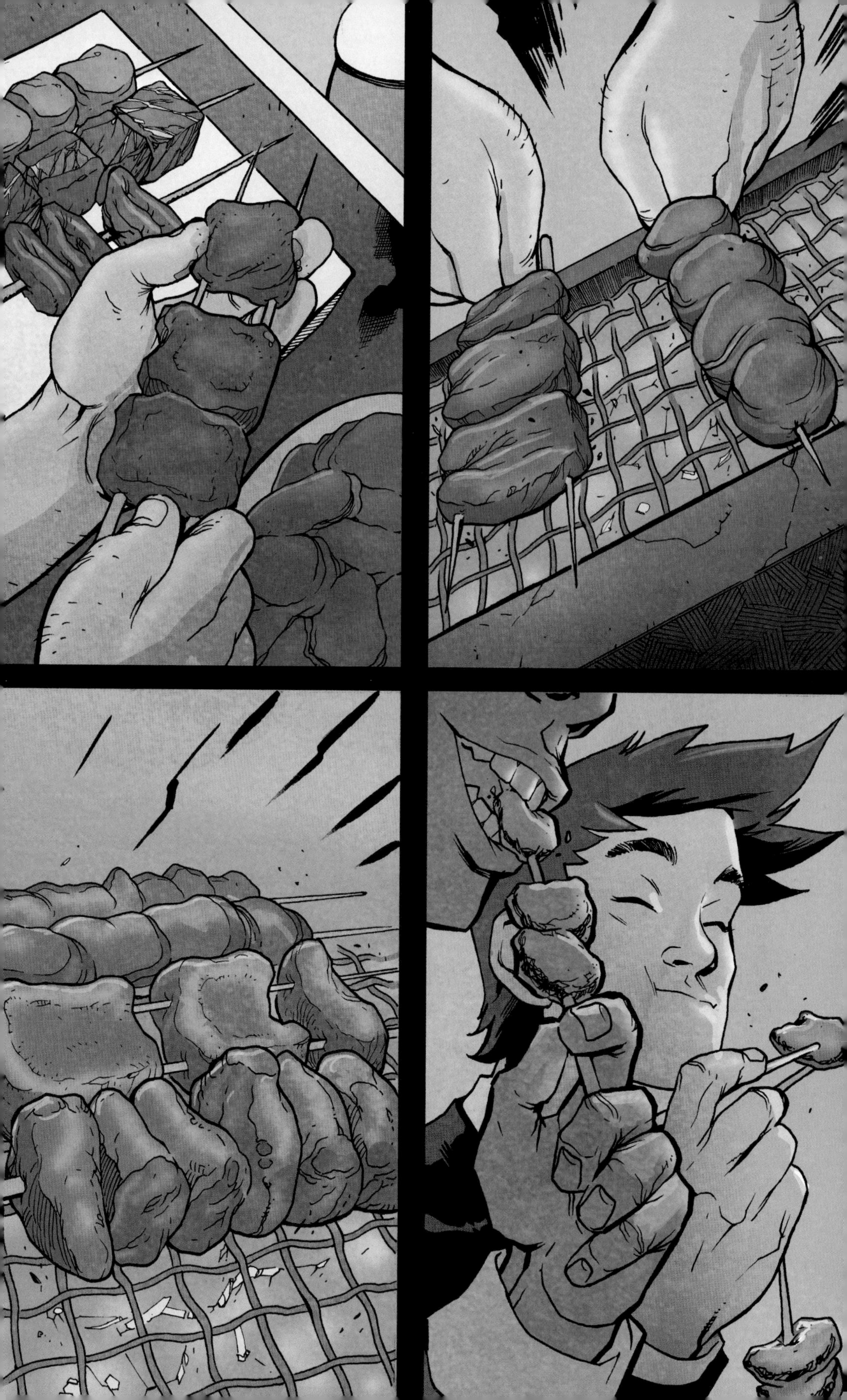

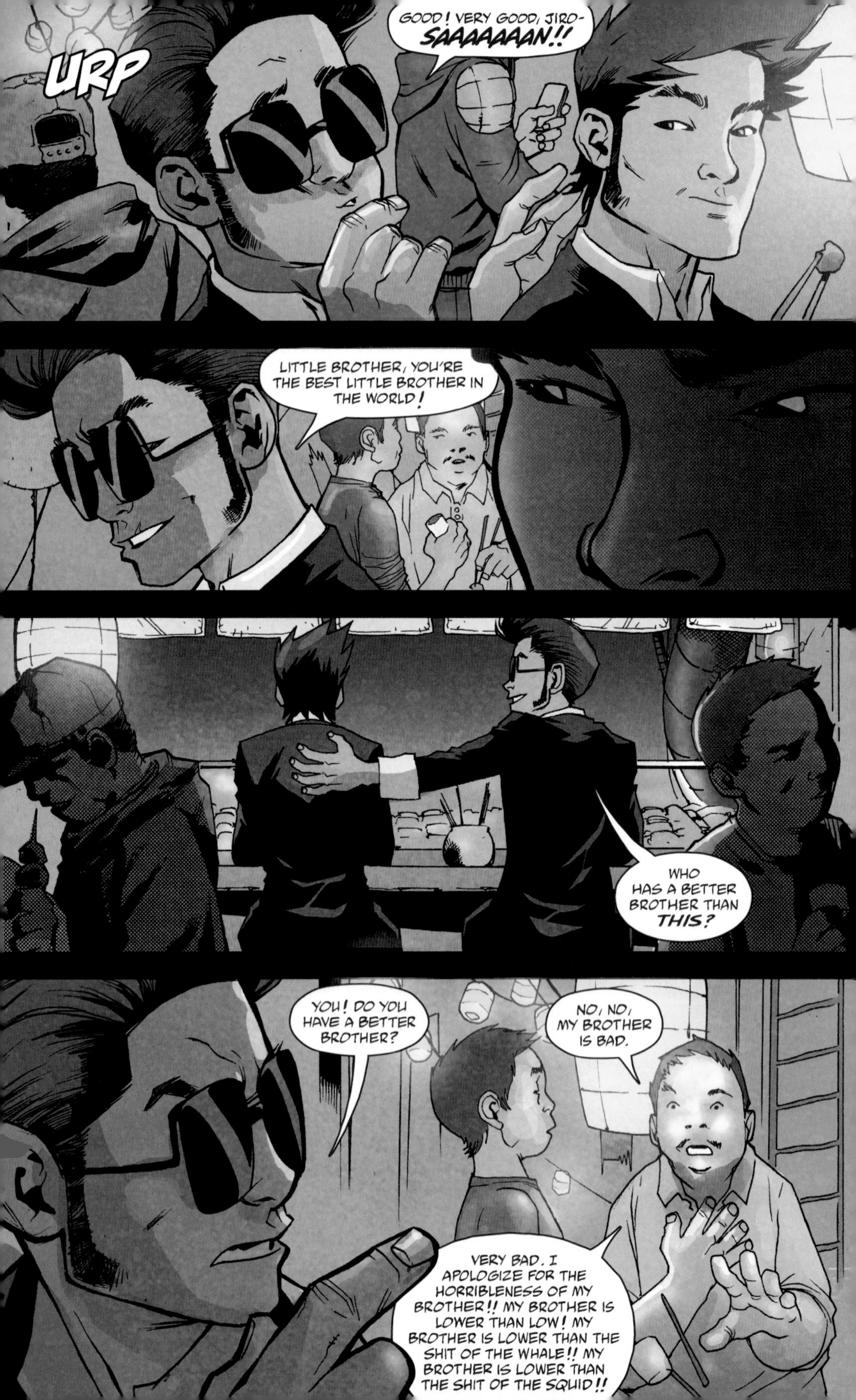
URP
GOOD! VERY GOOD, JIRO-SAAAAAAAN!!
LITTLE BROTHER, YOU'RE THE BEST LITTLE BROTHER IN THE WORLD!
WHO HAS A BETTER BROTHER THAN THIS?
YOU! DO YOU HAVE A BETTER BROTHER?
NO, NO, MY BROTHER IS BAD.
VERY BAD. I APOLOGIZE FOR THE HORRIBLENESS OF MY BROTHER!! MY BROTHER IS LOWER THAN LOW! MY BROTHER IS LOWER THAN THE SHIT OF THE WHALE!! MY BROTHER IS LOWER THAN THE SHIT OF THE SQUID!!

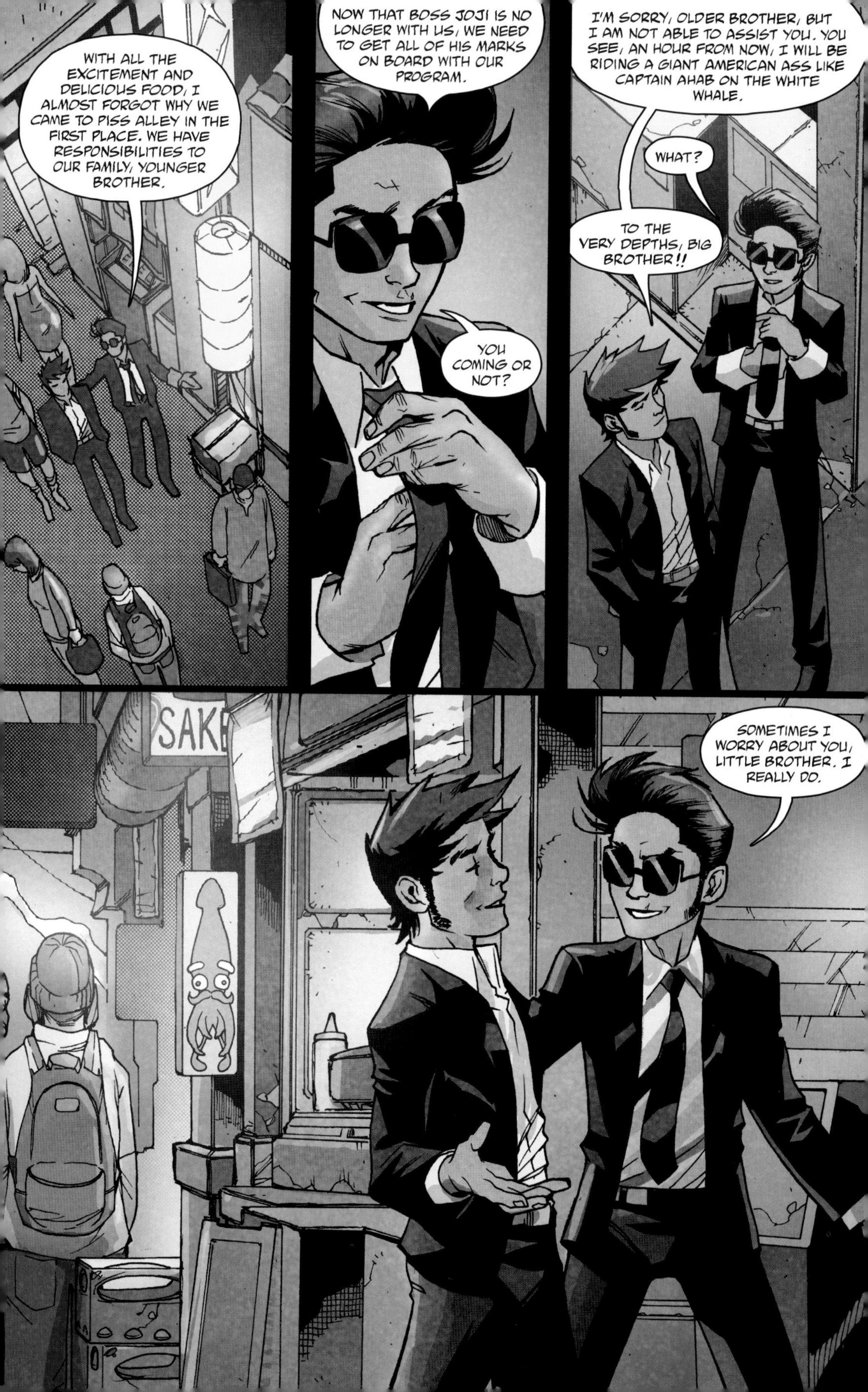
WITH ALL THE EXCITEMENT AND DELICIOUS FOOD, I ALMOST FORGOT WHY WE CAME TO PISS ALLEY IN THE FIRST PLACE. WE HAVE RESPONSIBILITIES TO OUR FAMILY, YOUNGER BROTHER.
NOW THAT BOSS JOJI IS NO LONGER WITH US, WE NEED TO GET ALL OF HIS MARKS ON BOARD WITH OUR PROGRAM.
YOU COMING OR NOT?
I'M SORRY, OLDER BROTHER, BUT I AM NOT ABLE TO ASSIST YOU. YOU SEE, AN HOUR FROM NOW, I WILL BE RIDING A GIANT AMERICAN ASS LIKE CAPTAIN AHAB ON THE WHITE WHALE.
WHAT?
TO THE VERY DEPTHS, BIG BROTHER!!
SAKE
SOMETIMES I WORRY ABOUT YOU, LITTLE BROTHER. I REALLY DO.

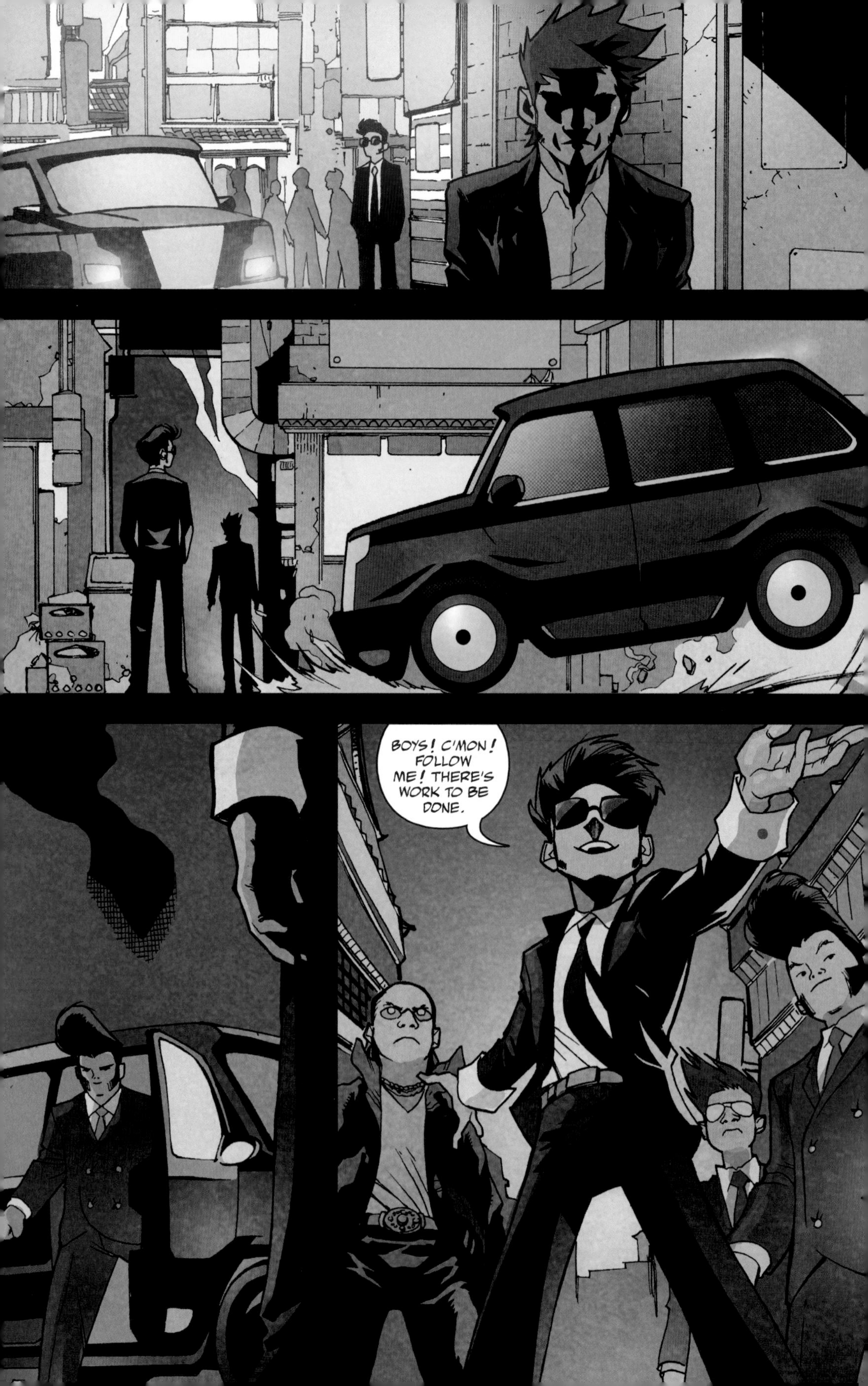
BOYS! C'MON! FOLLOW ME! THERE'S WORK TO BE DONE.

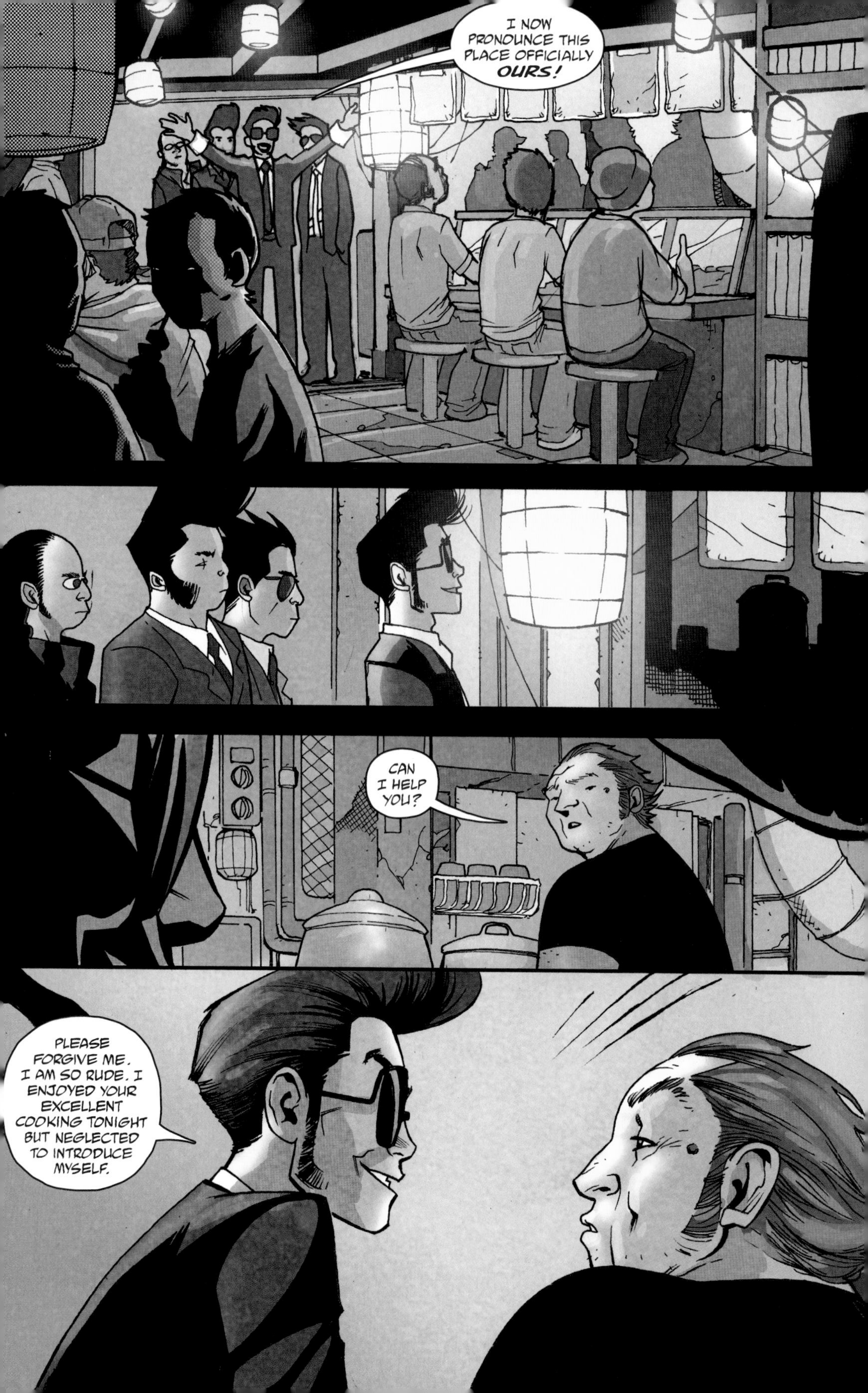
I NOW PRONOUNCE THIS PLACE OFFICIALLY OURS!
CAN I HELP YOU?
PLEASE FORGIVE ME. I AM SO RUDE. I ENJOYED YOUR EXCELLENT COOKING TONIGHT BUT NEGLECTED TO INTRODUCE MYSELF.

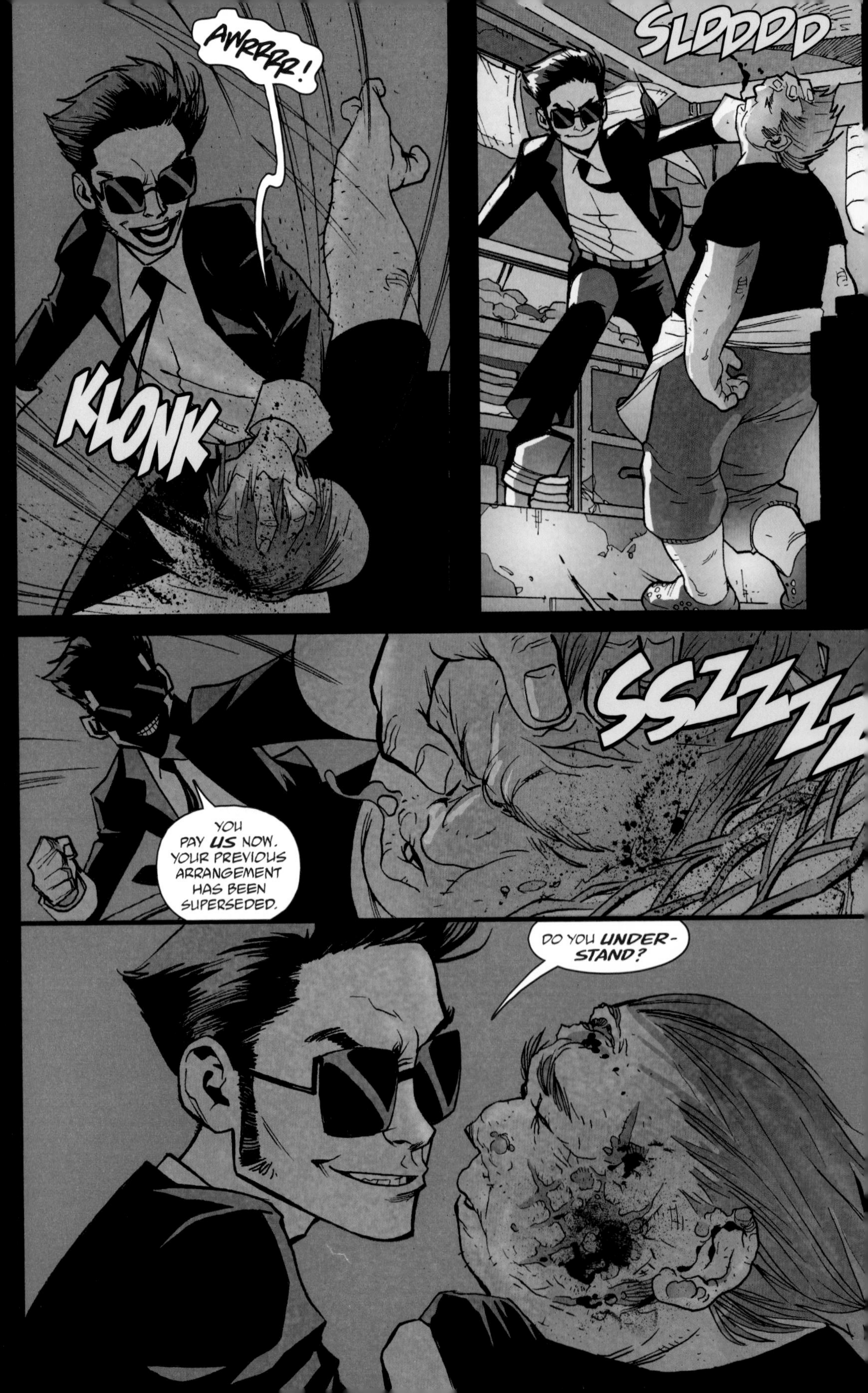
AWRRRR!
KLONK
SLDDDD
SSZZZZ
YOU PAY US NOW. YOUR PREVIOUS ARRANGEMENT HAS BEEN SUPERSEDED.
DO YOU UNDERSTAND?

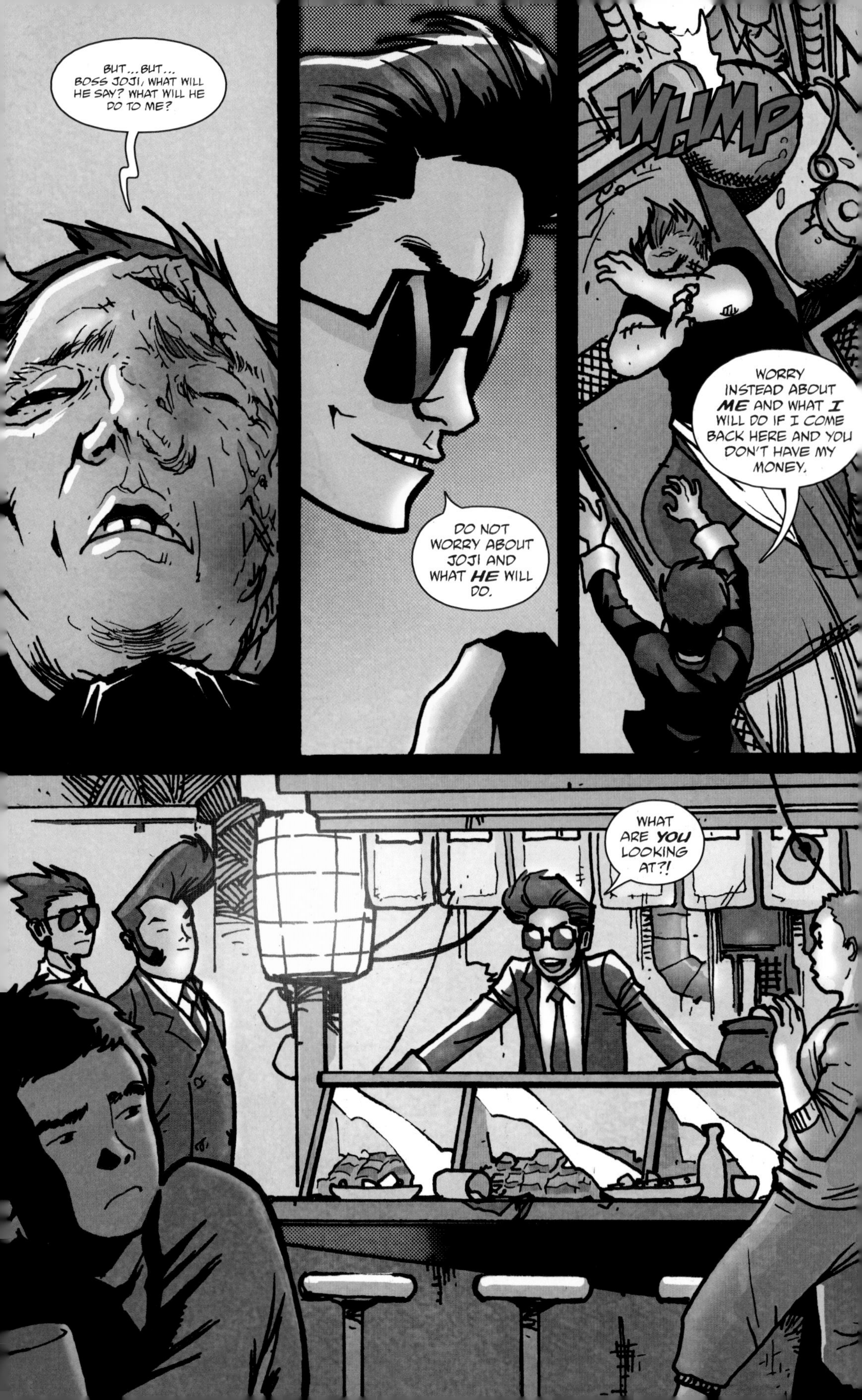
BUT... BUT... BOSS JOJI, WHAT WILL HE SAY? WHAT WILL HE DO TO ME?
DO NOT WORRY ABOUT JOJI AND WHAT HE WILL DO.
WHMP
WORRY INSTEAD ABOUT ME AND WHAT I WILL DO IF I COME BACK HERE AND YOU DON'T HAVE MY MONEY.
WHAT ARE YOU LOOKING AT?!

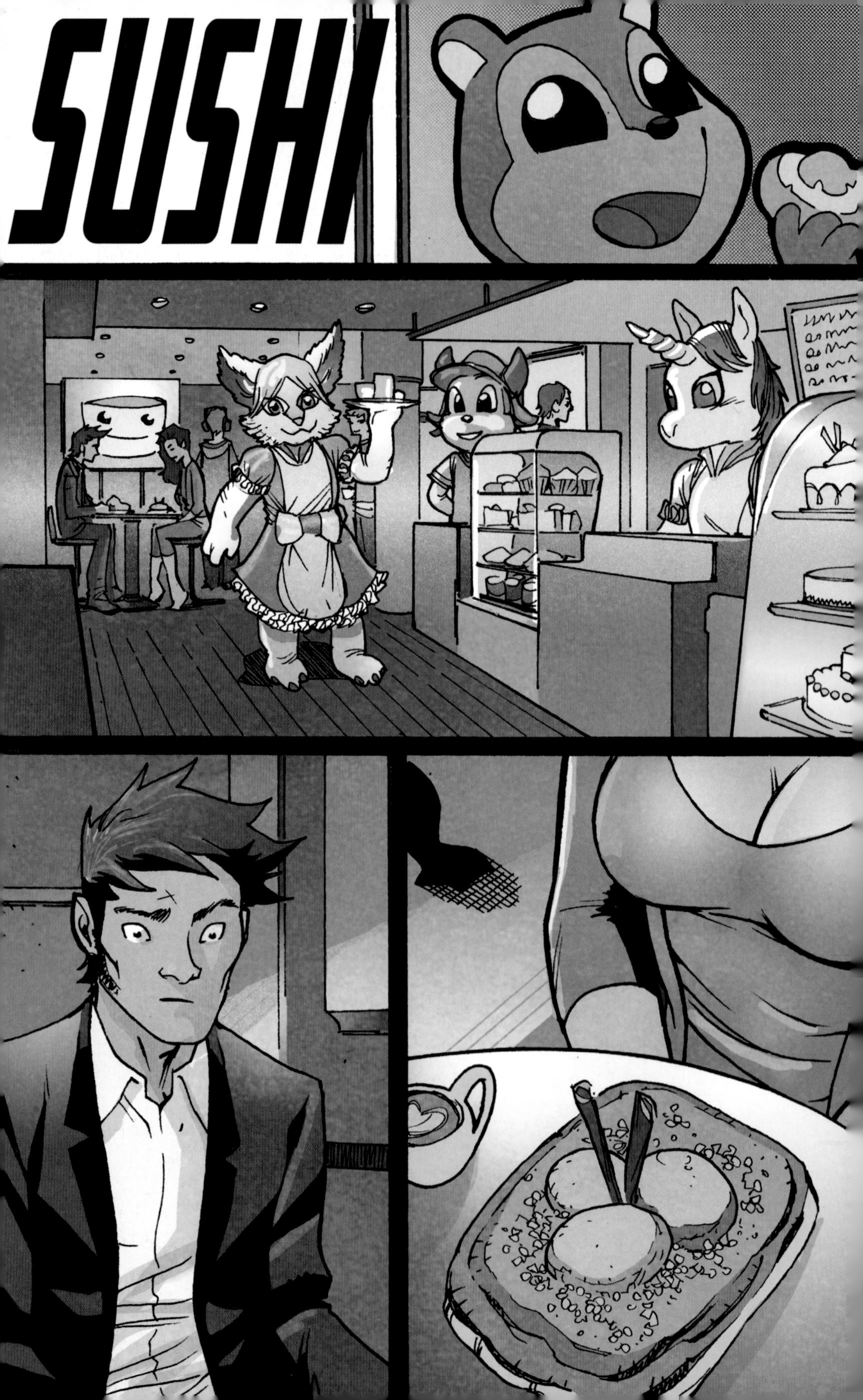
SUSHI

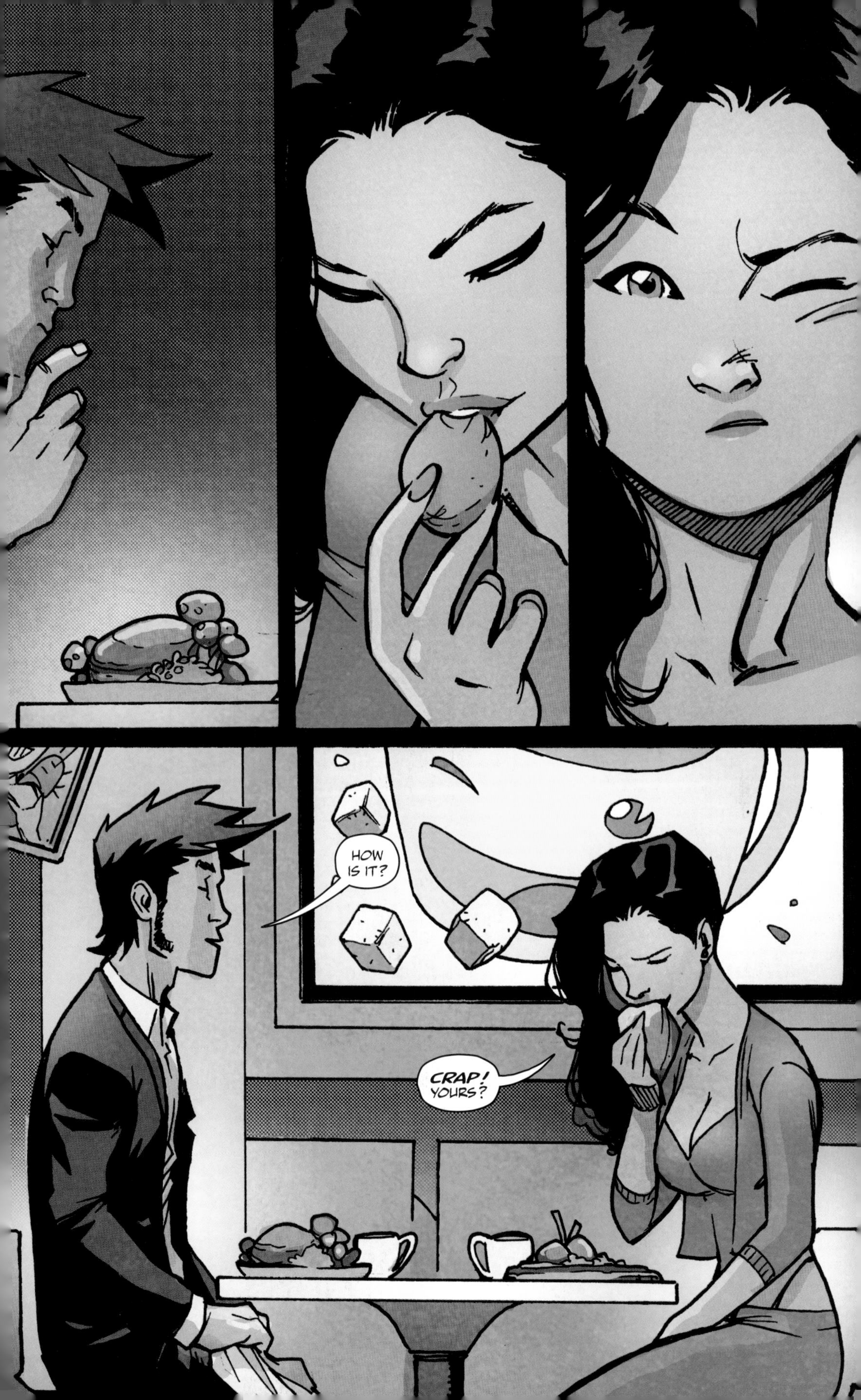
HOW IS IT?
CRAP! YOURS?

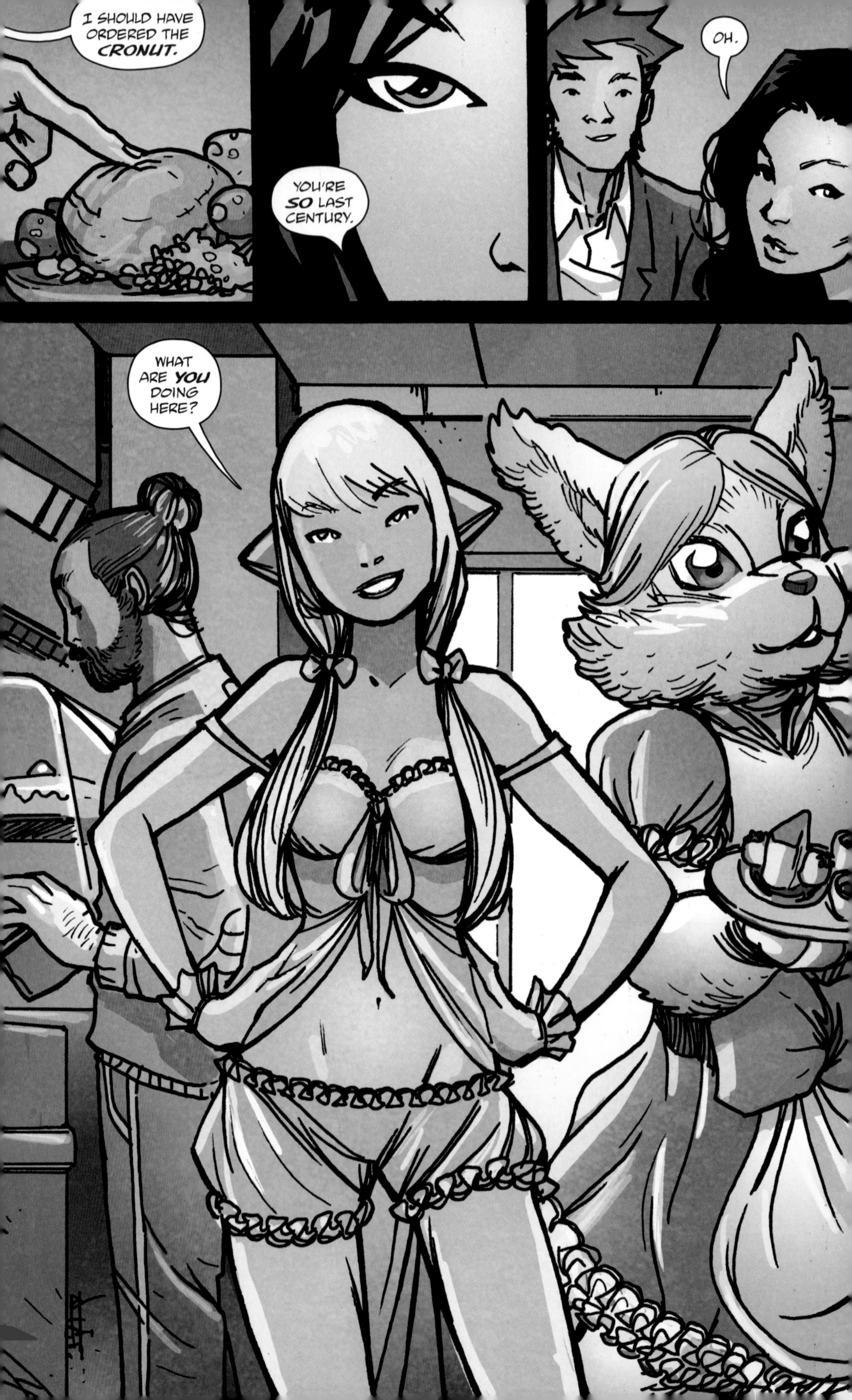
I SHOULD HAVE ORDERED THE **CRONUT.**
YOU'RE **SO** LAST CENTURY.
OH.
WHAT ARE **YOU** DOING HERE?

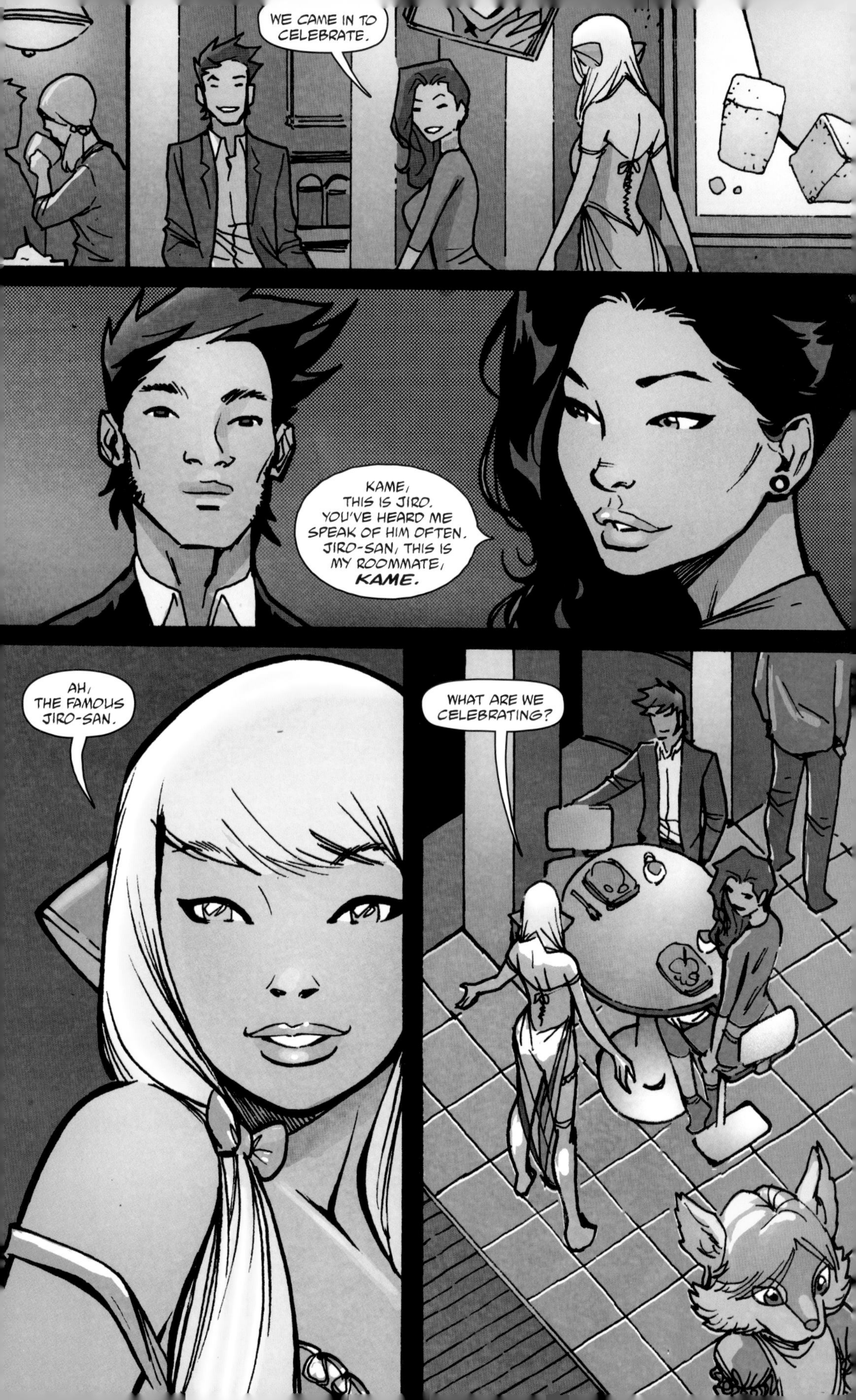
WE CAME IN TO CELEBRATE.
KAME, THIS IS JIRO. YOU'VE HEARD ME SPEAK OF HIM OFTEN. JIRO-SAN, THIS IS MY ROOMMATE, **KAME.**
AH, THE FAMOUS JIRO-SAN.
WHAT ARE WE CELEBRATING?

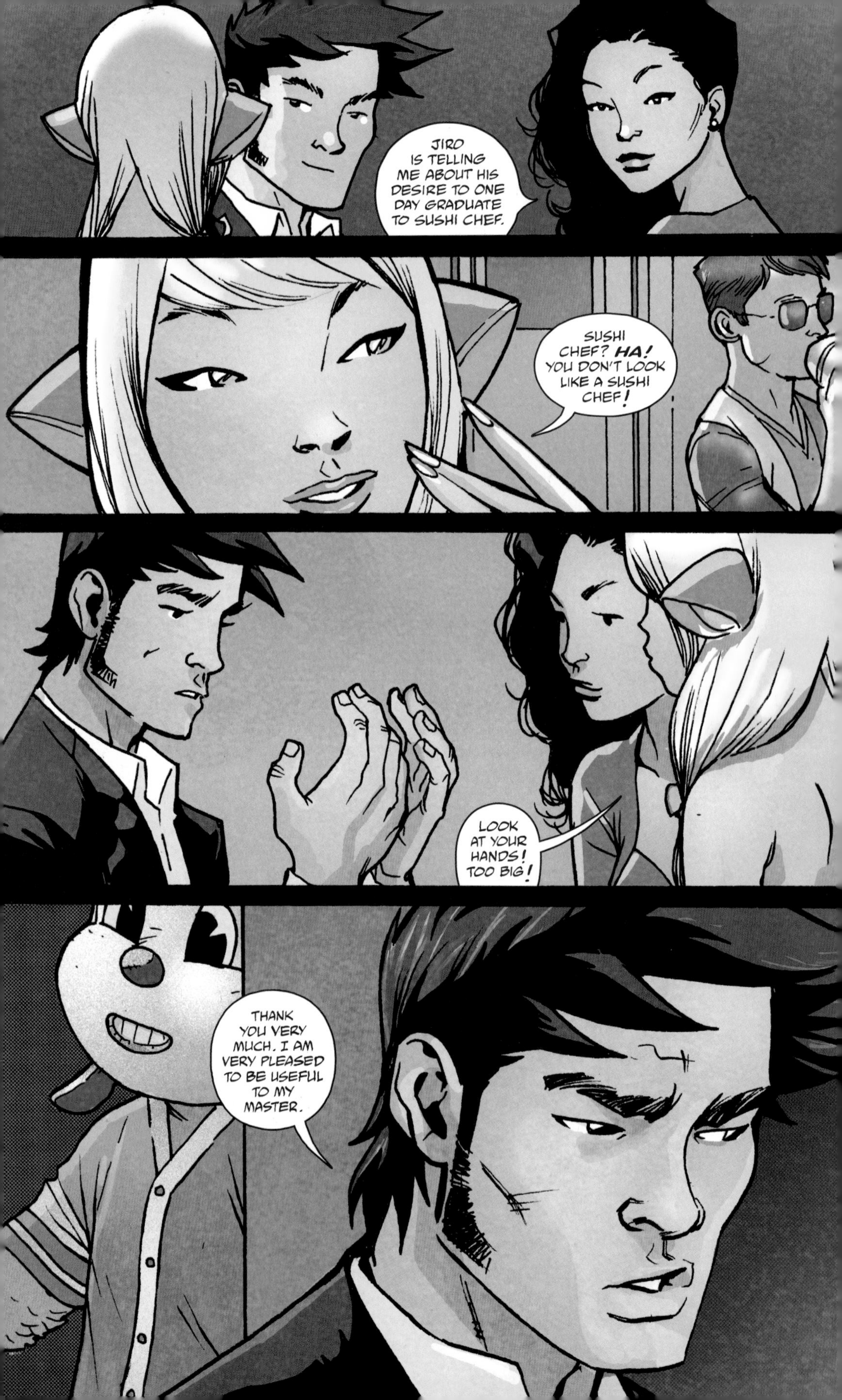
JIRO IS TELLING ME ABOUT HIS DESIRE TO ONE DAY GRADUATE TO SUSHI CHEF.
SUSHI CHEF? HA! YOU DON'T LOOK LIKE A SUSHI CHEF!
LOOK AT YOUR HANDS! TOO BIG!
THANK YOU VERY MUCH. I AM VERY PLEASED TO BE USEFUL TO MY MASTER.

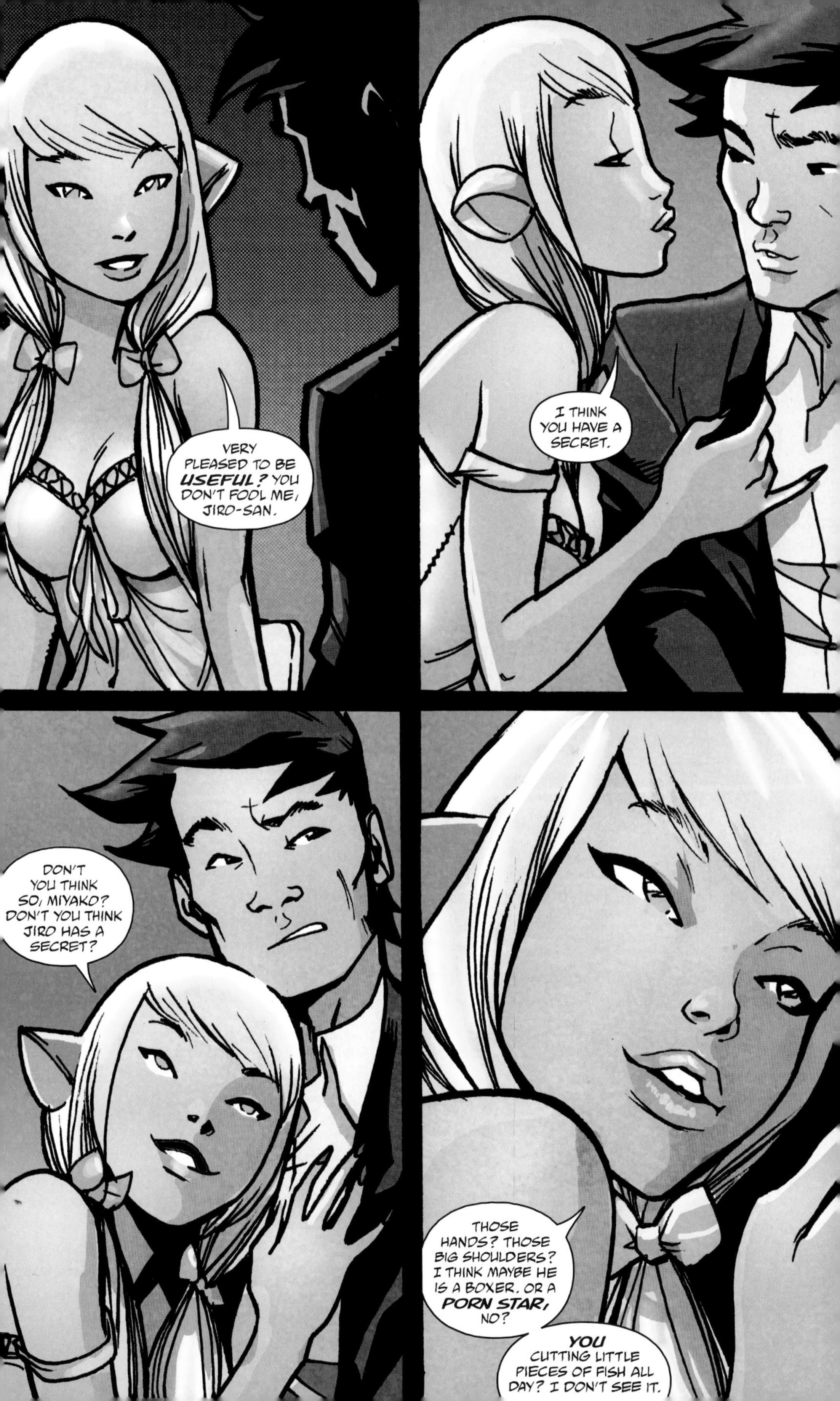
VERY PLEASED TO BE USEFUL? YOU DON'T FOOL ME, JIRO-SAN.
I THINK YOU HAVE A SECRET.
DON'T YOU THINK SO, MIYAKO? DON'T YOU THINK JIRO HAS A SECRET?
THOSE HANDS? THOSE BIG SHOULDERS? I THINK MAYBE HE IS A BOXER. OR A PORN STAR, NO?
YOU CUTTING LITTLE PIECES OF FISH ALL DAY? I DON'T SEE IT.

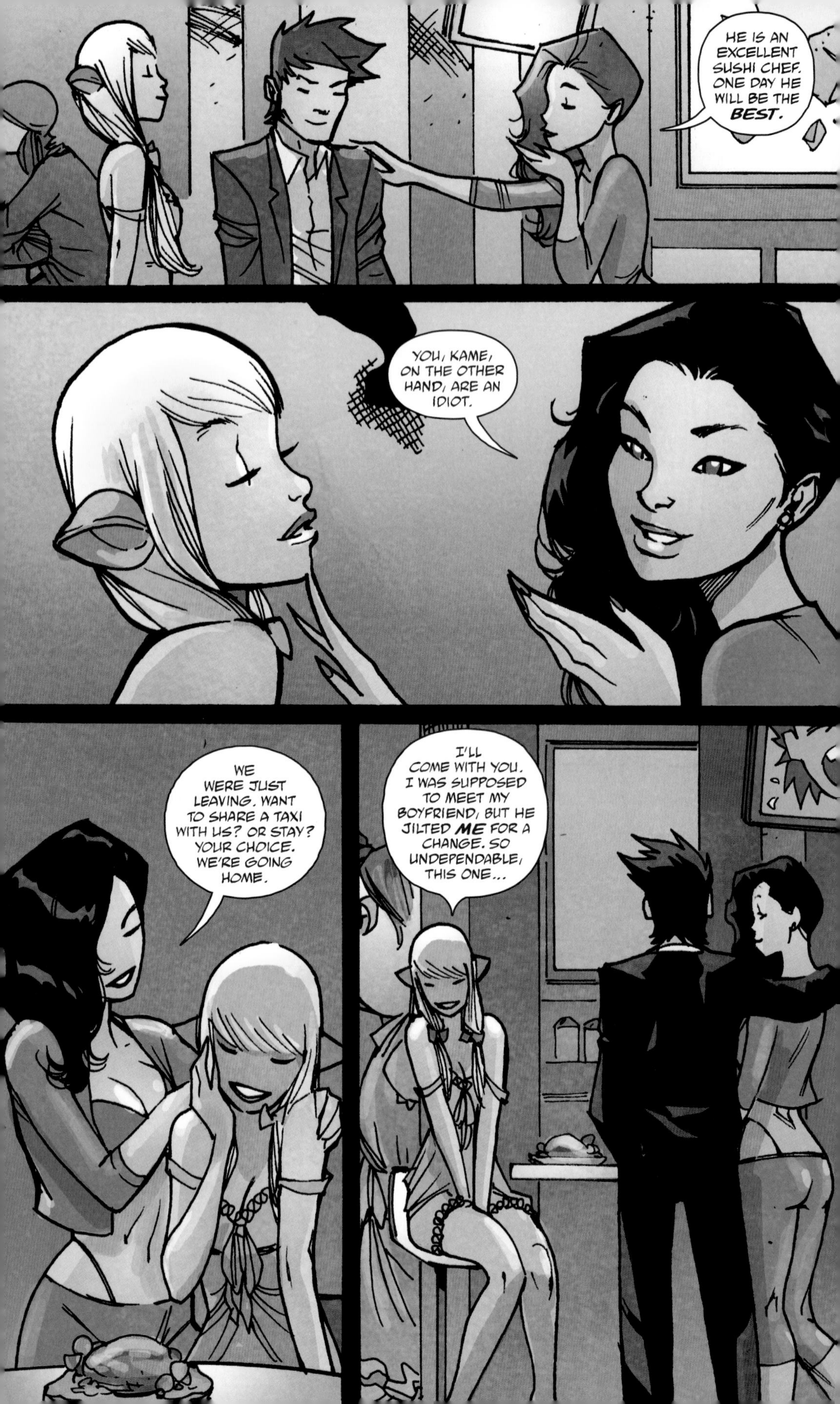
HE IS AN EXCELLENT SUSHI CHEF. ONE DAY HE WILL BE THE BEST.
YOU, KAME, ON THE OTHER HAND, ARE AN IDIOT.
WE WERE JUST LEAVING. WANT TO SHARE A TAXI WITH US? OR STAY? YOUR CHOICE. WE'RE GOING HOME.
I'LL COME WITH YOU. I WAS SUPPOSED TO MEET MY BOYFRIEND, BUT HE JILTED ME FOR A CHANGE. SO UNDEPENDABLE, THIS ONE...

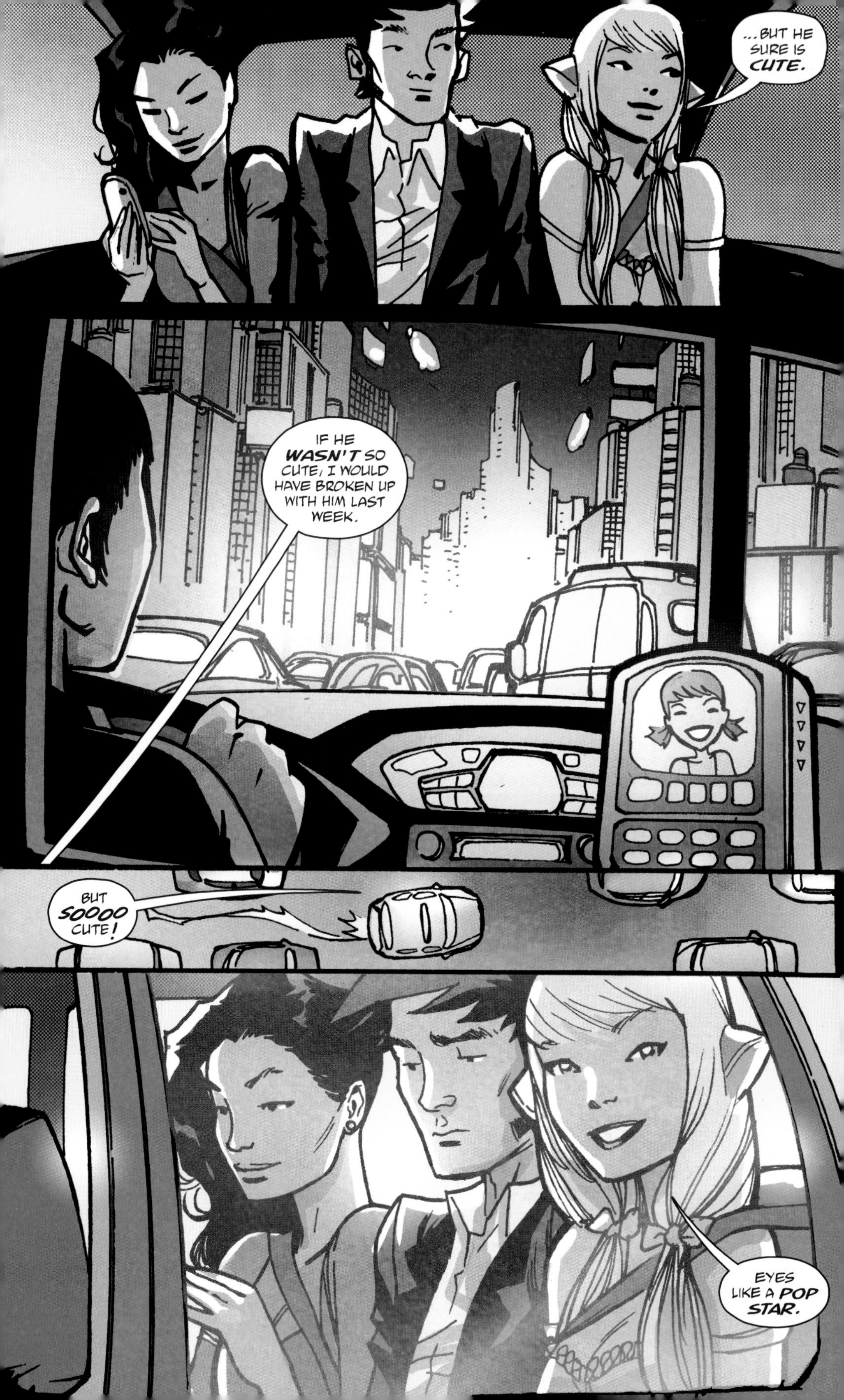
...BUT HE SURE IS CUTE.
IF HE WASN'T SO CUTE, I WOULD HAVE BROKEN UP WITH HIM LAST WEEK.
BUT SOOOO CUTE!
EYES LIKE A POP STAR.

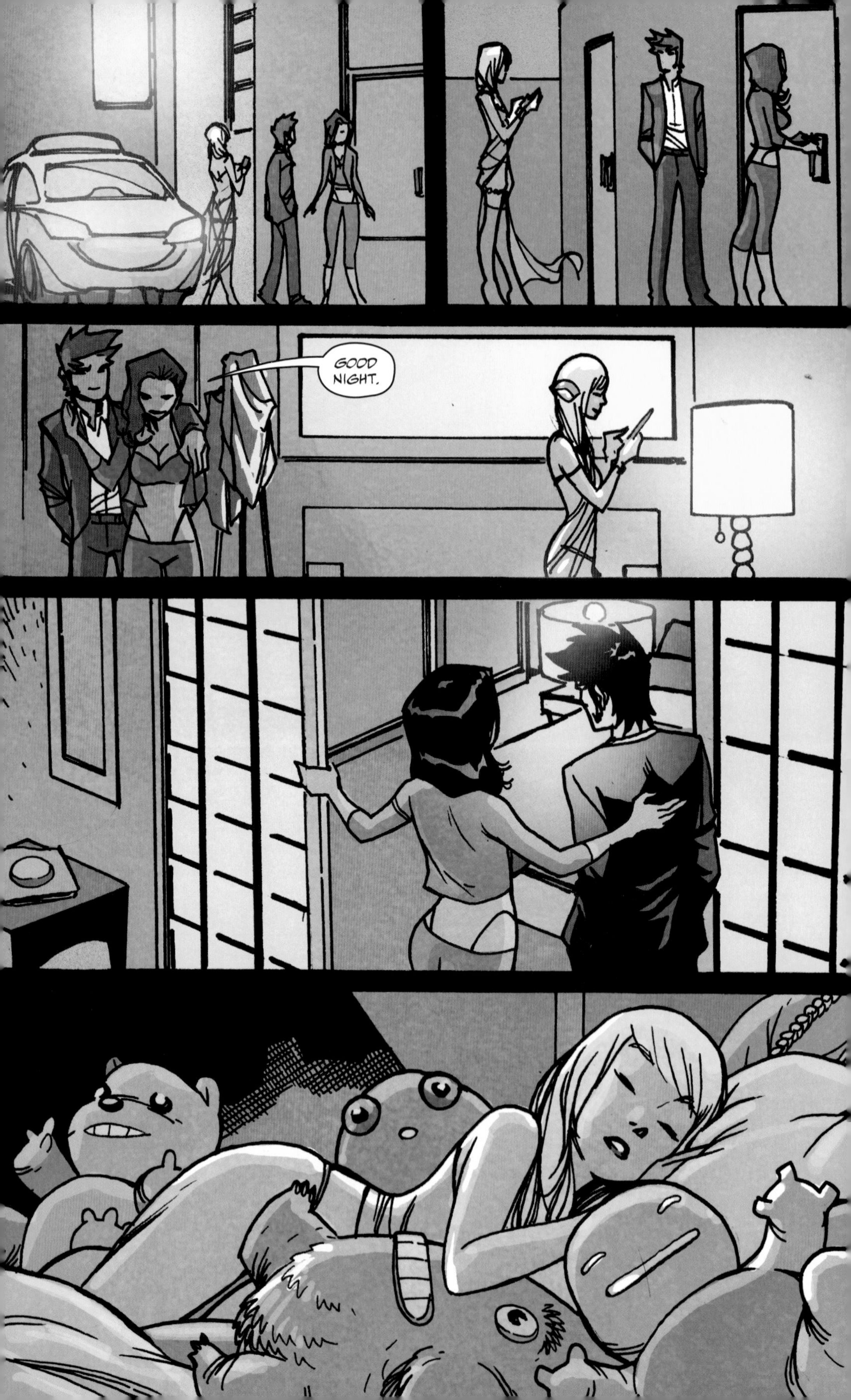
GOOD NIGHT.

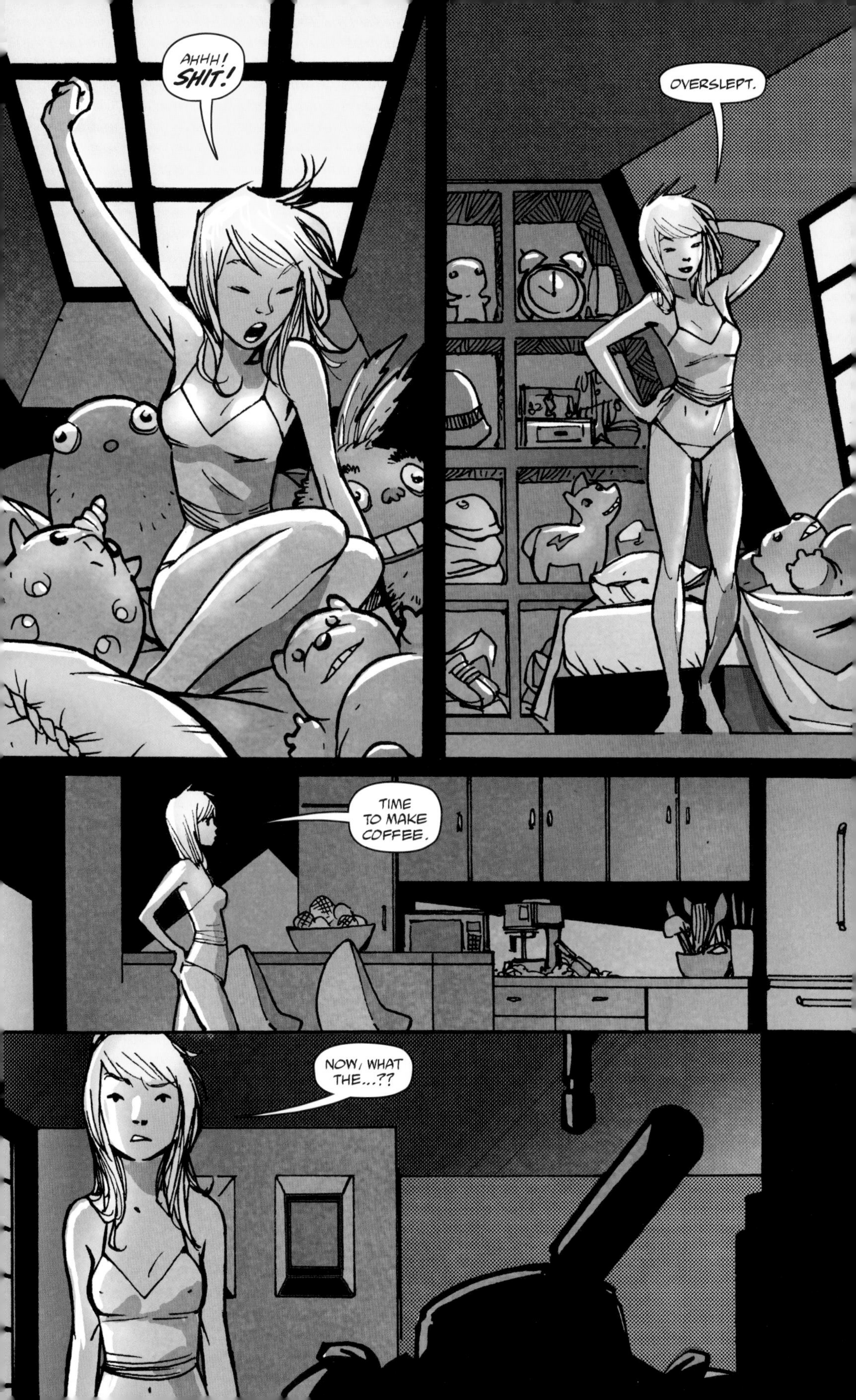
AHHH! SHIT!
OVERSLEPT.
TIME TO MAKE COFFEE.
NOW, WHAT THE...??

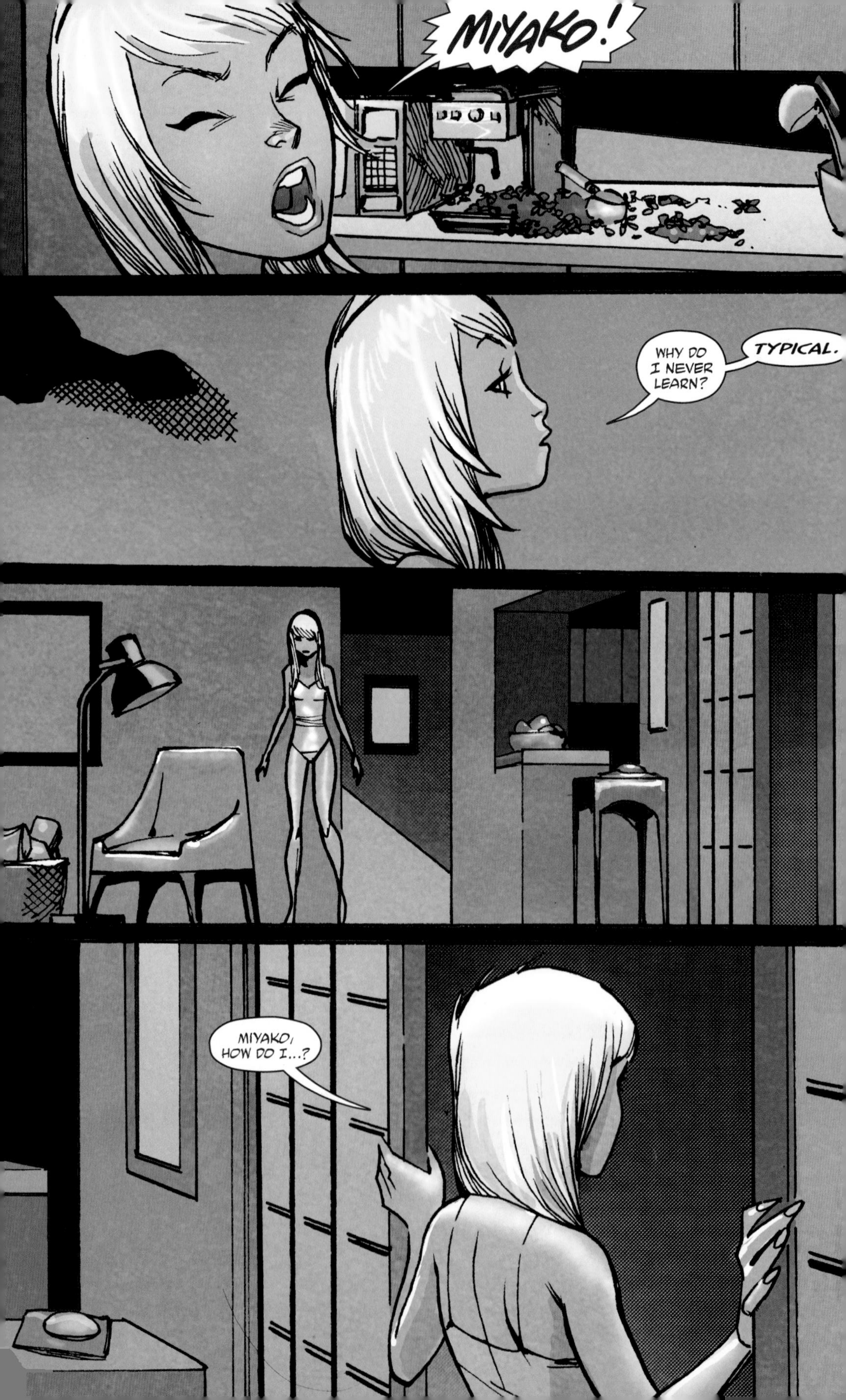
MIYAKO!
WHY DO I NEVER LEARN?
TYPICAL.
MIYAKO, HOW DO I...?

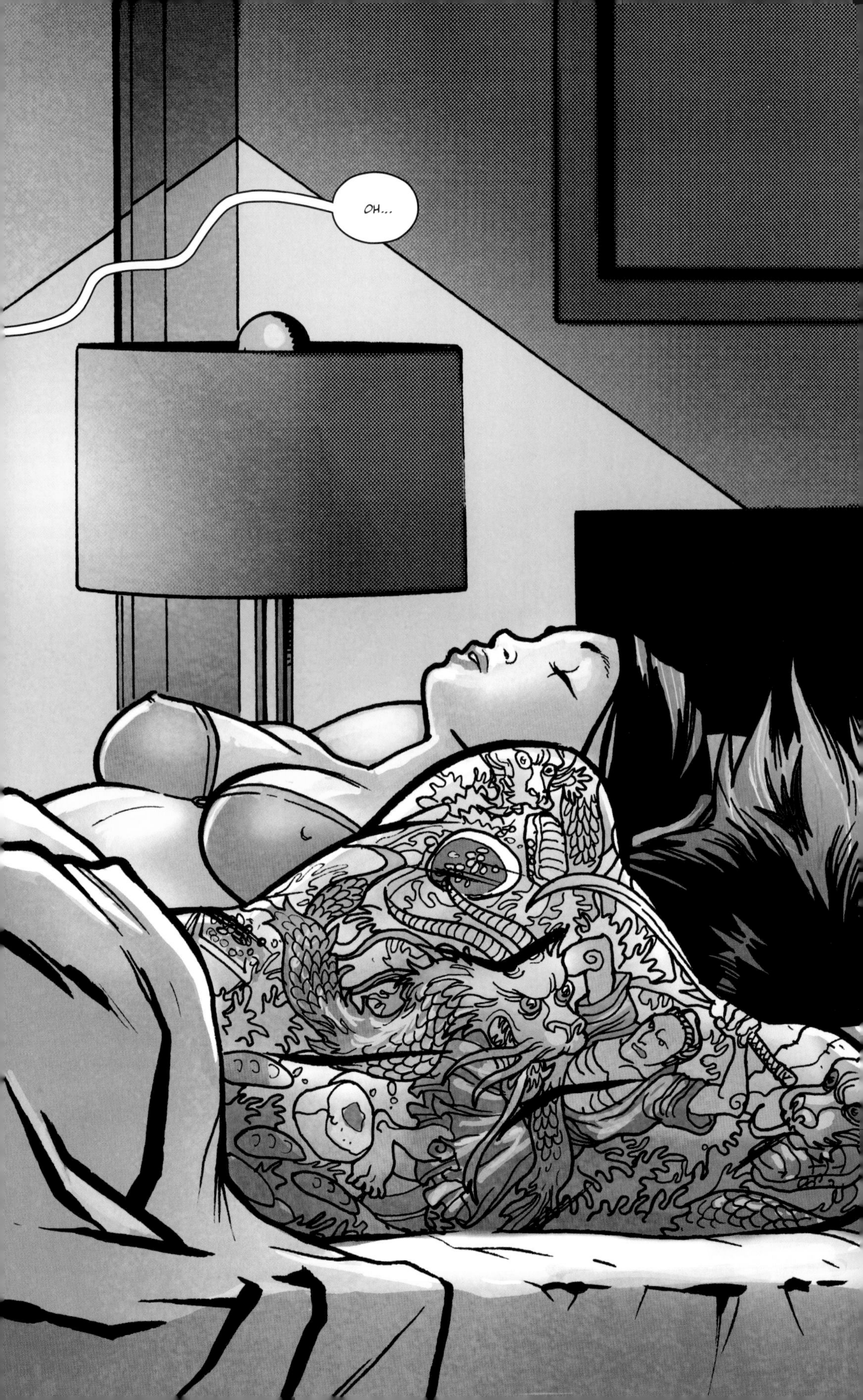
OH...

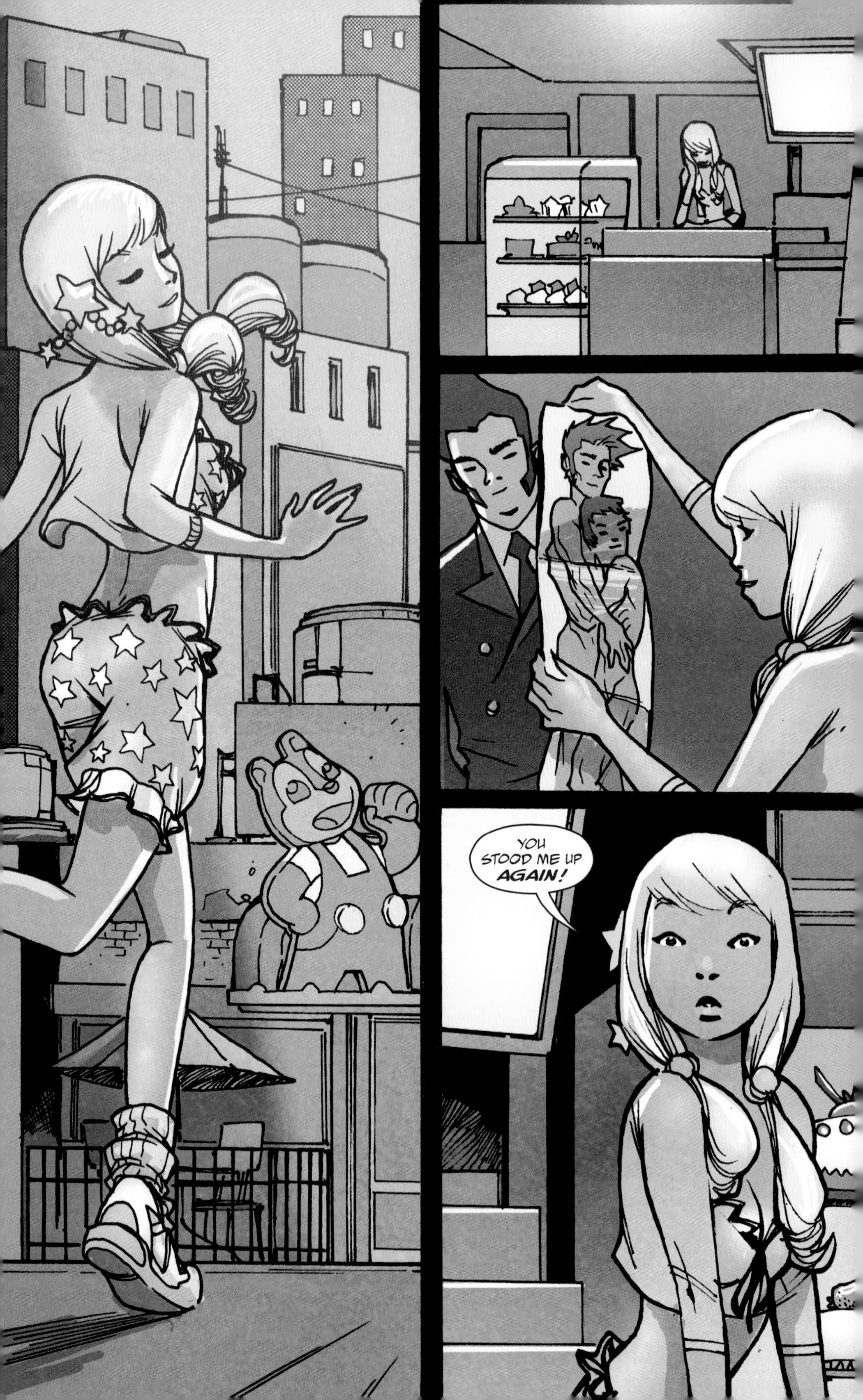
YOU STOOD ME UP AGAIN!

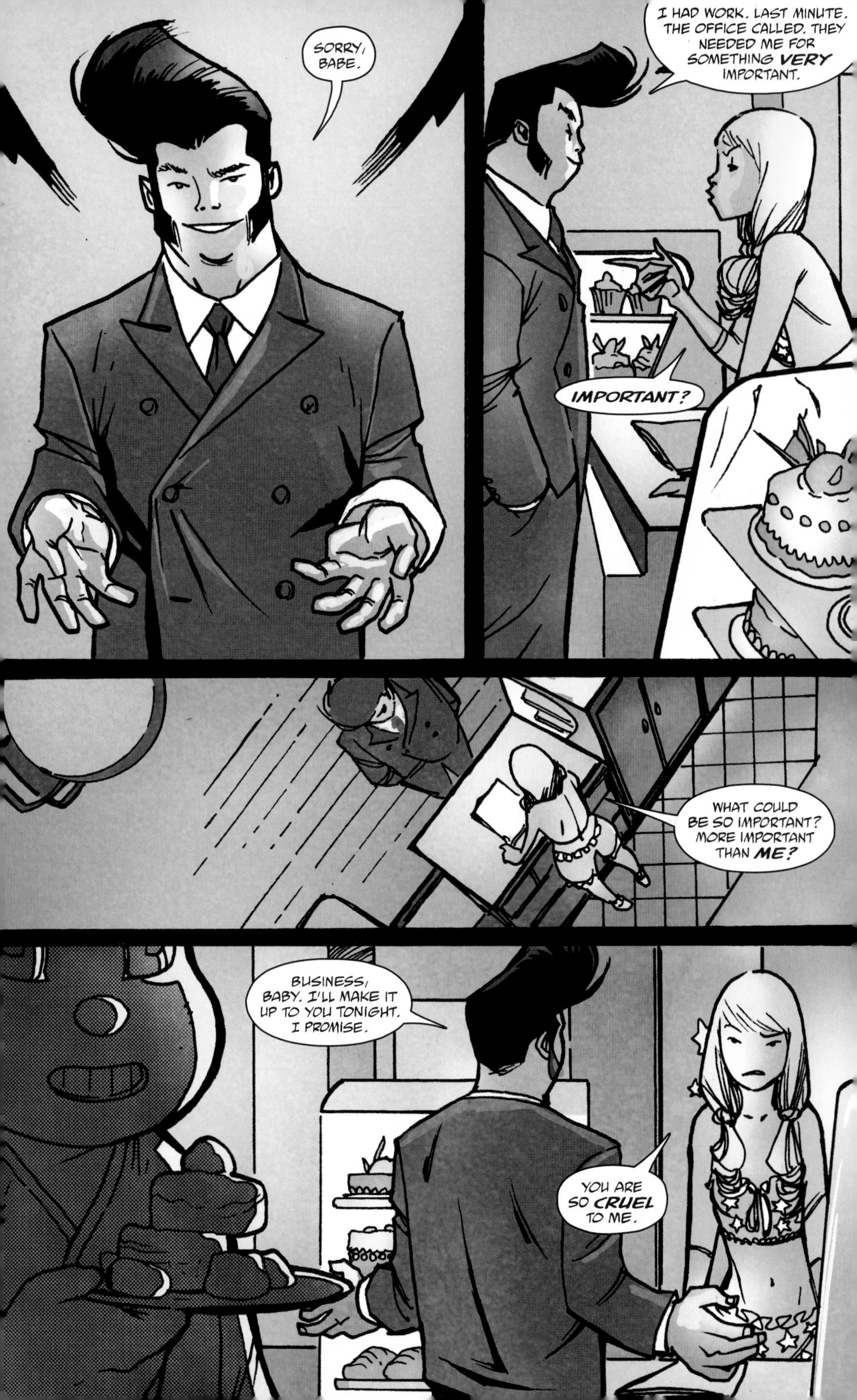
SORRY, BABE.
I HAD WORK. LAST MINUTE. THE OFFICE CALLED. THEY NEEDED ME FOR SOMETHING VERY IMPORTANT.
IMPORTANT?
WHAT COULD BE SO IMPORTANT? MORE IMPORTANT THAN ME?
BUSINESS, BABY. I'LL MAKE IT UP TO YOU TONIGHT. I PROMISE.
YOU ARE SO CRUEL TO ME.

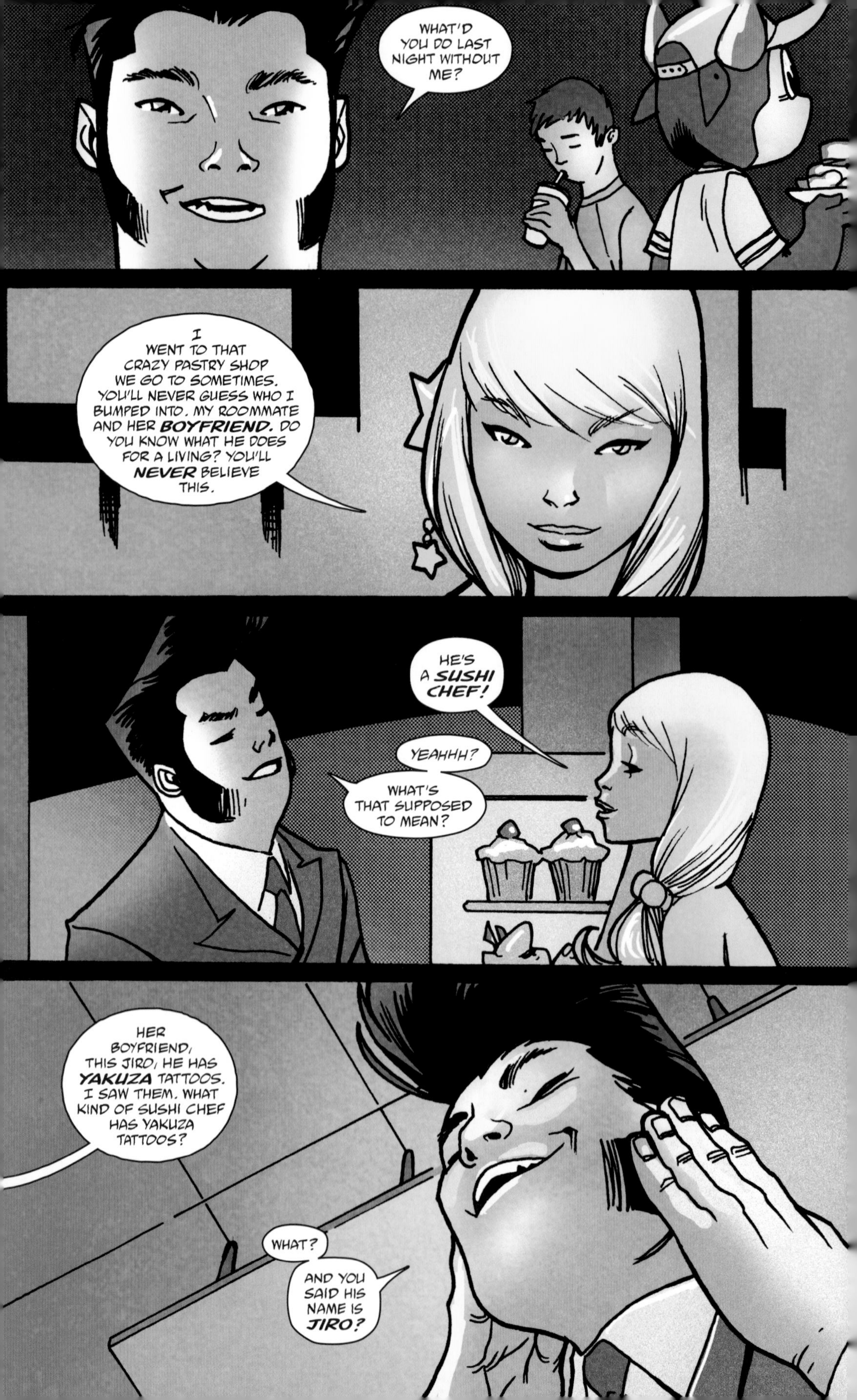

WHAT'D YOU DO LAST NIGHT WITHOUT ME?
I WENT TO THAT CRAZY PASTRY SHOP WE GO TO SOMETIMES. YOU'LL NEVER GUESS WHO I BUMPED INTO. MY ROOMMATE AND HER BOYFRIEND. DO YOU KNOW WHAT HE DOES FOR A LIVING? YOU'LL NEVER BELIEVE THIS.
HE'S A SUSHI CHEF!
YEAHHH?
WHAT'S THAT SUPPOSED TO MEAN?
HER BOYFRIEND, THIS JIRO, HE HAS YAKUZA TATTOOS. I SAW THEM. WHAT KIND OF SUSHI CHEF HAS YAKUZA TATTOOS?
WHAT?
AND YOU SAID HIS NAME IS JIRO?

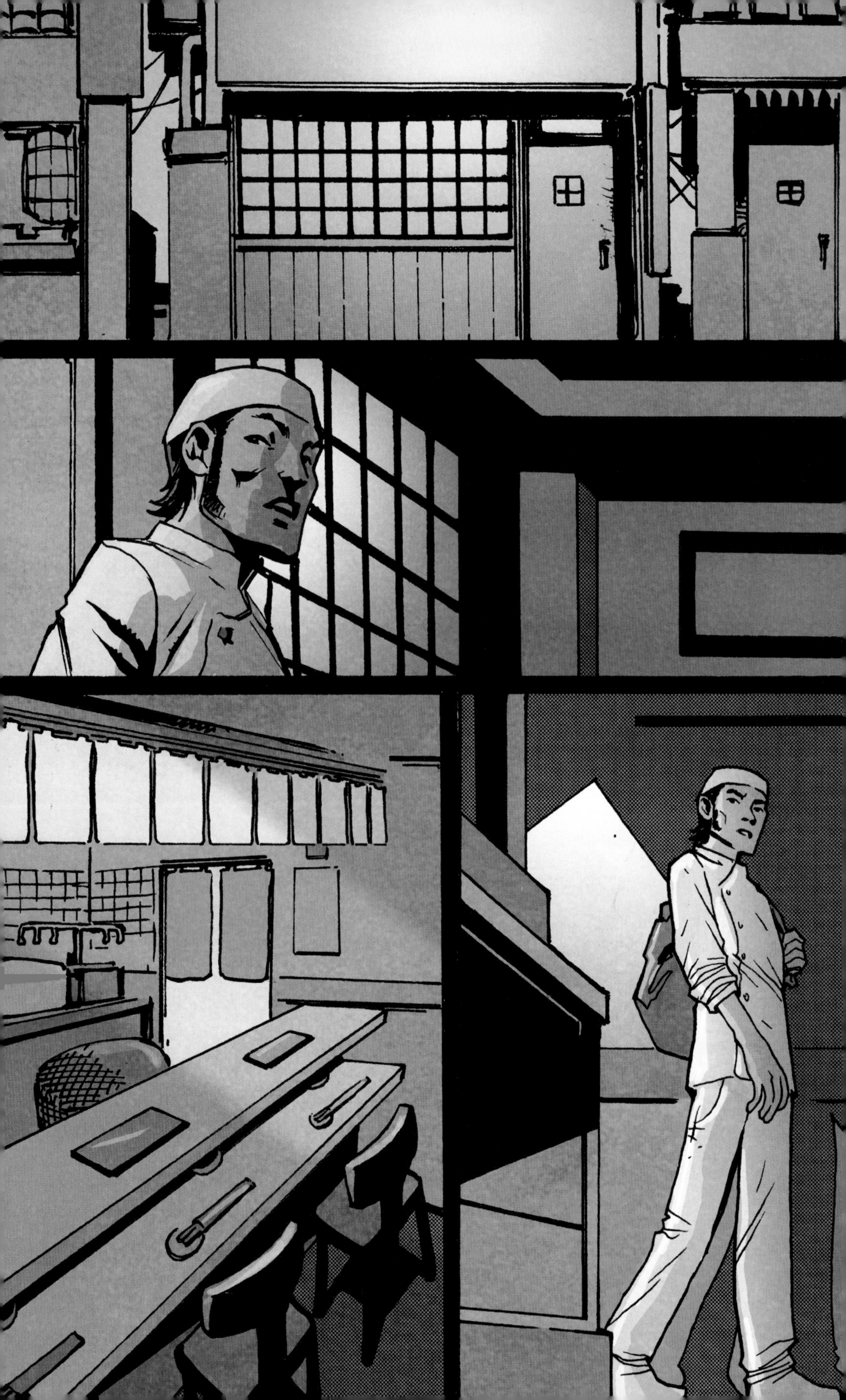

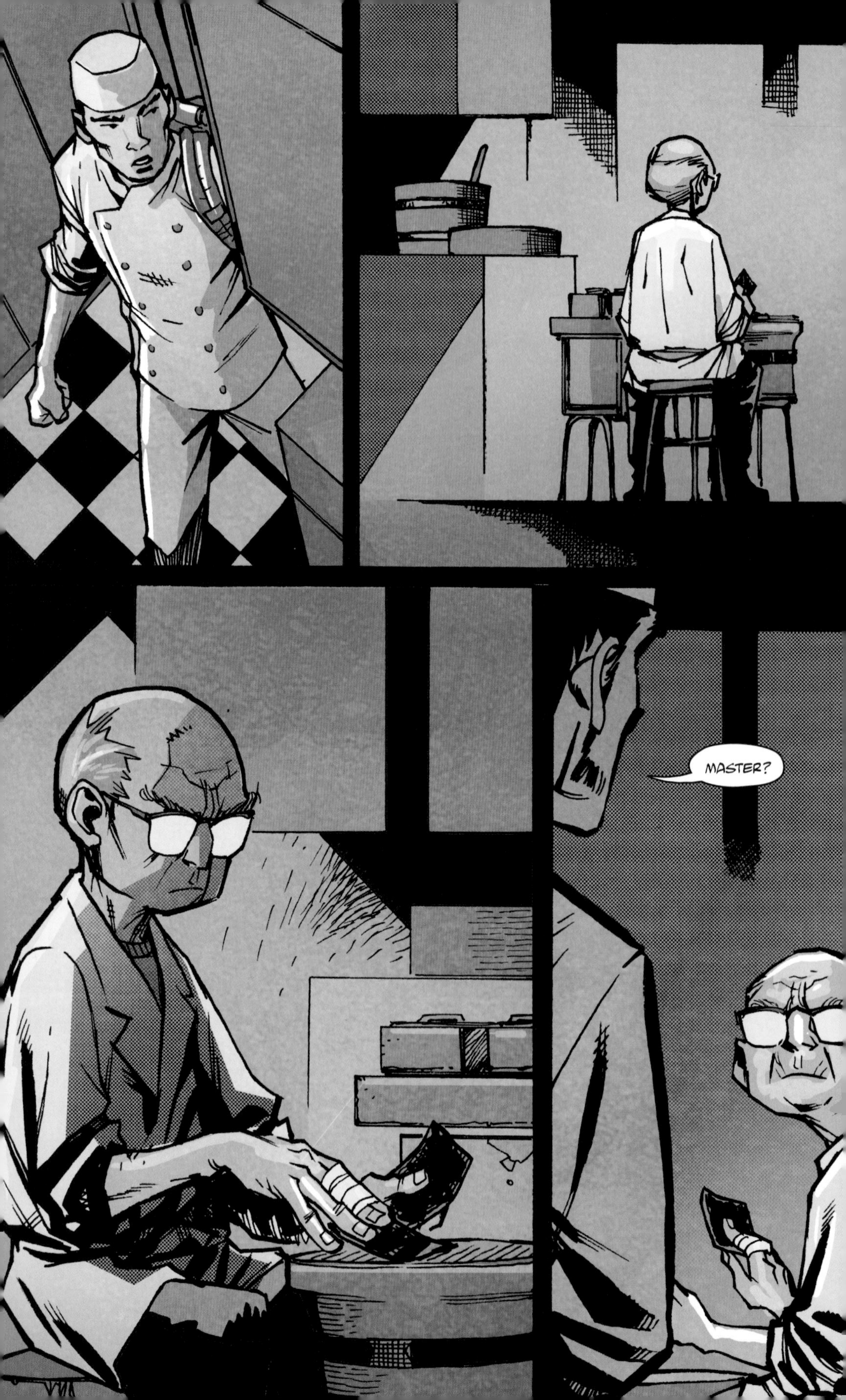
MASTER?

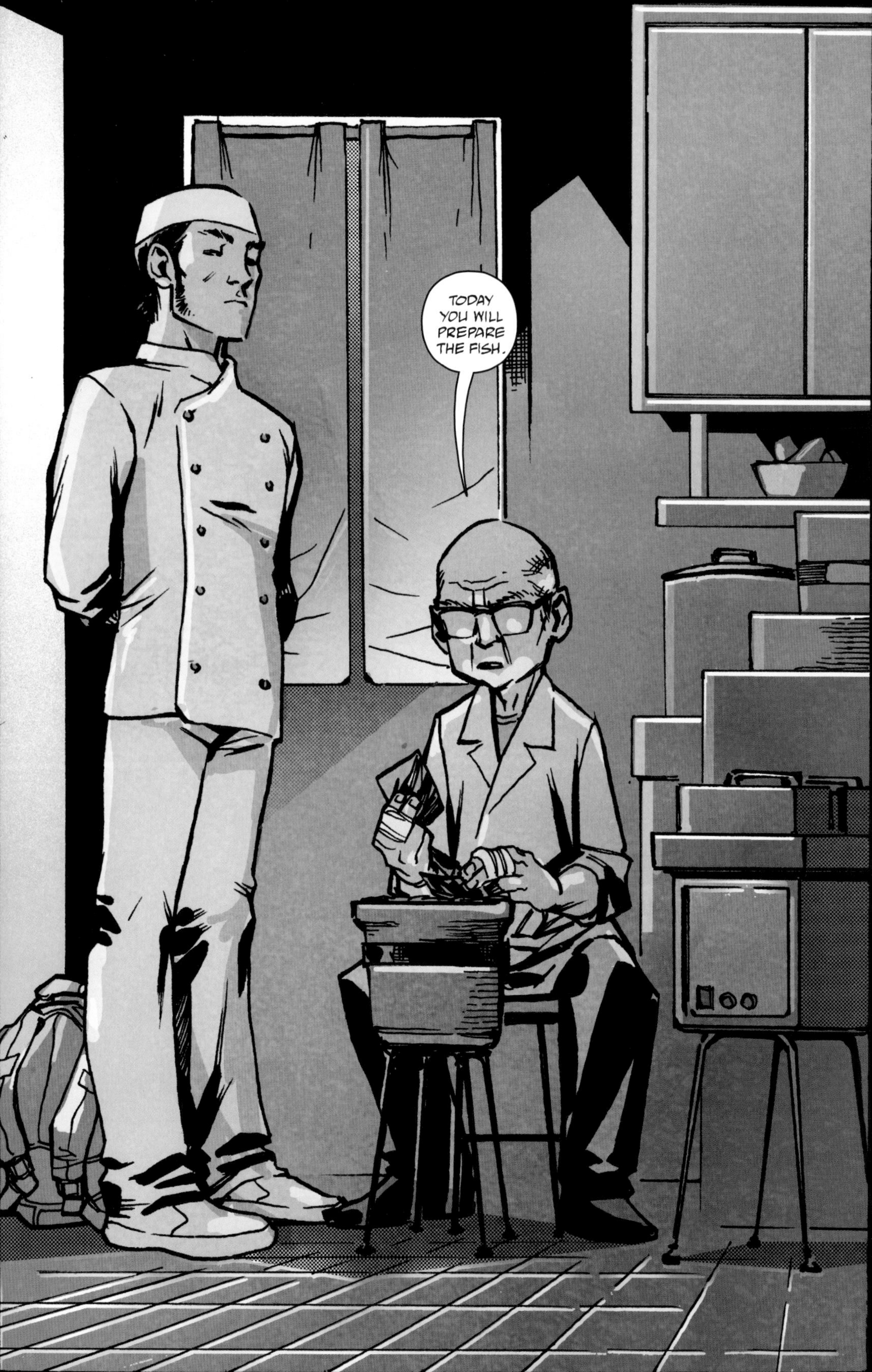
TODAY YOU WILL PREPARE THE FISH.

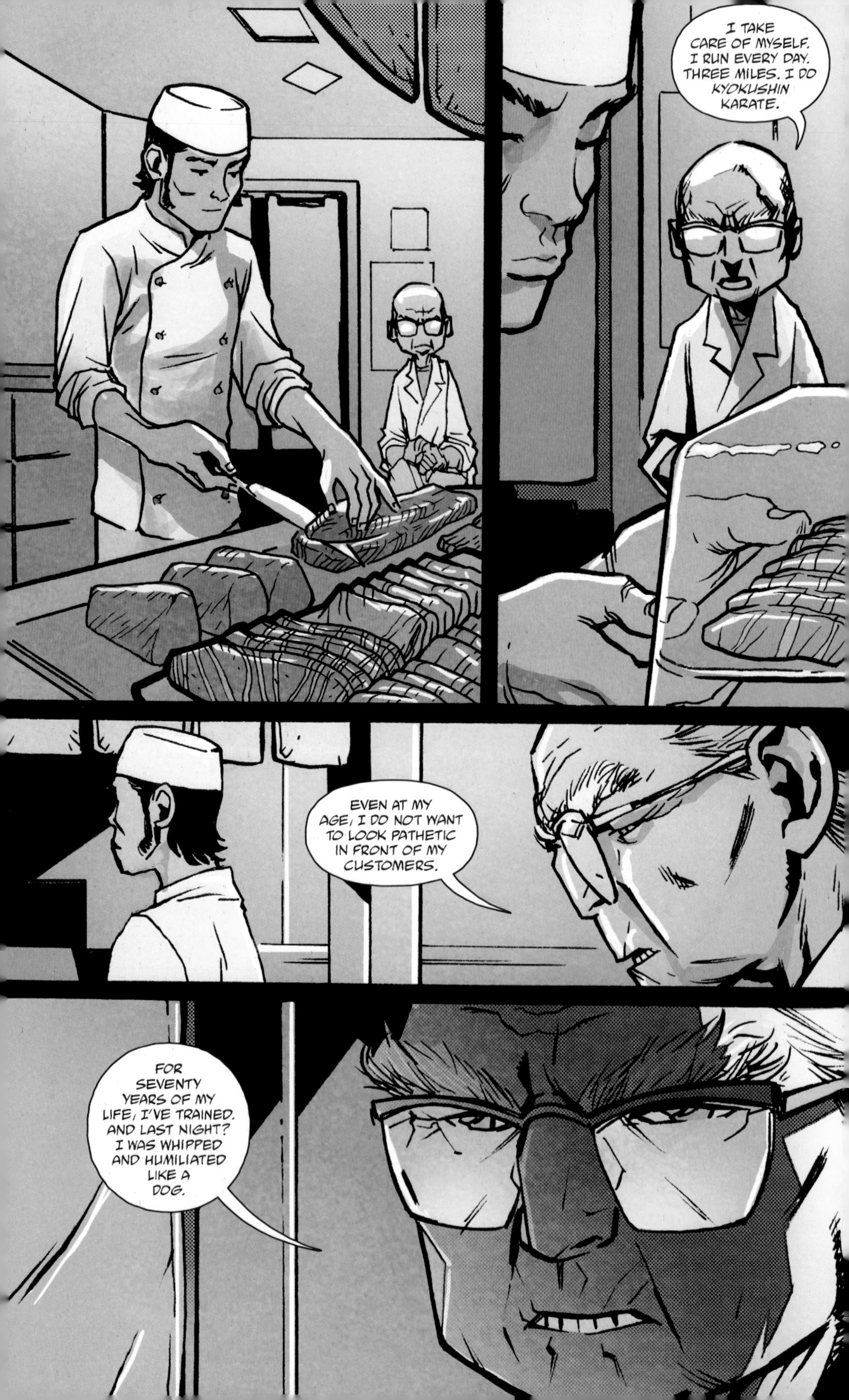
I TAKE CARE OF MYSELF. I RUN EVERY DAY. THREE MILES. I DO KYOKUSHIN KARATE.
EVEN AT MY AGE, I DO NOT WANT TO LOOK PATHETIC IN FRONT OF MY CUSTOMERS.
FOR SEVENTY YEARS OF MY LIFE, I'VE TRAINED. AND LAST NIGHT? I WAS WHIPPED AND HUMILIATED LIKE A DOG.

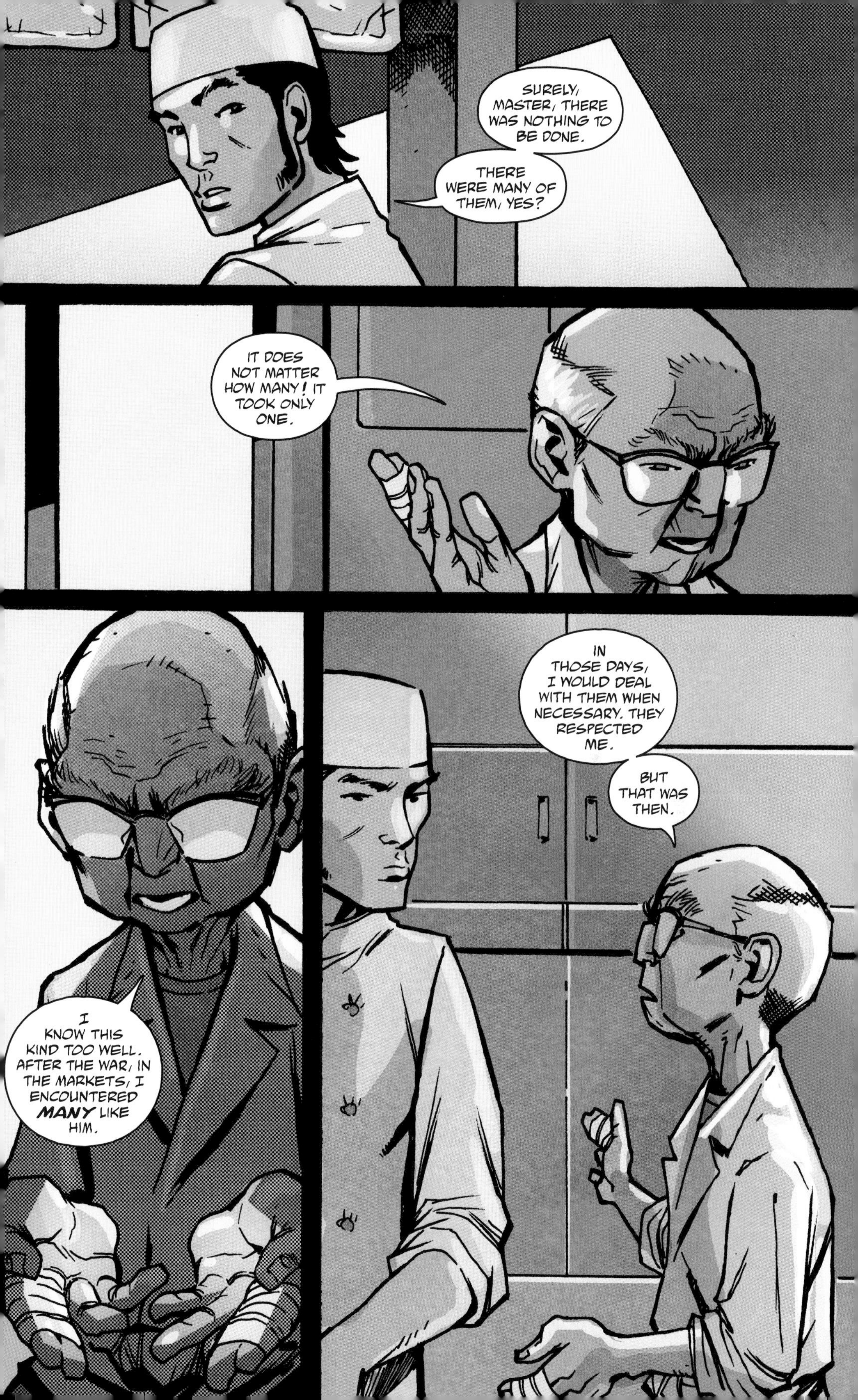
SURELY, MASTER, THERE WAS NOTHING TO BE DONE.
THERE WERE MANY OF THEM, YES?
IT DOES NOT MATTER HOW MANY! IT TOOK ONLY ONE.
I KNOW THIS KIND TOO WELL. AFTER THE WAR, IN THE MARKETS, I ENCOUNTERED **MANY** LIKE HIM.
IN THOSE DAYS, I WOULD DEAL WITH THEM WHEN NECESSARY. THEY RESPECTED ME.
BUT THAT WAS THEN.

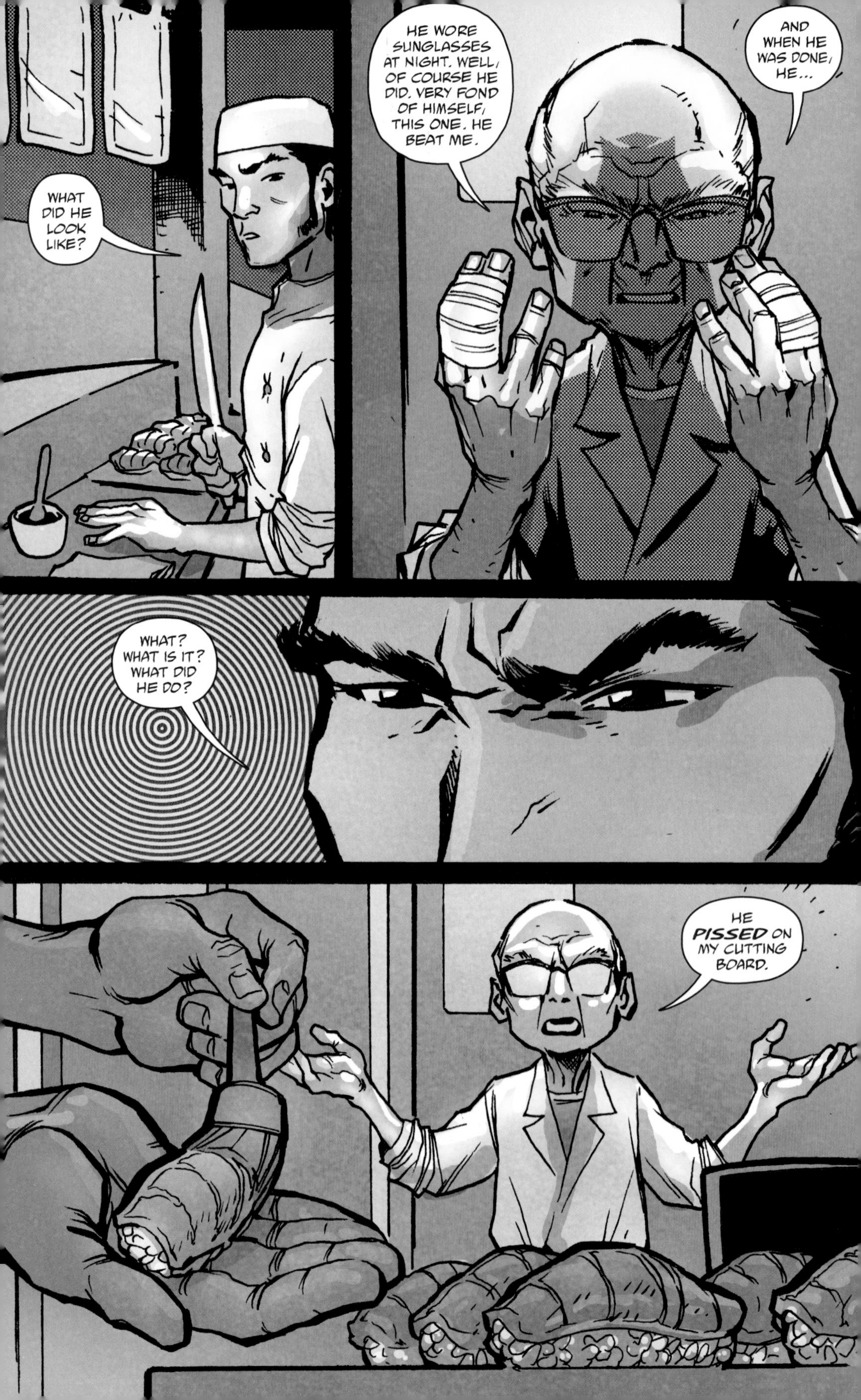
WHAT DID HE LOOK LIKE?
HE WORE SUNGLASSES AT NIGHT. WELL, OF COURSE HE DID. VERY FOND OF HIMSELF, THIS ONE. HE BEAT ME.
AND WHEN HE WAS DONE, HE...
WHAT? WHAT IS IT? WHAT DID HE DO?
HE **PISSED** ON MY CUTTING BOARD.

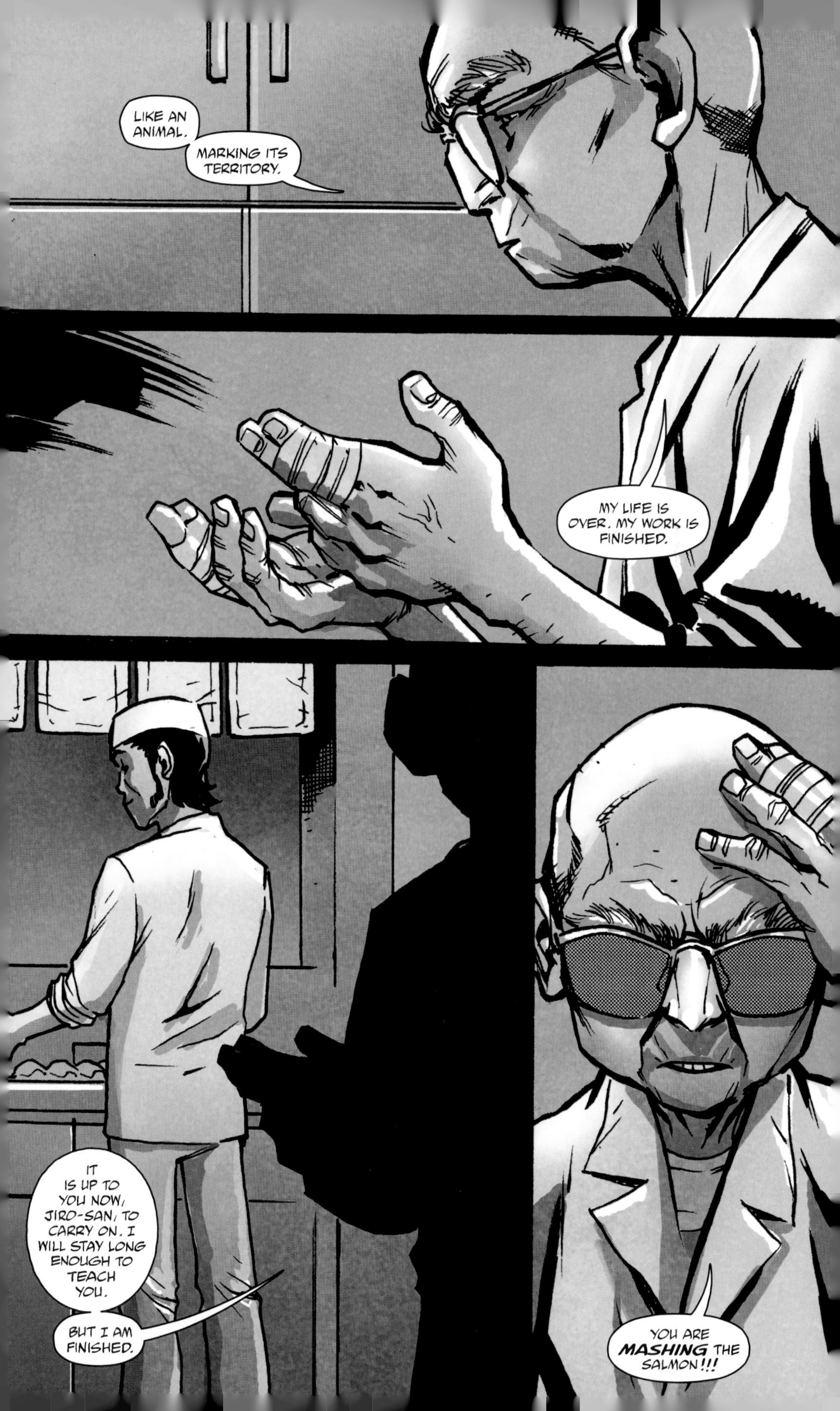
LIKE AN ANIMAL.
MARKING ITS TERRITORY.
MY LIFE IS OVER. MY WORK IS FINISHED.
IT IS UP TO YOU NOW, JIRO-SAN, TO CARRY ON. I WILL STAY LONG ENOUGH TO TEACH YOU.
BUT I AM FINISHED.
YOU ARE MASHING THE SALMON!!!

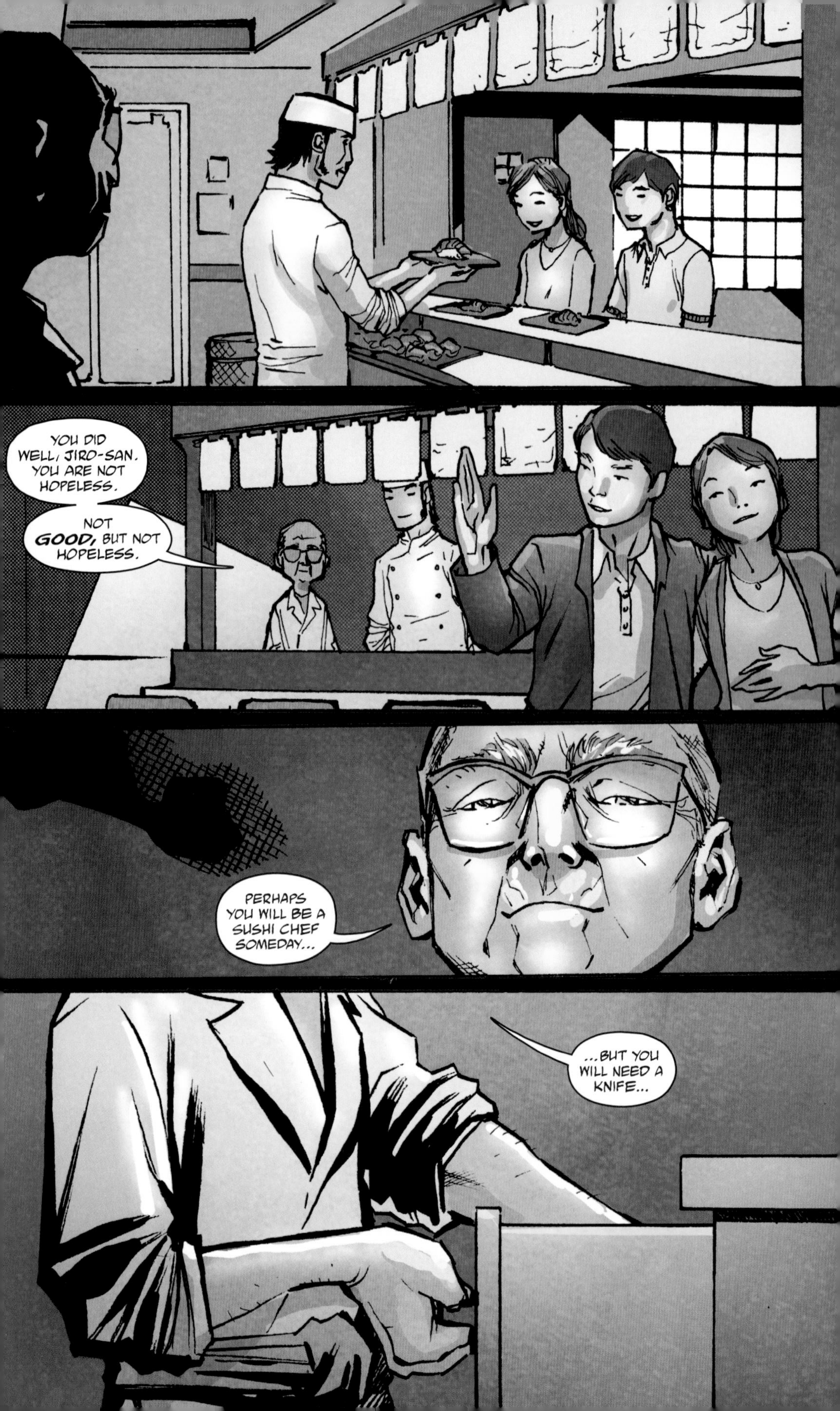
YOU DID WELL, JIRO-SAN. YOU ARE NOT HOPELESS.
NOT GOOD, BUT NOT HOPELESS.
PERHAPS YOU WILL BE A SUSHI CHEF SOMEDAY...
...BUT YOU WILL NEED A KNIFE...

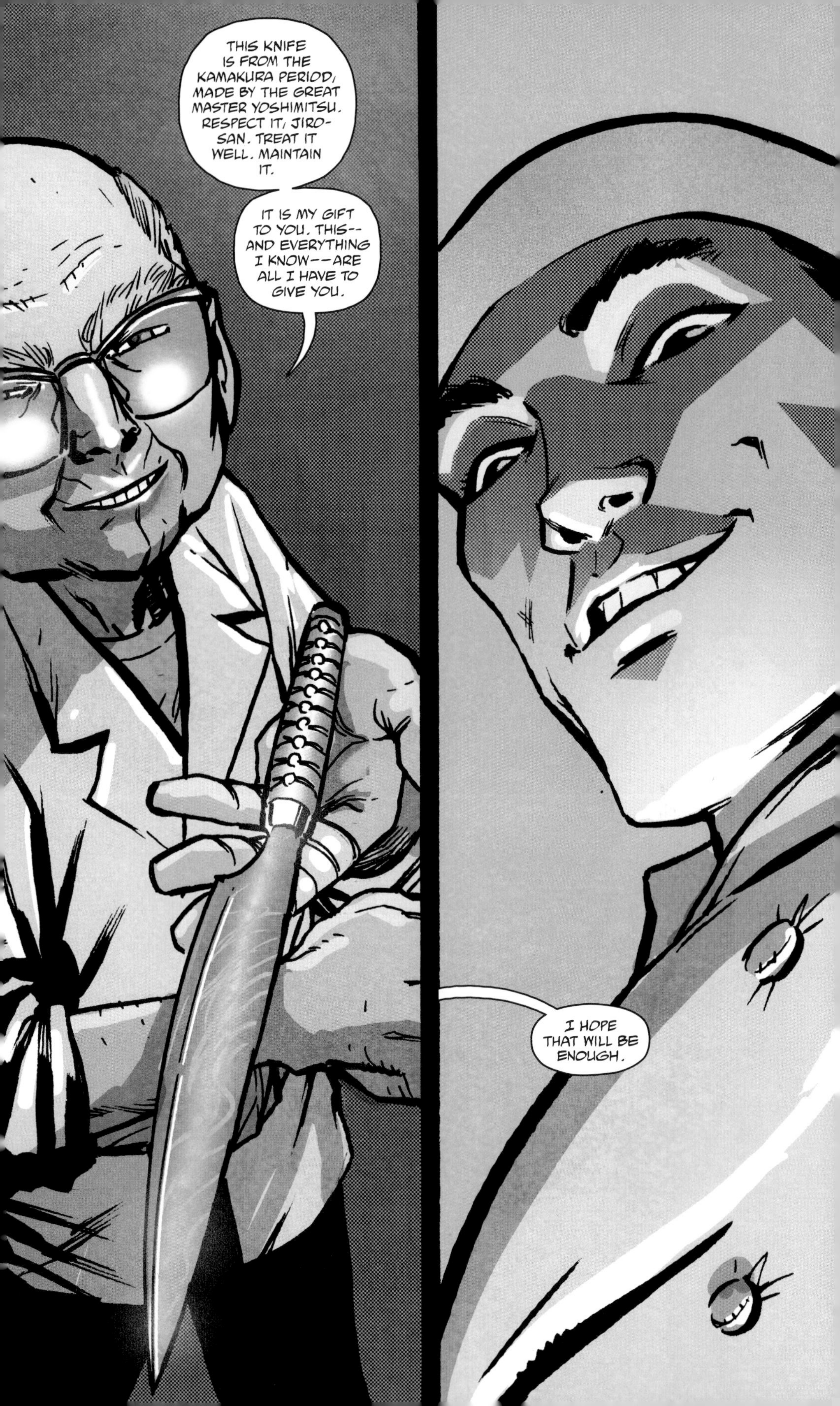
THIS KNIFE IS FROM THE KAMAKURA PERIOD, MADE BY THE GREAT MASTER YOSHIMITSU. RESPECT IT, JIRO-SAN. TREAT IT WELL. MAINTAIN IT.
IT IS MY GIFT TO YOU. THIS--AND EVERYTHING I KNOW--ARE ALL I HAVE TO GIVE YOU.
I HOPE THAT WILL BE ENOUGH.

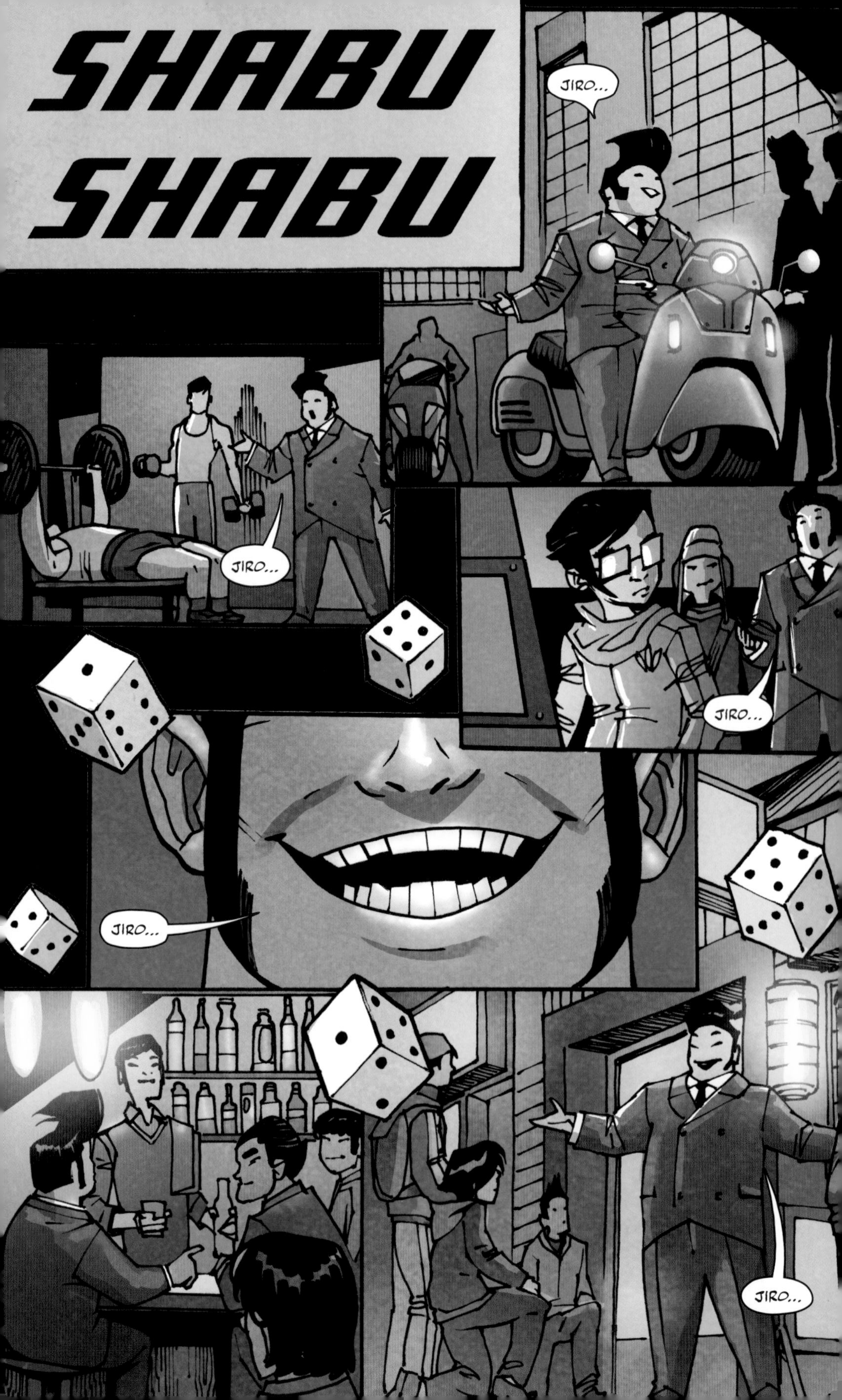

SHABU SHABU
JIRO...
JIRO...
JIRO...
JIRO...
JIRO...

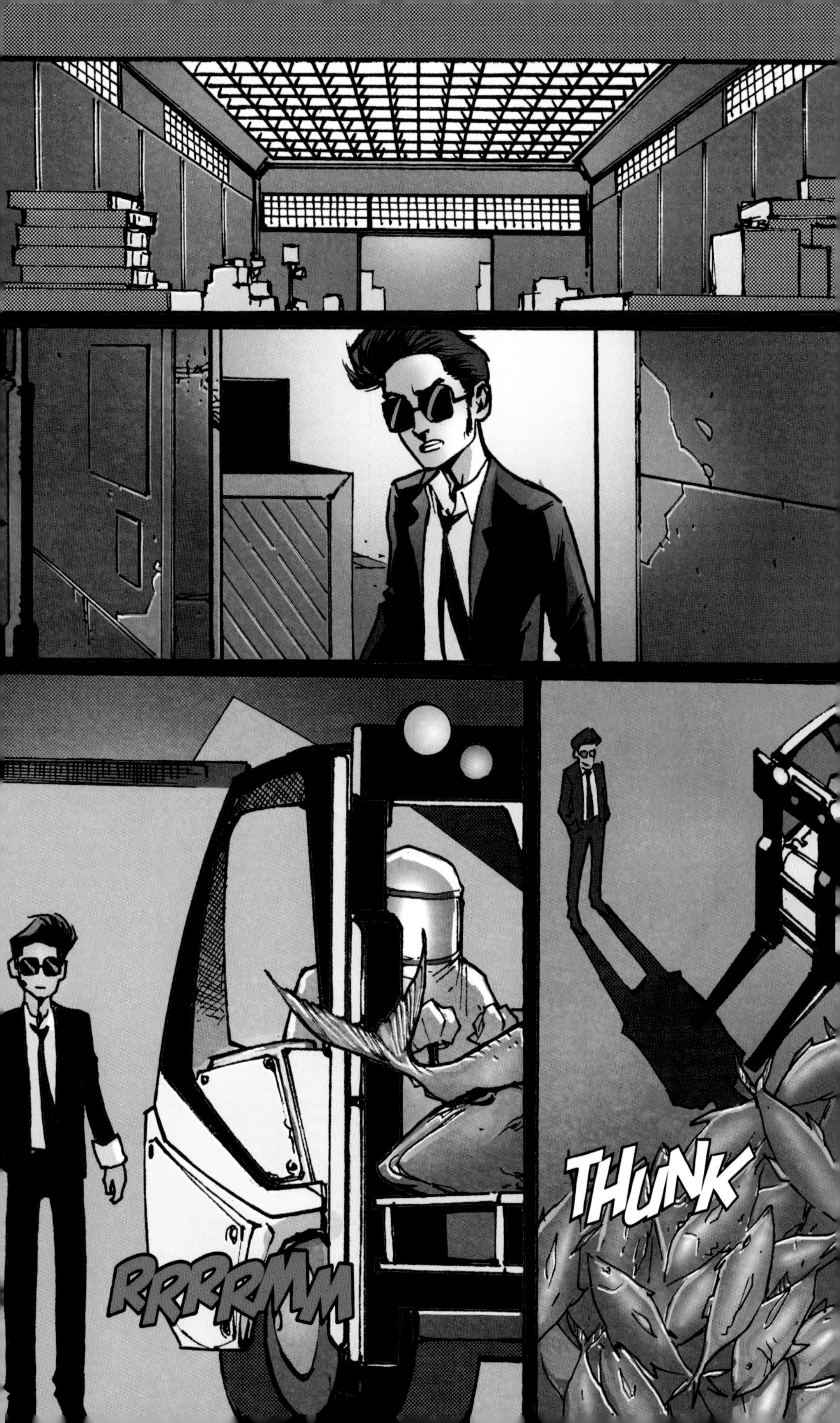
RRRRMMM
THUNK

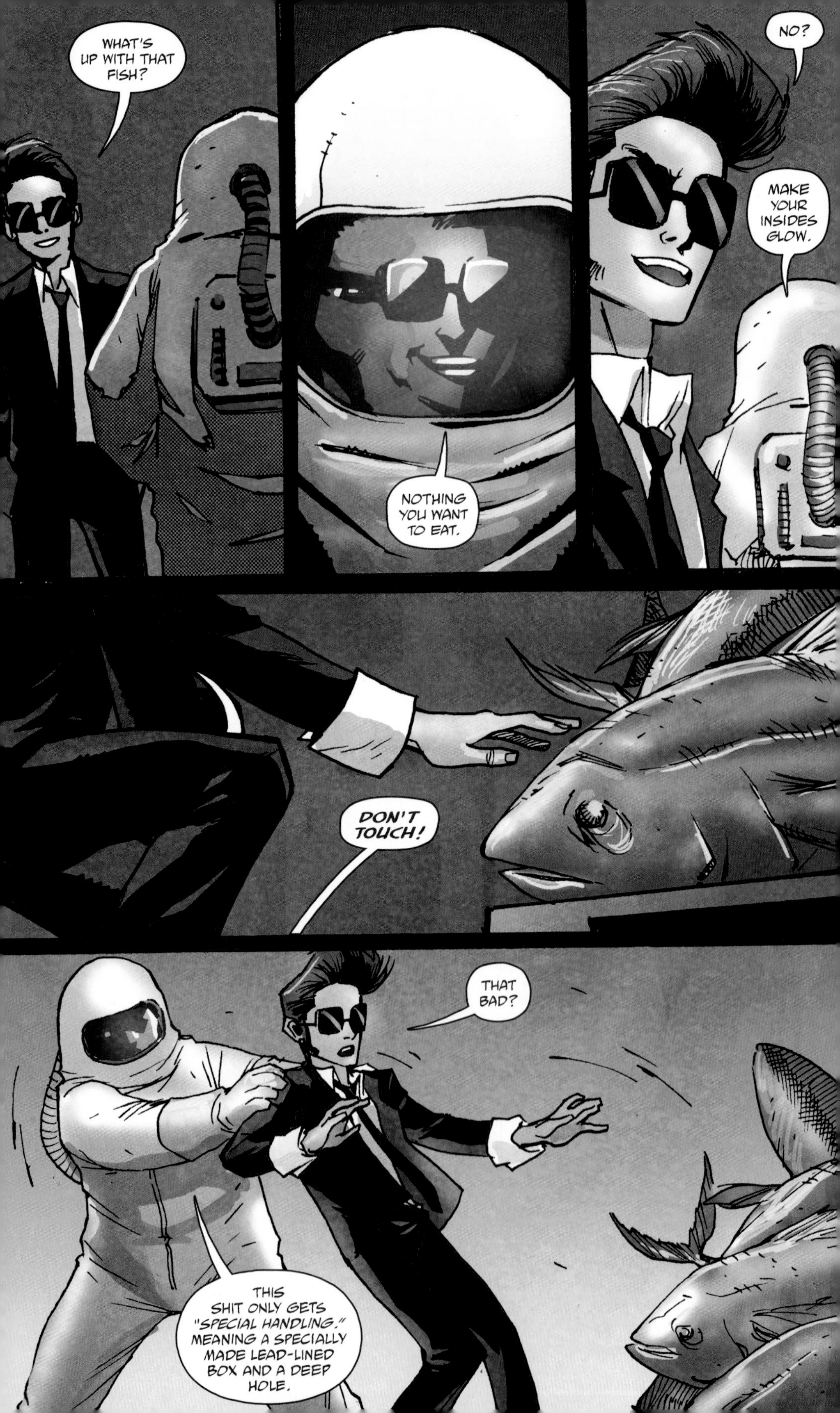
WHAT'S UP WITH THAT FISH?
NOTHING YOU WANT TO EAT.
NO?
MAKE YOUR INSIDES GLOW.
DON'T TOUCH!
THAT BAD?
THIS SHIT ONLY GETS "SPECIAL HANDLING." MEANING A SPECIALLY MADE LEAD-LINED BOX AND A DEEP HOLE.

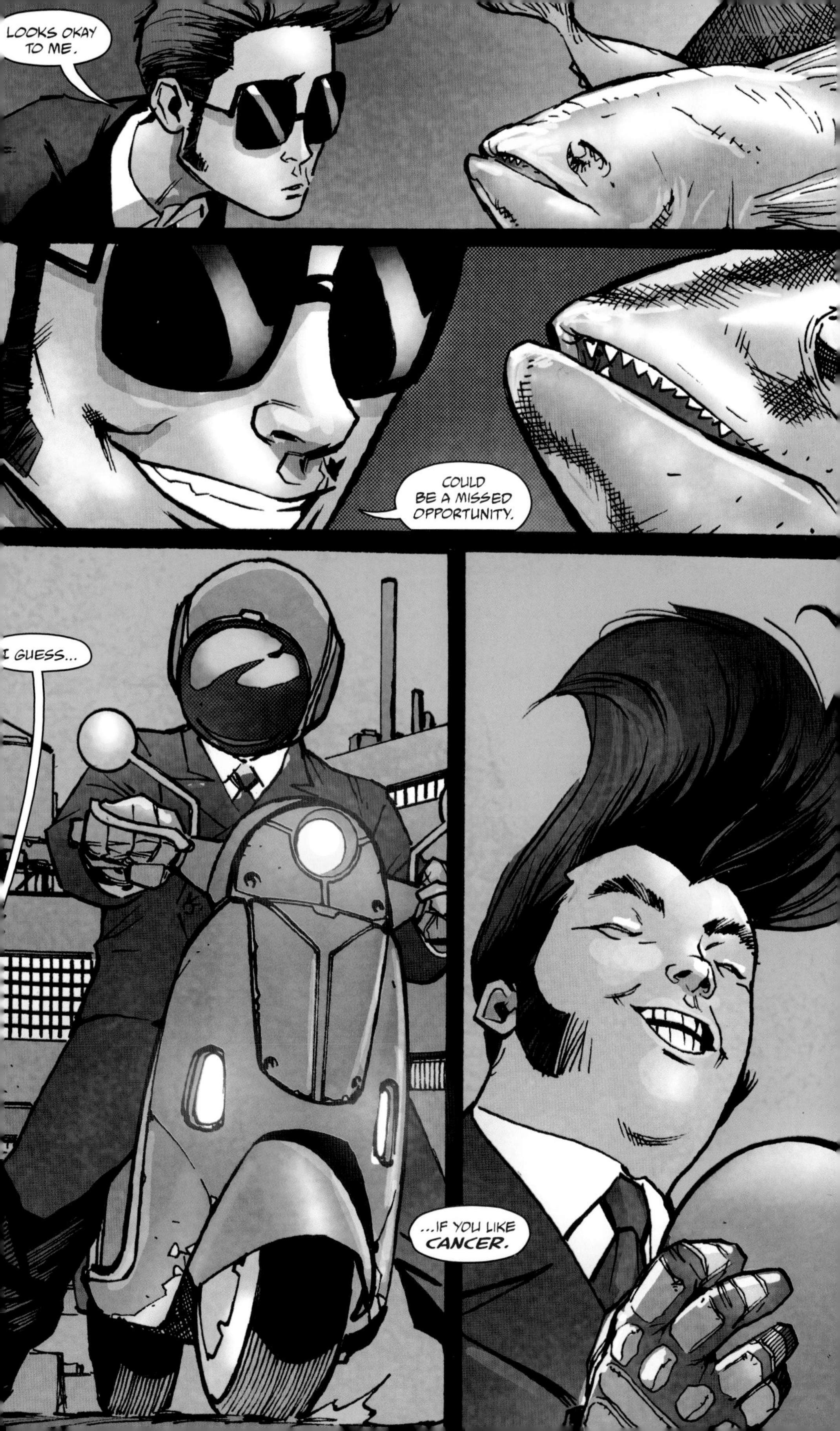
LOOKS OKAY TO ME.
COULD BE A MISSED OPPORTUNITY.
I GUESS...
...IF YOU LIKE CANCER.

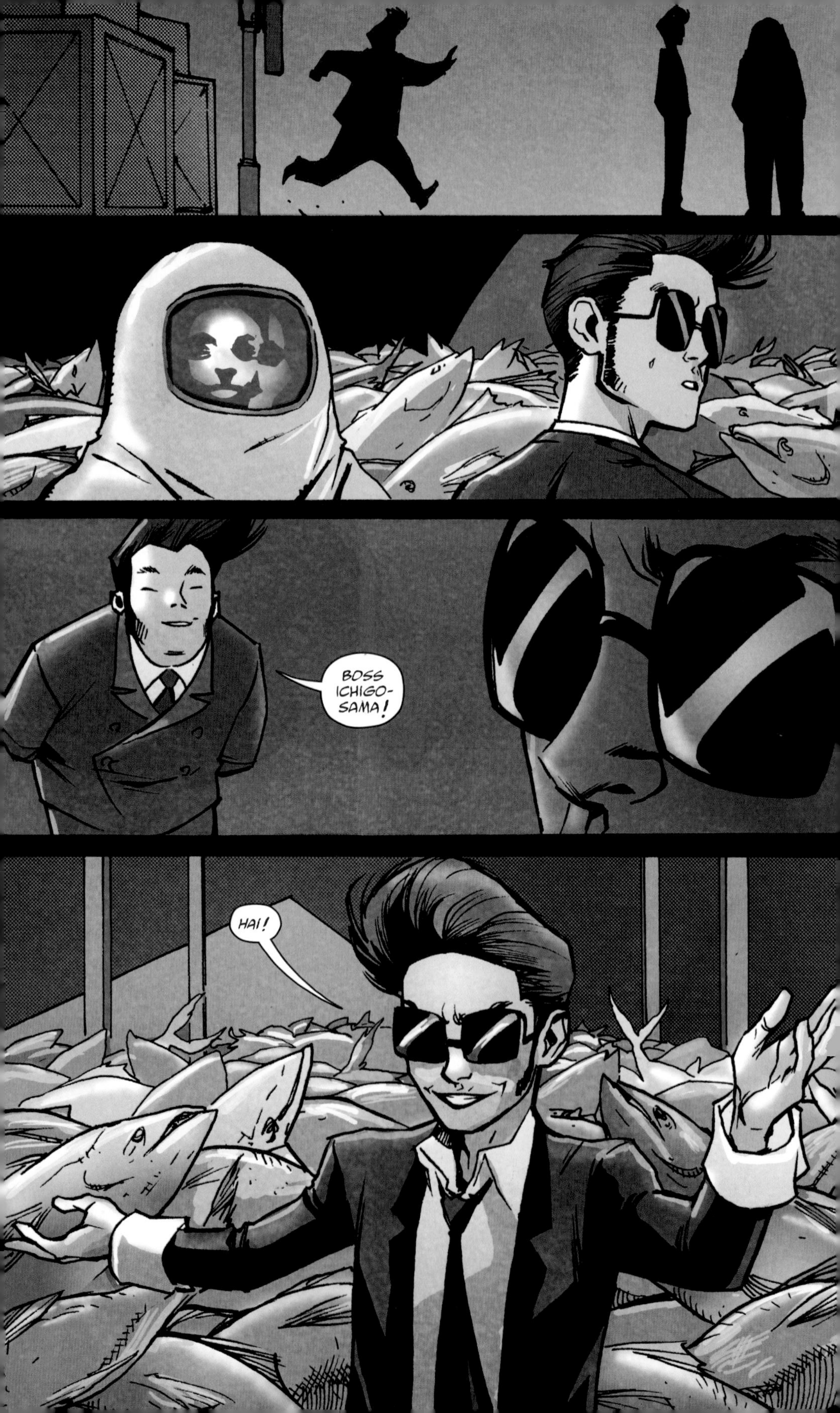
BOSS ICHIGO-SAMA!
HAI!

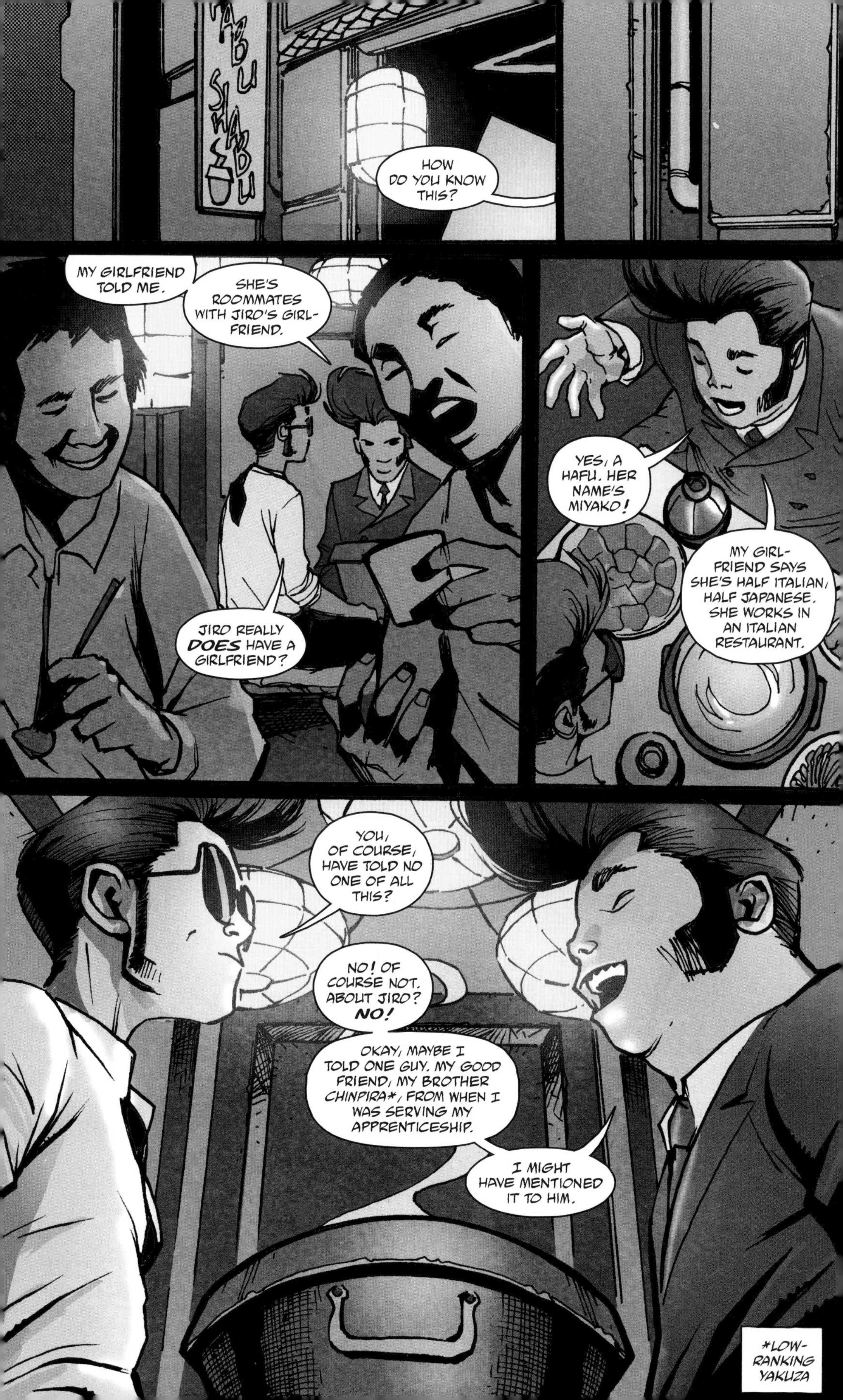
YABU SHABU SHABU
HOW DO YOU KNOW THIS?
MY GIRLFRIEND TOLD ME.
SHE'S ROOMMATES WITH JIRO'S GIRLFRIEND.
JIRO REALLY **DOES** HAVE A GIRLFRIEND?
YES, A HAFU. HER NAME'S MIYAKO!
MY GIRLFRIEND SAYS SHE'S HALF ITALIAN, HALF JAPANESE. SHE WORKS IN AN ITALIAN RESTAURANT.
YOU, OF COURSE, HAVE TOLD NO ONE OF ALL THIS?
NO! OF COURSE NOT. ABOUT JIRO? **NO!**
OKAY, MAYBE I TOLD ONE GUY. MY GOOD FRIEND, MY BROTHER *CHINPIRA**, FROM WHEN I WAS SERVING MY APPRENTICESHIP.
I MIGHT HAVE MENTIONED IT TO HIM.
*LOW-RANKING YAKUZA

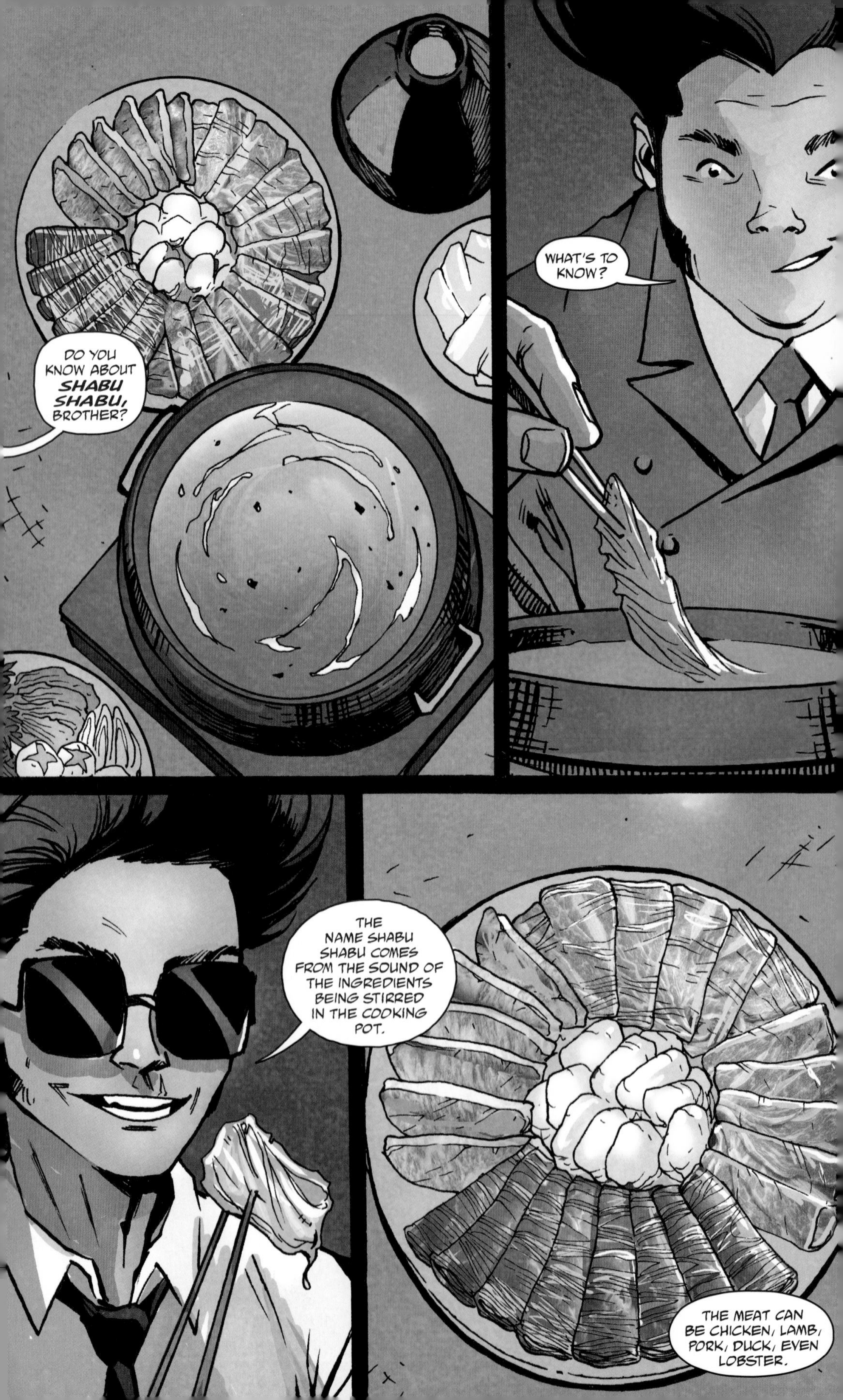
DO YOU KNOW ABOUT **SHABU SHABU,** BROTHER?
WHAT'S TO KNOW?
THE NAME SHABU SHABU COMES FROM THE SOUND OF THE INGREDIENTS BEING STIRRED IN THE COOKING POT.
THE MEAT CAN BE CHICKEN, LAMB, PORK, DUCK, EVEN LOBSTER.

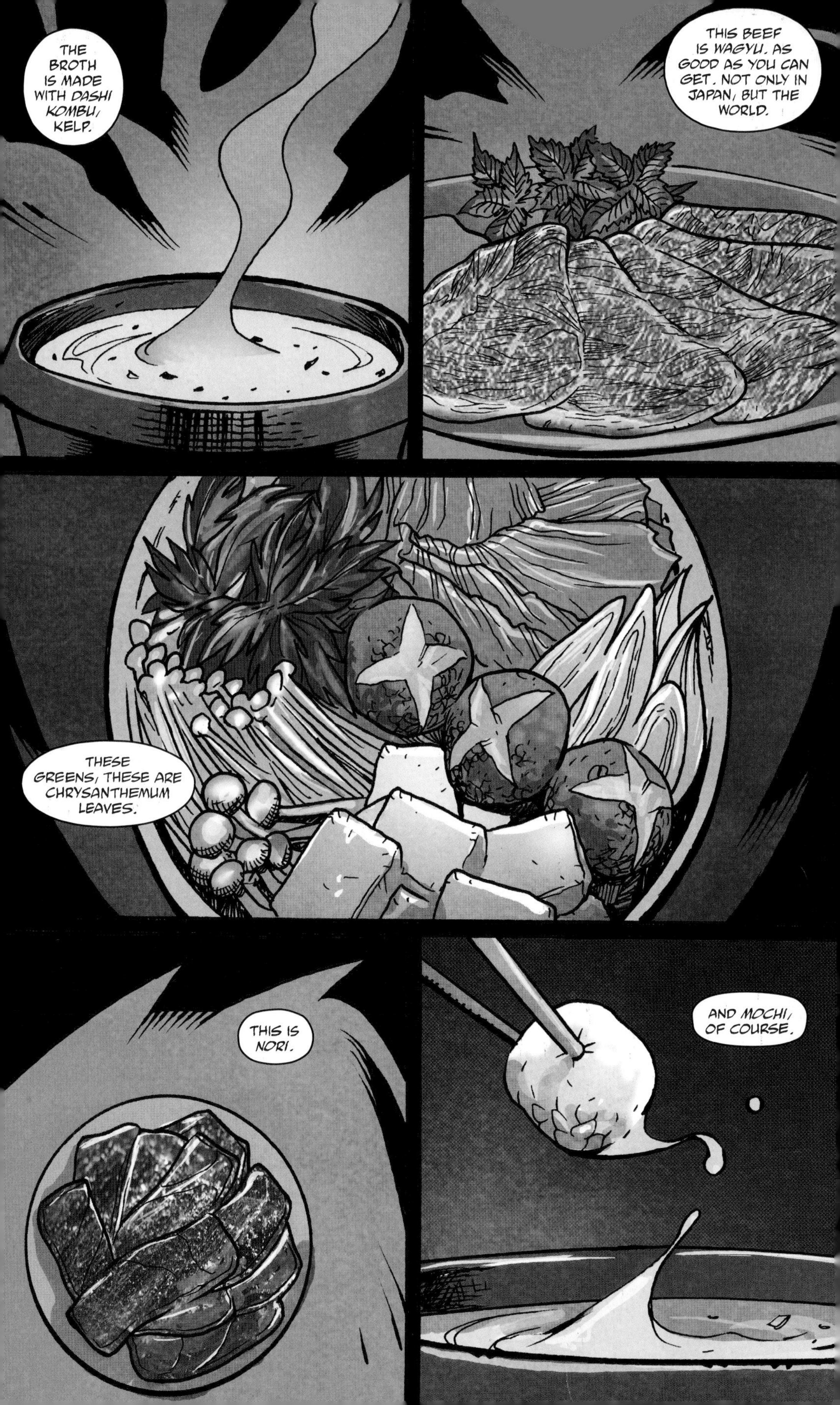
THE BROTH IS MADE WITH DASHI KOMBU, KELP.
THIS BEEF IS WAGYU. AS GOOD AS YOU CAN GET. NOT ONLY IN JAPAN, BUT THE WORLD.
THESE GREENS, THESE ARE CHRYSANTHEMUM LEAVES.
THIS IS NORI.
AND MOCHI, OF COURSE.

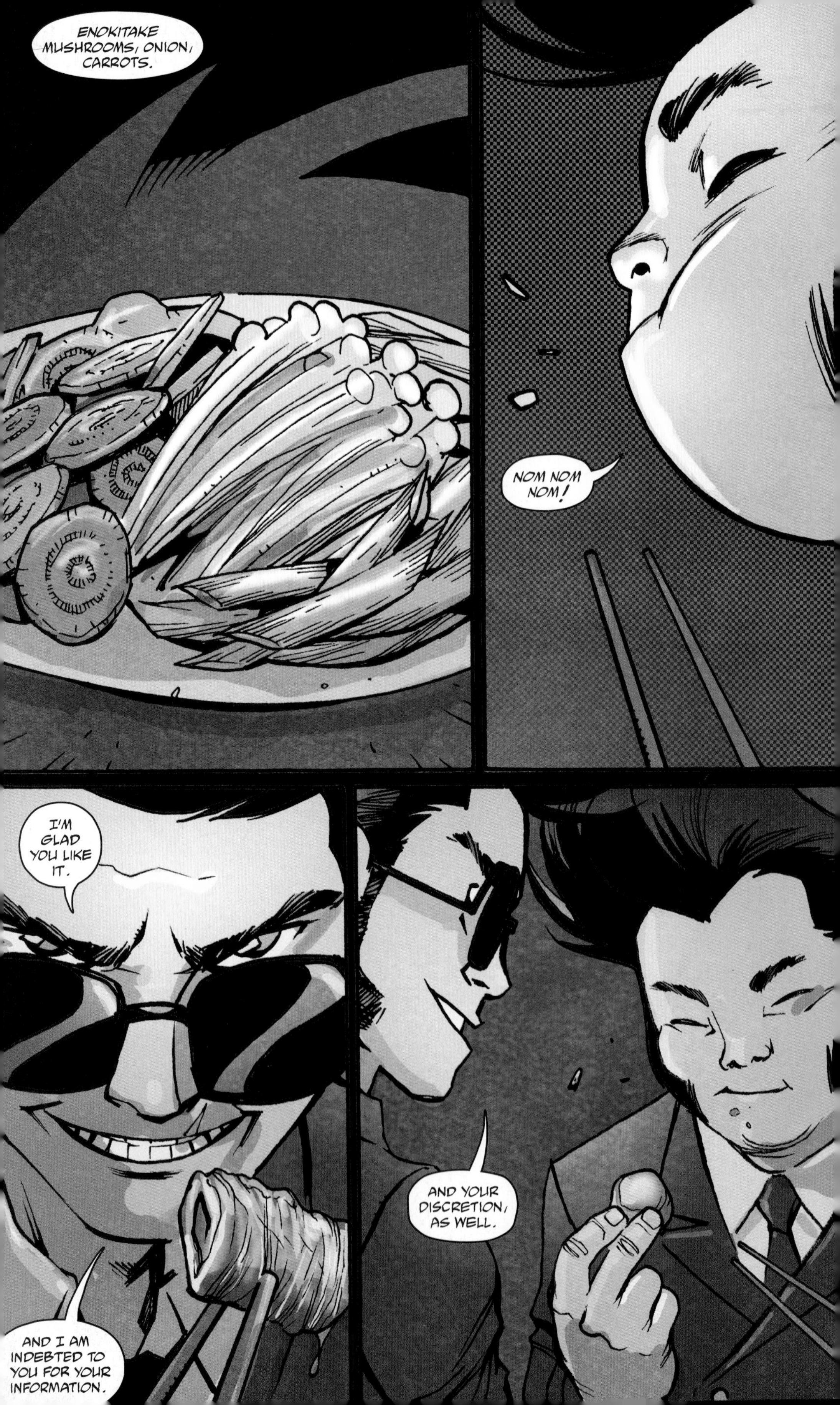
ENOKITAKE MUSHROOMS, ONION, CARROTS.
NOM NOM NOM!
I'M GLAD YOU LIKE IT.
AND I AM INDEBTED TO YOU FOR YOUR INFORMATION.
AND YOUR DISCRETION, AS WELL.

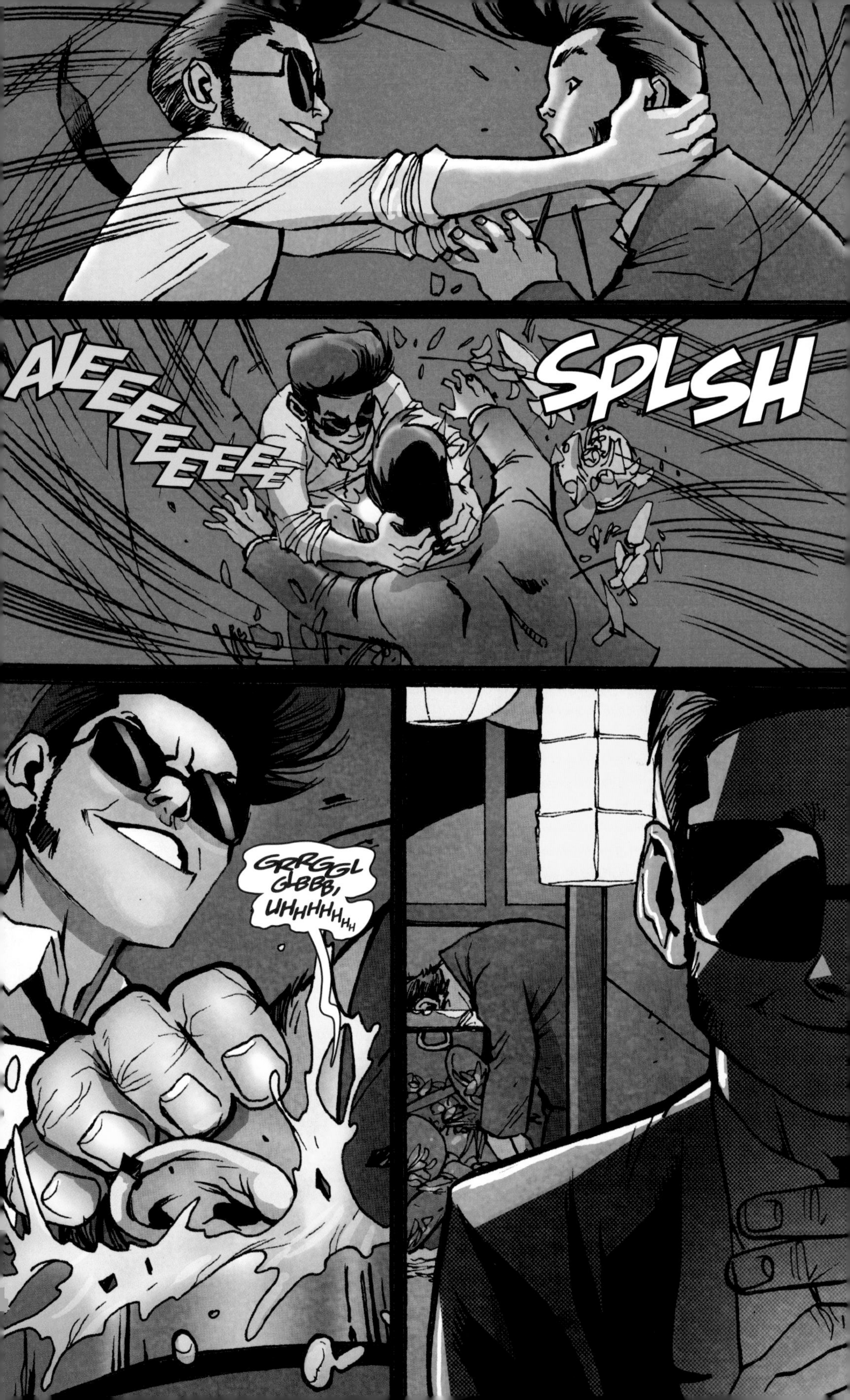
AIEEEEEEEEE
SPLSH
GRRGGL GLBBB, UHHHHHHH

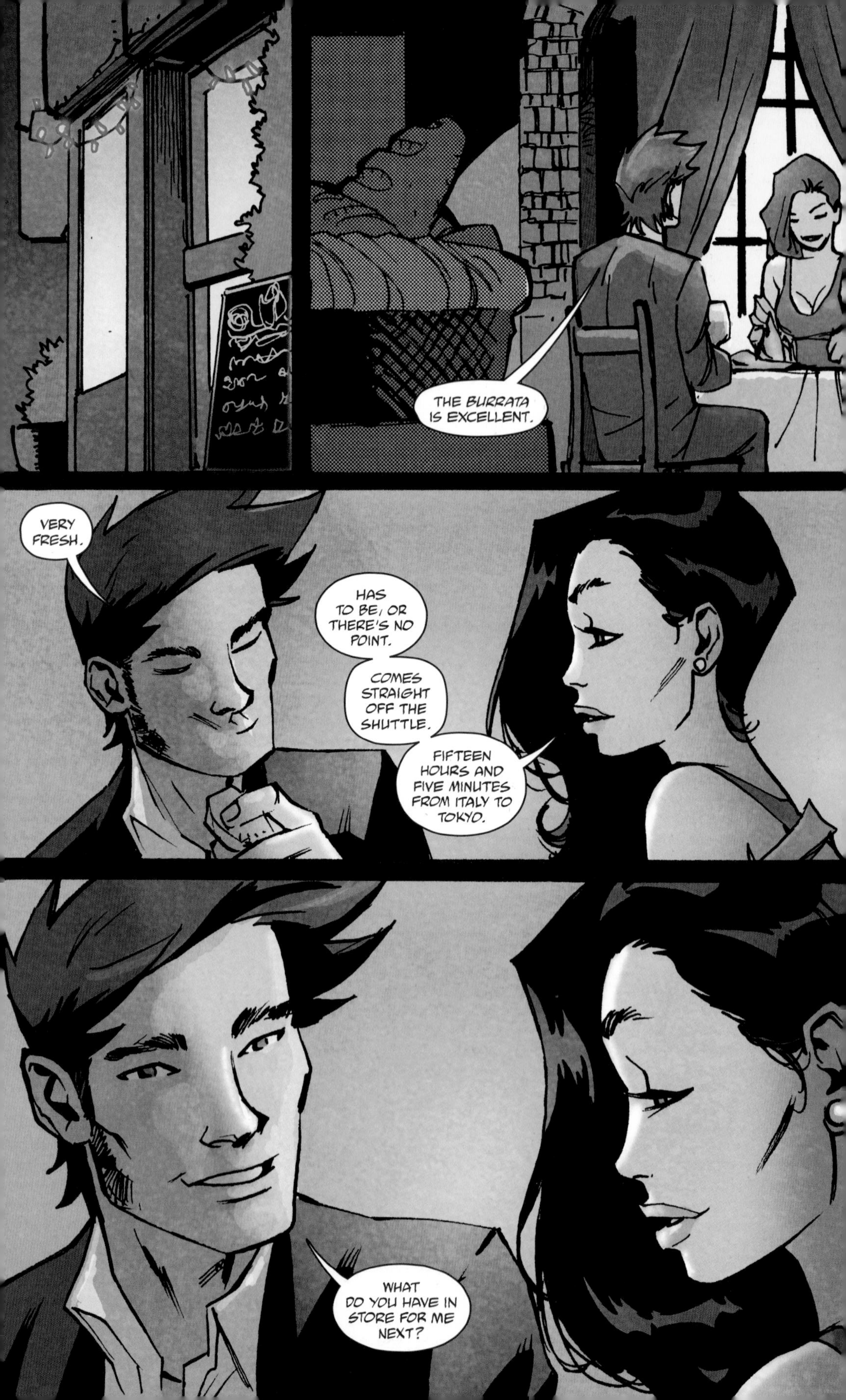
THE BURRATA IS EXCELLENT.
VERY FRESH.
HAS TO BE, OR THERE'S NO POINT.
COMES STRAIGHT OFF THE SHUTTLE.
FIFTEEN HOURS AND FIVE MINUTES FROM ITALY TO TOKYO.
WHAT DO YOU HAVE IN STORE FOR ME NEXT?

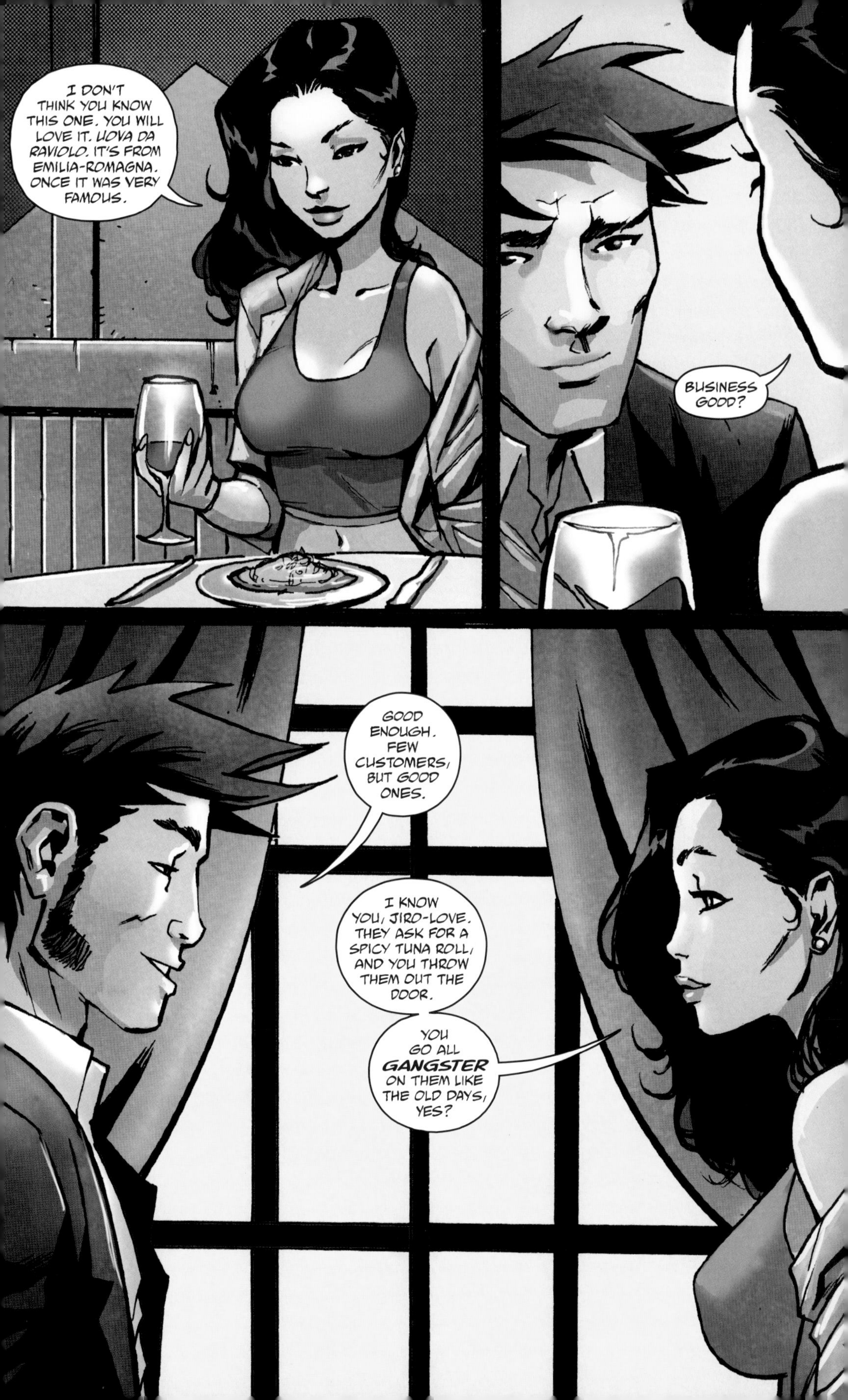
I DON'T THINK YOU KNOW THIS ONE. YOU WILL LOVE IT. *UOVA DA RAVIOLO*. IT'S FROM EMILIA-ROMAGNA. ONCE IT WAS VERY FAMOUS.
BUSINESS GOOD?
GOOD ENOUGH. FEW CUSTOMERS, BUT GOOD ONES.
I KNOW YOU, JIRO-LOVE. THEY ASK FOR A SPICY TUNA ROLL, AND YOU THROW THEM OUT THE DOOR.
YOU GO ALL **GANGSTER** ON THEM LIKE THE OLD DAYS, YES?

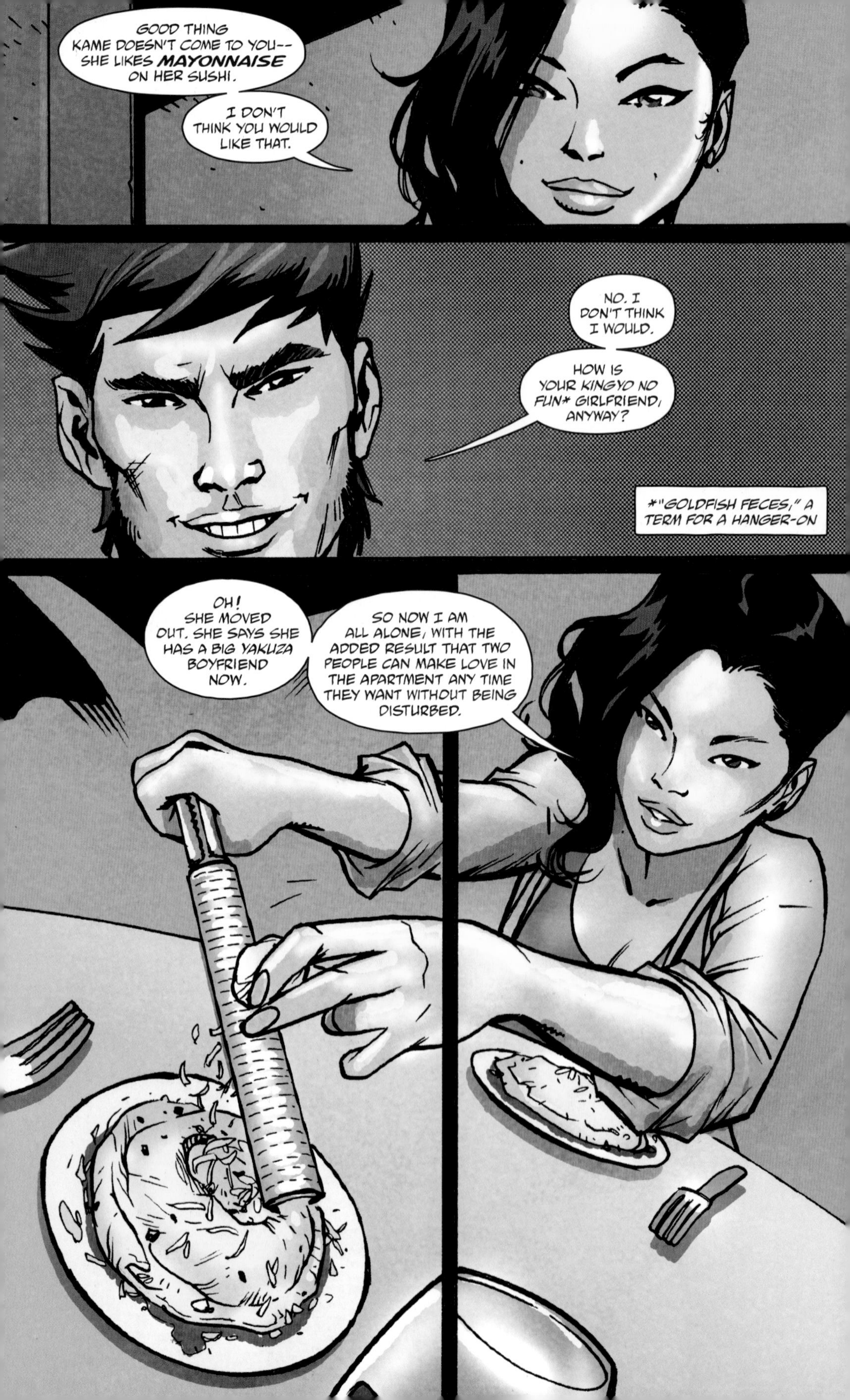
GOOD THING KAME DOESN'T COME TO YOU-- SHE LIKES **MAYONNAISE** ON HER SUSHI.
I DON'T THINK YOU WOULD LIKE THAT.
NO. I DON'T THINK I WOULD.
HOW IS YOUR *KINGYO NO FUN** GIRLFRIEND, ANYWAY?
*"GOLDFISH FECES," A TERM FOR A HANGER-ON
OH! SHE MOVED OUT. SHE SAYS SHE HAS A BIG *YAKUZA* BOYFRIEND NOW.
SO NOW I AM ALL ALONE, WITH THE ADDED RESULT THAT TWO PEOPLE CAN MAKE LOVE IN THE APARTMENT ANY TIME THEY WANT WITHOUT BEING DISTURBED.

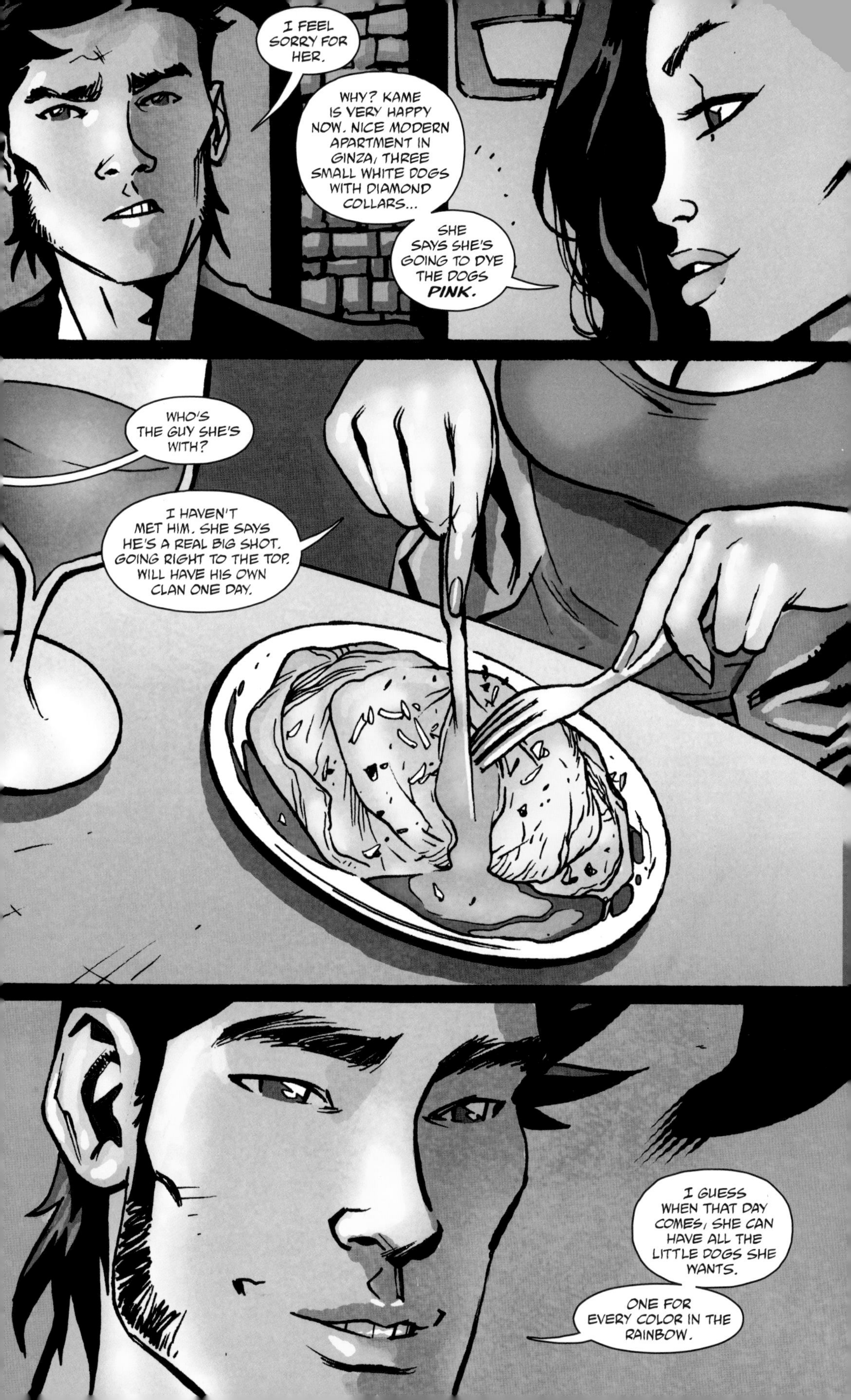
I FEEL SORRY FOR HER.
WHY? KAME IS VERY HAPPY NOW. NICE MODERN APARTMENT IN GINZA, THREE SMALL WHITE DOGS WITH DIAMOND COLLARS...
SHE SAYS SHE'S GOING TO DYE THE DOGS **PINK.**
WHO'S THE GUY SHE'S WITH?
I HAVEN'T MET HIM. SHE SAYS HE'S A REAL BIG SHOT. GOING RIGHT TO THE TOP. WILL HAVE HIS OWN CLAN ONE DAY.
I GUESS WHEN THAT DAY COMES, SHE CAN HAVE ALL THE LITTLE DOGS SHE WANTS.
ONE FOR EVERY COLOR IN THE RAINBOW.

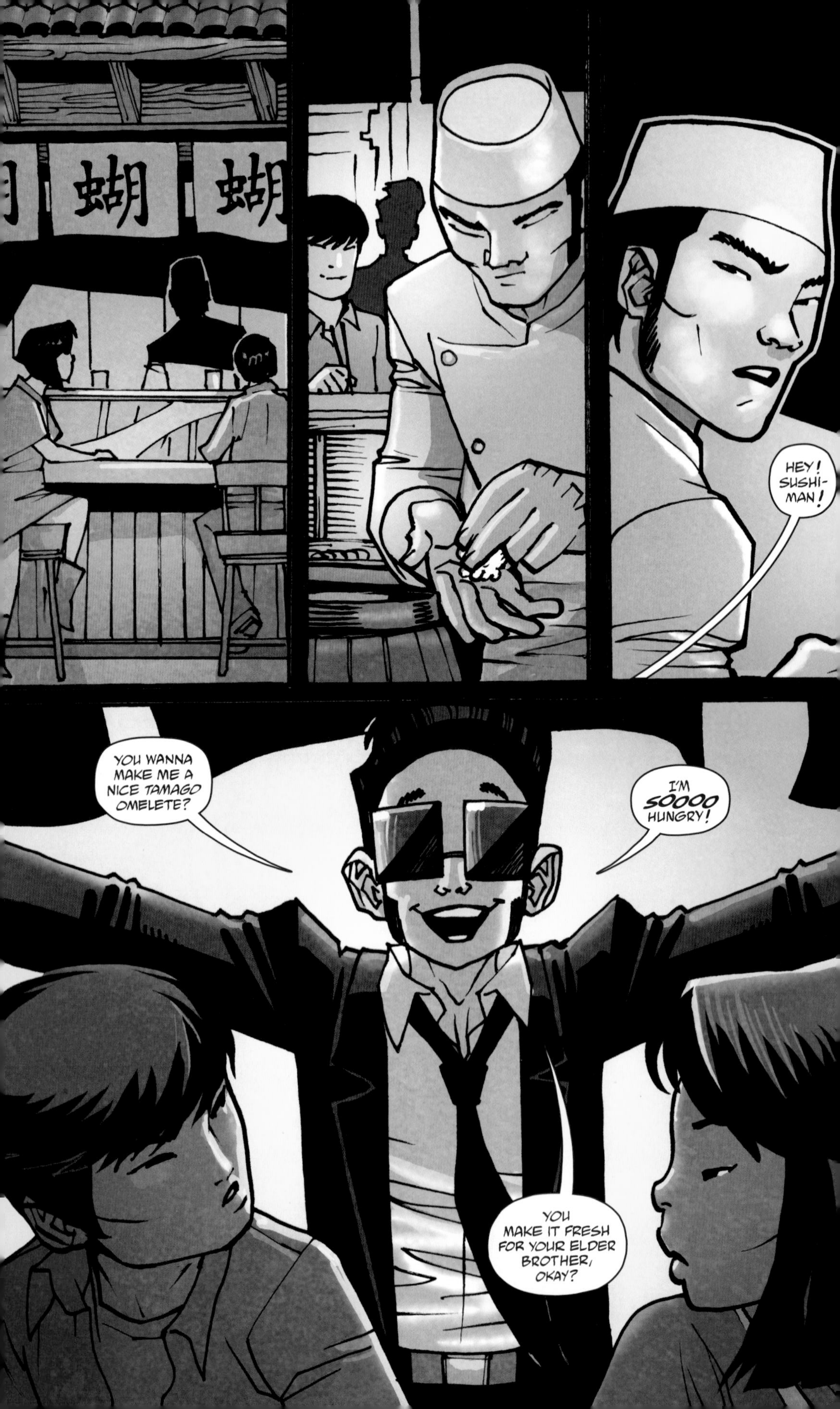
蝴 蝴
HEY! SUSHI-MAN!
YOU WANNA MAKE ME A NICE *TAMAGO* OMELETE?
I'M *SOOOO* HUNGRY!
YOU MAKE IT FRESH FOR YOUR ELDER BROTHER, OKAY?

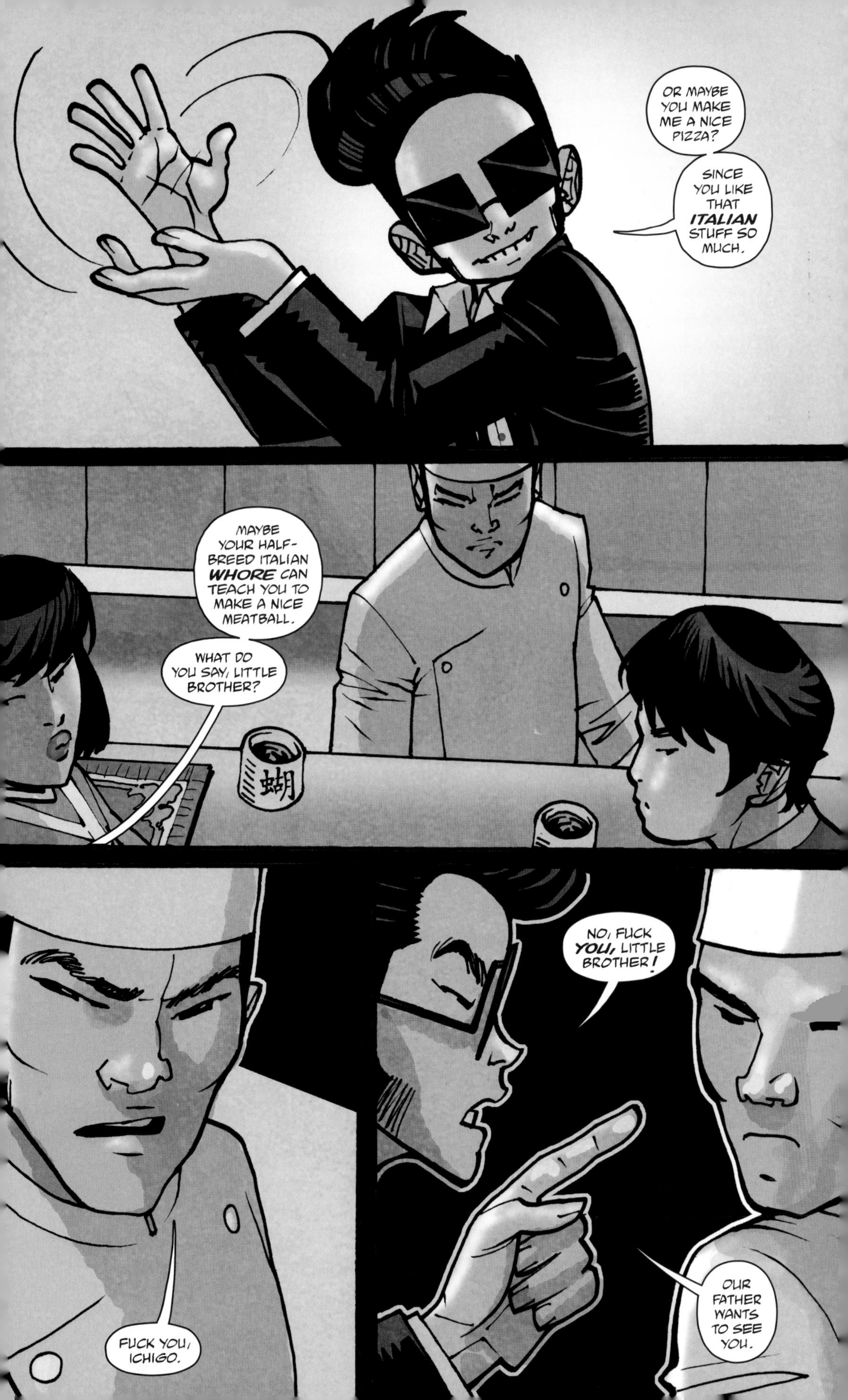
OR MAYBE YOU MAKE ME A NICE PIZZA?
SINCE YOU LIKE THAT *ITALIAN* STUFF SO MUCH.
MAYBE YOUR HALF-BREED ITALIAN *WHORE* CAN TEACH YOU TO MAKE A NICE MEATBALL.
WHAT DO YOU SAY, LITTLE BROTHER?
蝴
FUCK YOU, ICHIGO.
NO, FUCK *YOU,* LITTLE BROTHER!
OUR FATHER WANTS TO SEE YOU.

HORMONE YAKI

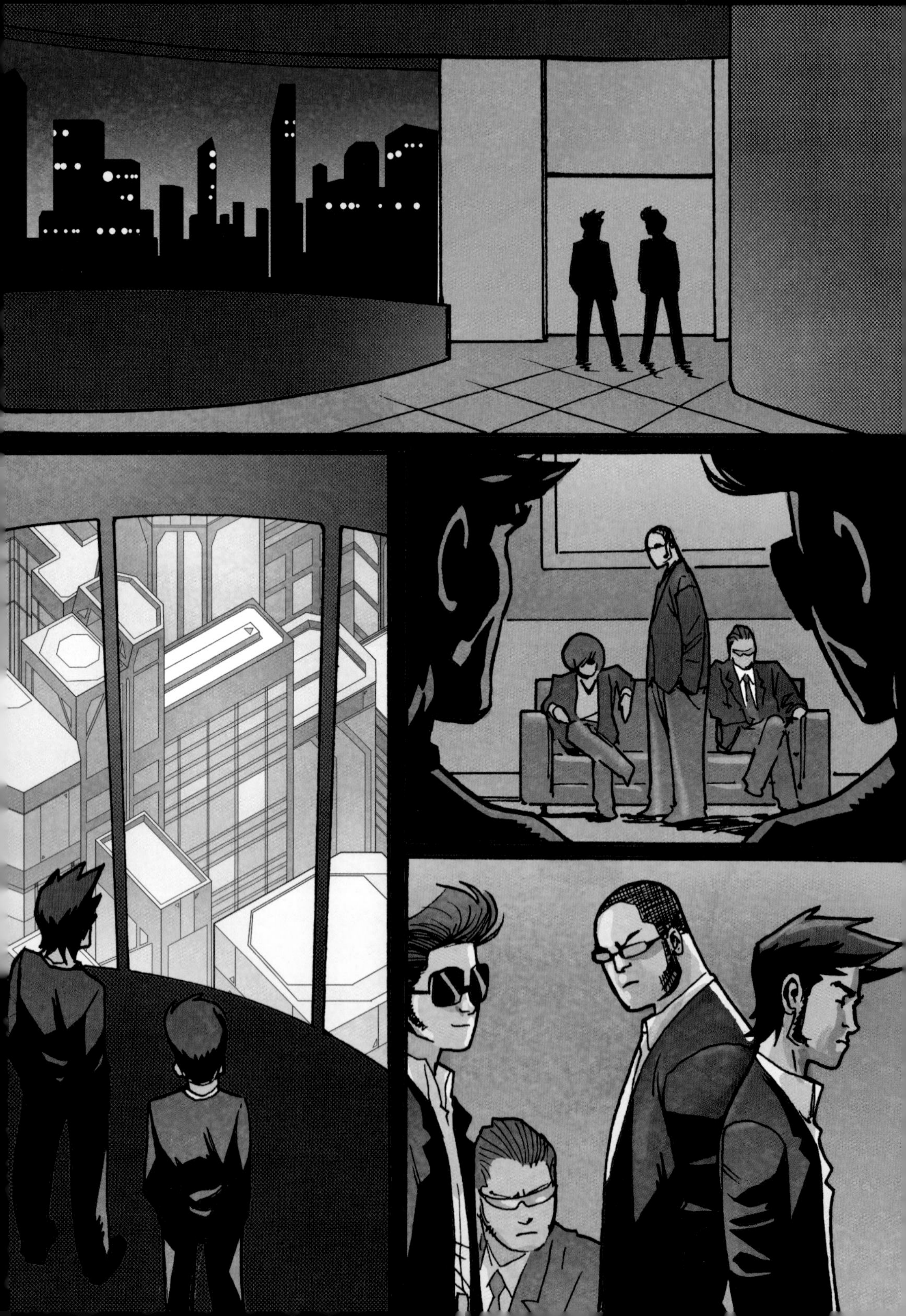

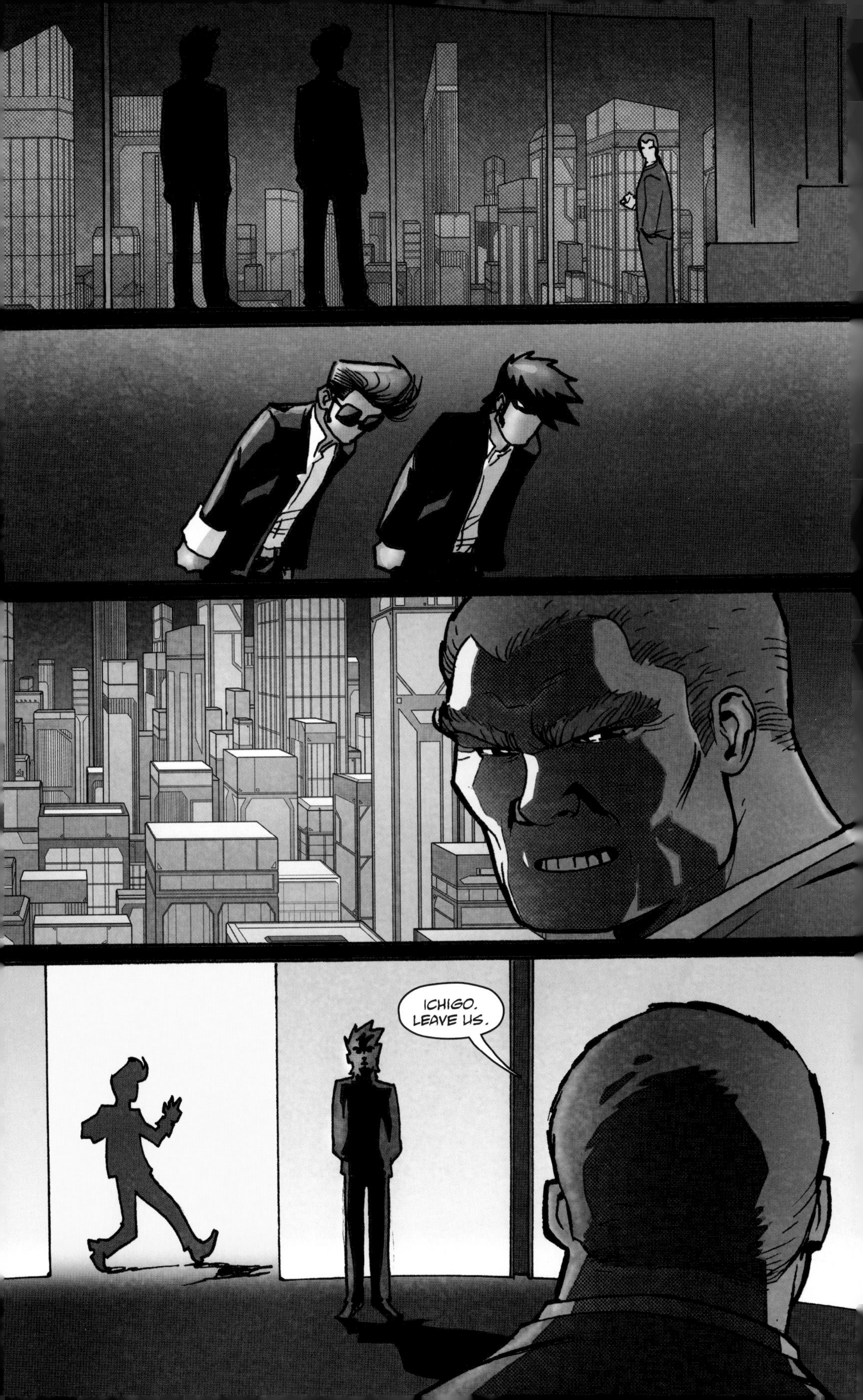
ICHIGO.
LEAVE US.

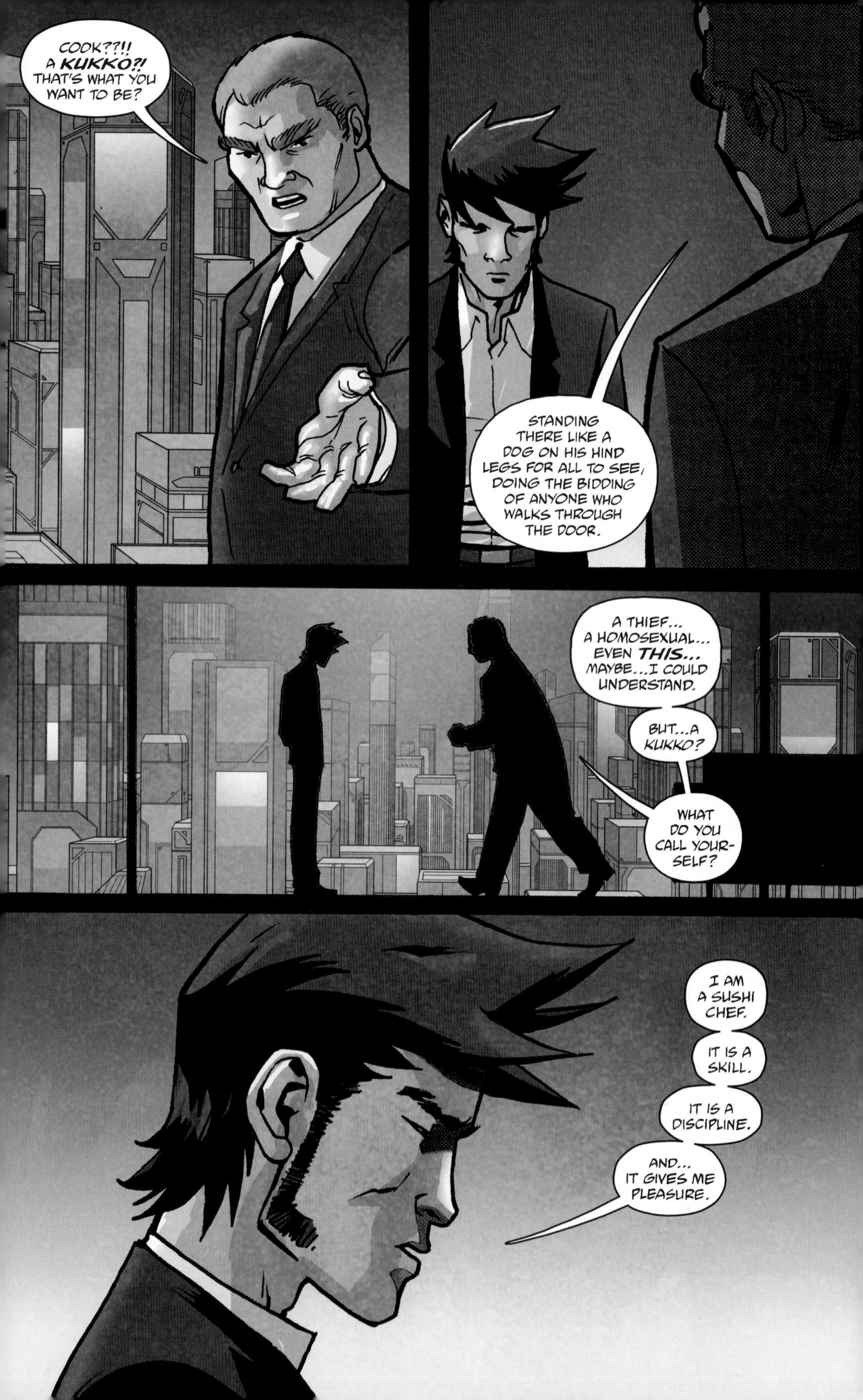
COOK??!! A **KUKKO?!** THAT'S WHAT YOU WANT TO BE?
STANDING THERE LIKE A DOG ON HIS HIND LEGS FOR ALL TO SEE, DOING THE BIDDING OF ANYONE WHO WALKS THROUGH THE DOOR.
A THIEF... A HOMOSEXUAL... EVEN **THIS...** MAYBE...I COULD UNDERSTAND.
BUT...A KUKKO?
WHAT DO YOU CALL YOURSELF?
I AM A SUSHI CHEF.
IT IS A SKILL.
IT IS A DISCIPLINE.
AND... IT GIVES ME PLEASURE.

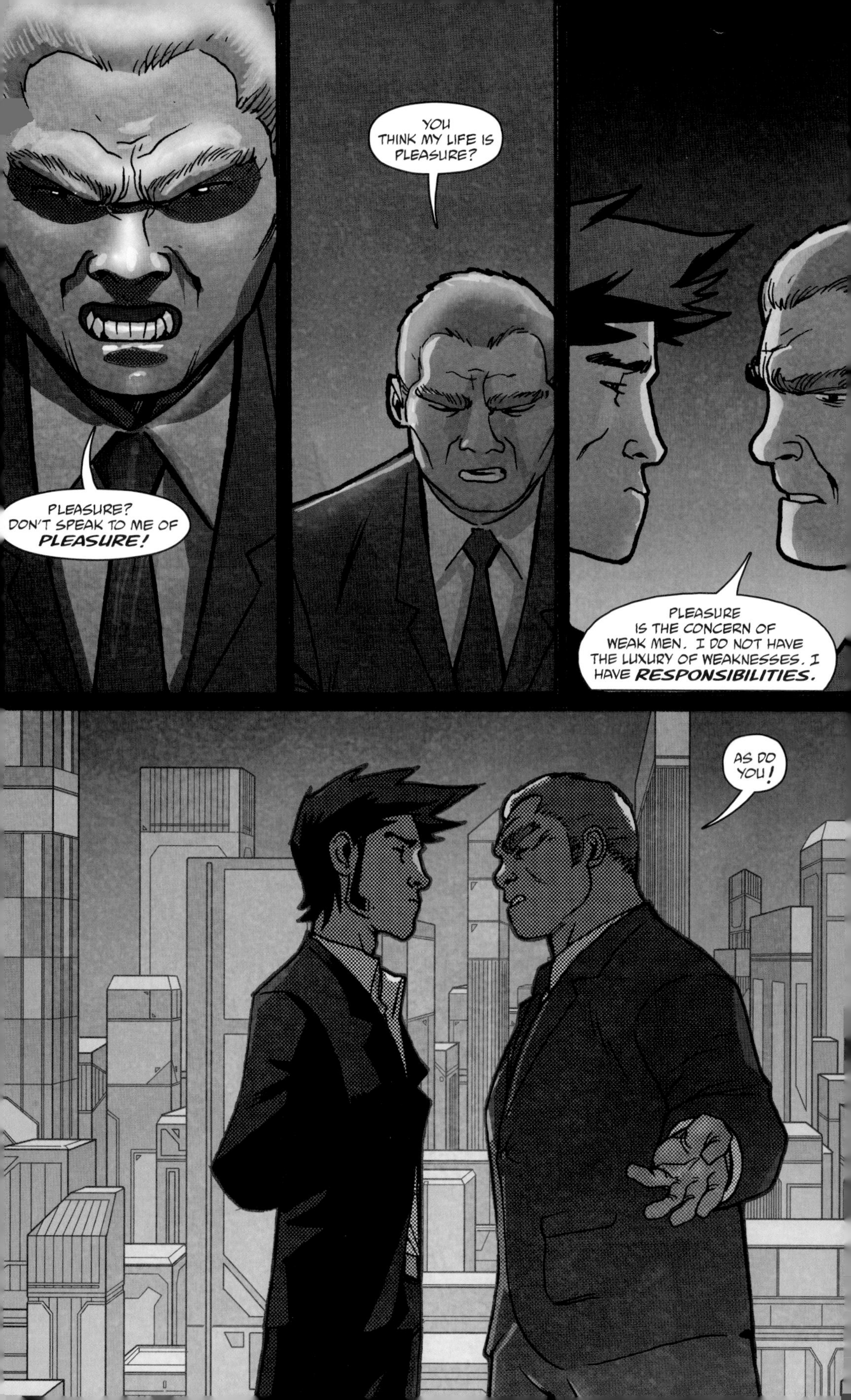
PLEASURE? DON'T SPEAK TO ME OF *PLEASURE!*
YOU THINK MY LIFE IS PLEASURE?
PLEASURE IS THE CONCERN OF WEAK MEN. I DO NOT HAVE THE LUXURY OF WEAKNESSES. I HAVE *RESPONSIBILITIES.*
AS DO YOU!

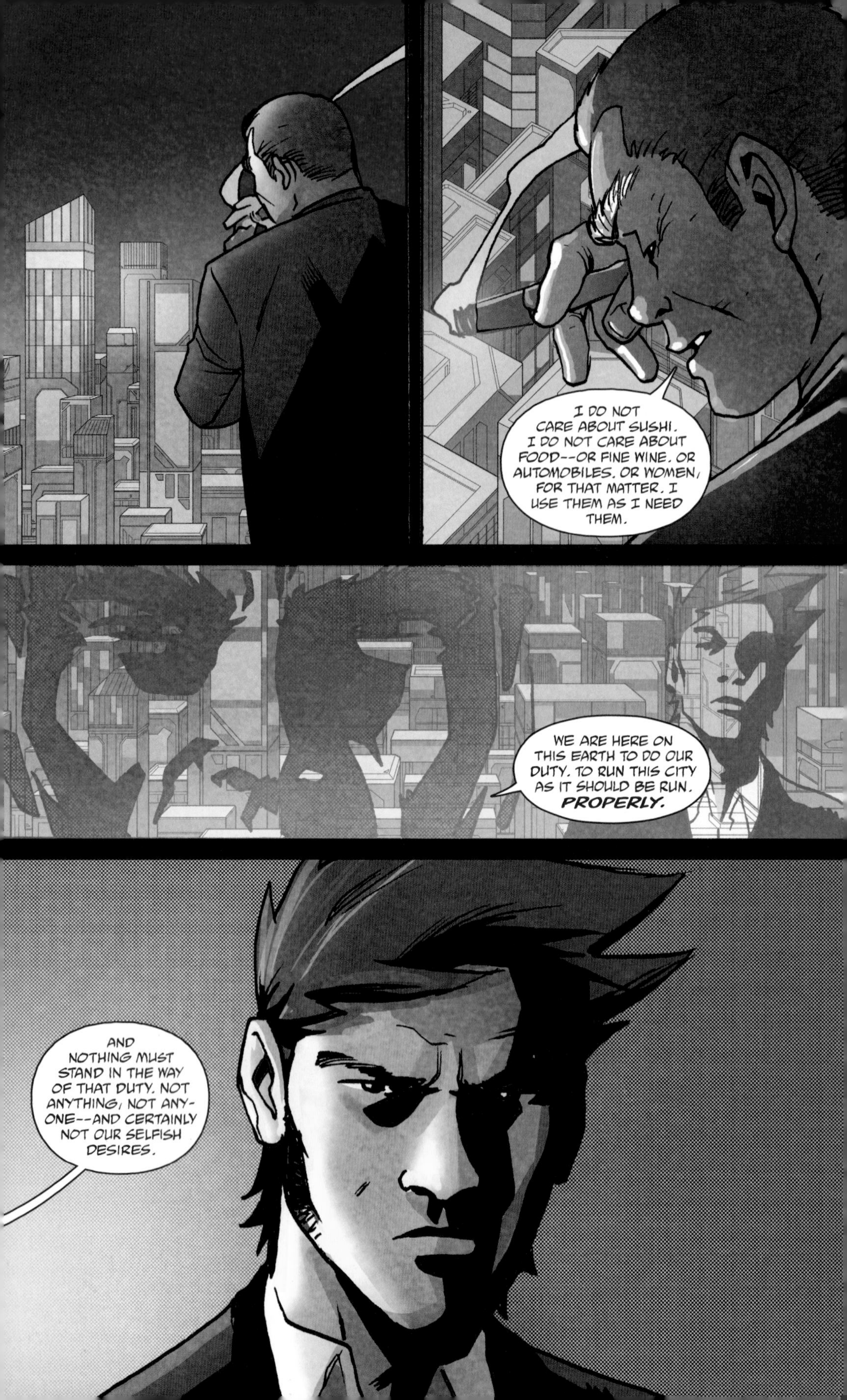
I DO NOT CARE ABOUT SUSHI. I DO NOT CARE ABOUT FOOD--OR FINE WINE. OR AUTOMOBILES. OR WOMEN, FOR THAT MATTER. I USE THEM AS I NEED THEM.
WE ARE HERE ON THIS EARTH TO DO OUR DUTY. TO RUN THIS CITY AS IT SHOULD BE RUN. PROPERLY.
AND NOTHING MUST STAND IN THE WAY OF THAT DUTY. NOT ANYTHING, NOT ANY-ONE--AND CERTAINLY NOT OUR SELFISH DESIRES.

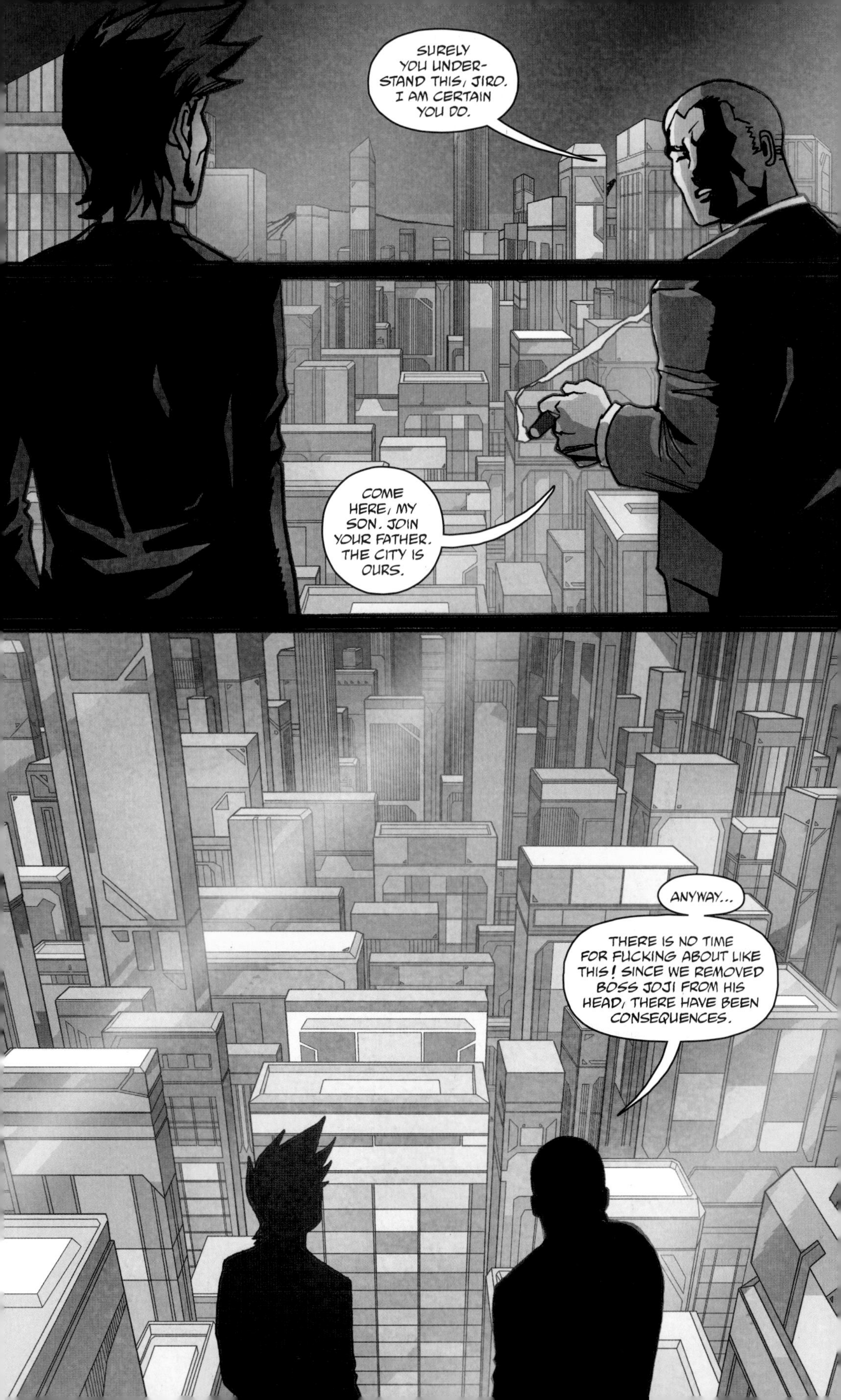
SURELY YOU UNDER-STAND THIS, JIRO. I AM CERTAIN YOU DO.
COME HERE, MY SON. JOIN YOUR FATHER. THE CITY IS OURS.
ANYWAY...
THERE IS NO TIME FOR FUCKING ABOUT LIKE THIS! SINCE WE REMOVED BOSS JOJI FROM HIS HEAD, THERE HAVE BEEN CONSEQUENCES.

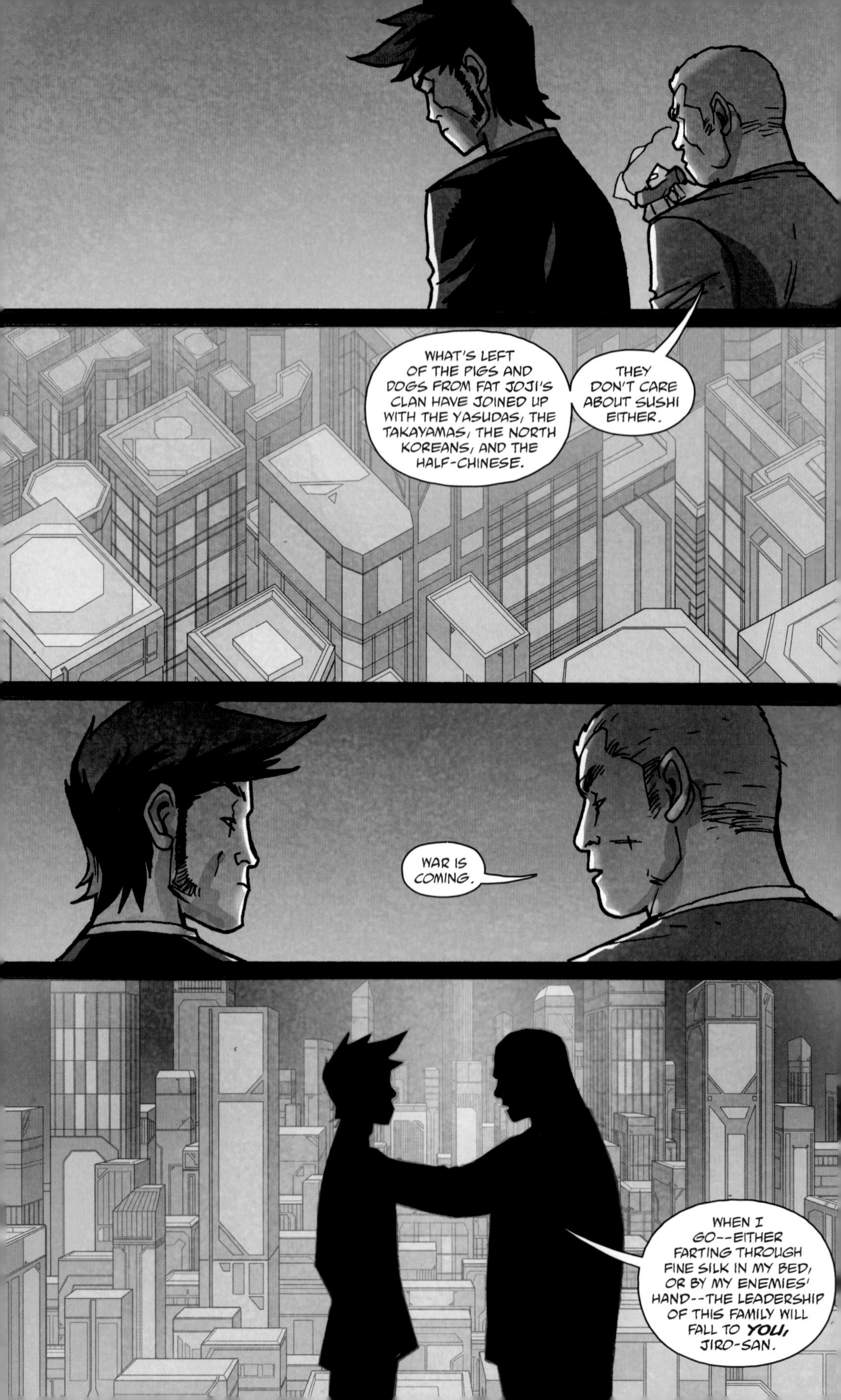
WHAT'S LEFT OF THE PIGS AND DOGS FROM FAT JOJI'S CLAN HAVE JOINED UP WITH THE YASUDAS, THE TAKAYAMAS, THE NORTH KOREANS, AND THE HALF-CHINESE.
THEY DON'T CARE ABOUT SUSHI EITHER.
WAR IS COMING.
WHEN I GO--EITHER FARTING THROUGH FINE SILK IN MY BED, OR BY MY ENEMIES' HAND--THE LEADERSHIP OF THIS FAMILY WILL FALL TO *YOU,* JIRO-SAN.

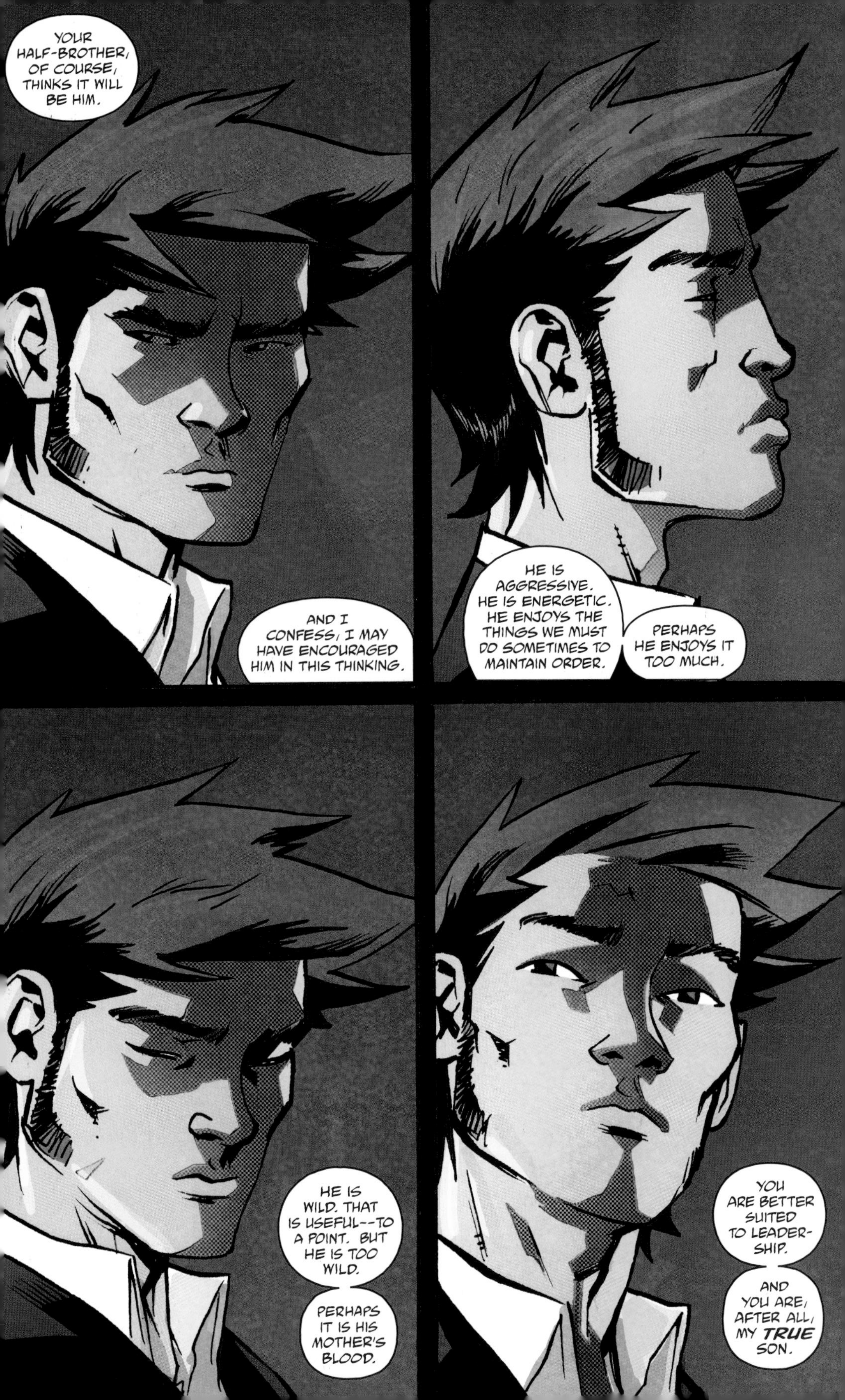
YOUR HALF-BROTHER, OF COURSE, THINKS IT WILL BE HIM.
AND I CONFESS, I MAY HAVE ENCOURAGED HIM IN THIS THINKING.
HE IS AGGRESSIVE. HE IS ENERGETIC. HE ENJOYS THE THINGS WE MUST DO SOMETIMES TO MAINTAIN ORDER.
PERHAPS HE ENJOYS IT TOO MUCH.
HE IS WILD. THAT IS USEFUL--TO A POINT. BUT HE IS TOO WILD.
PERHAPS IT IS HIS MOTHER'S BLOOD.
YOU ARE BETTER SUITED TO LEADER-SHIP.
AND YOU ARE, AFTER ALL, MY TRUE SON.

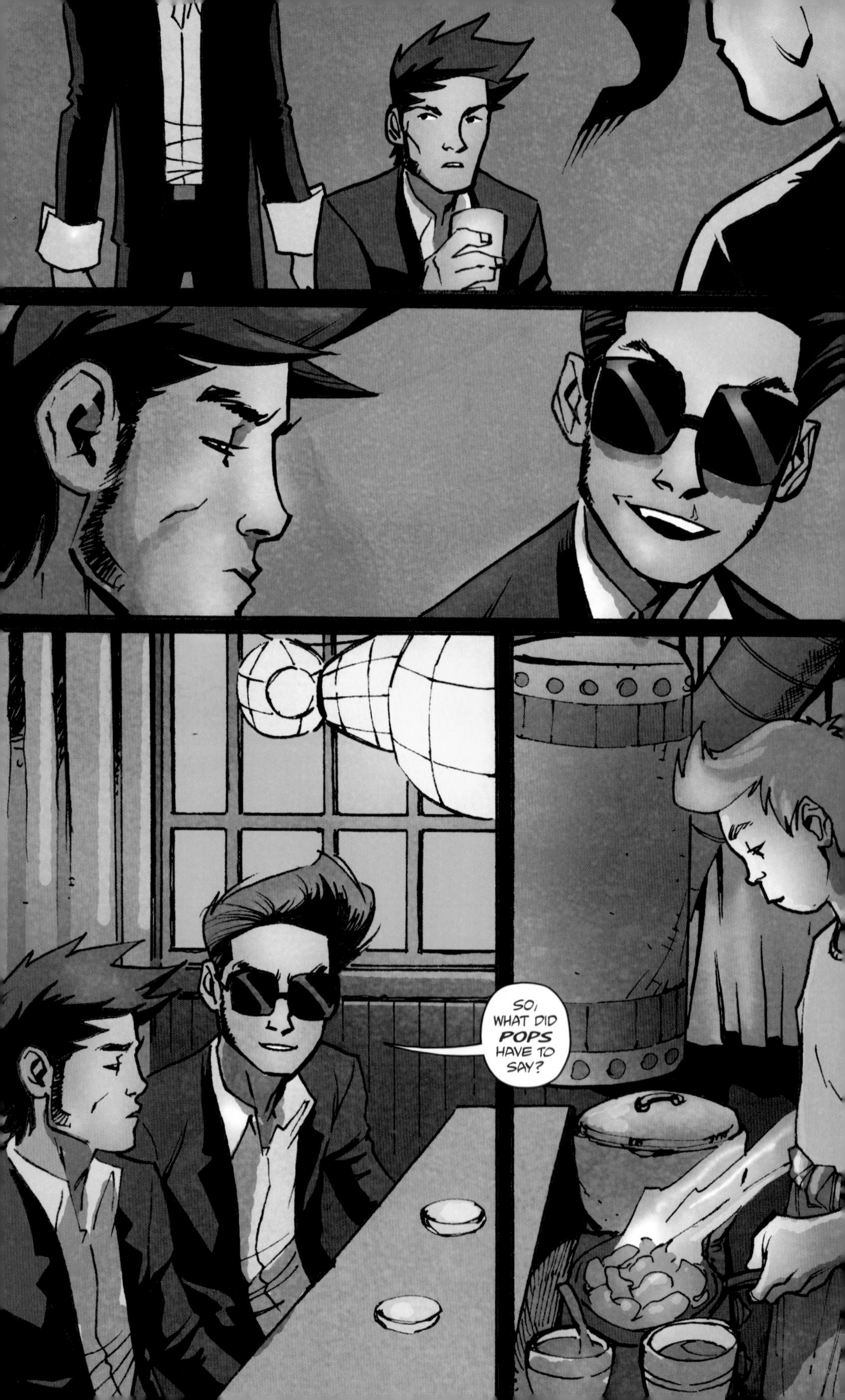
SO, WHAT DID POPS HAVE TO SAY?

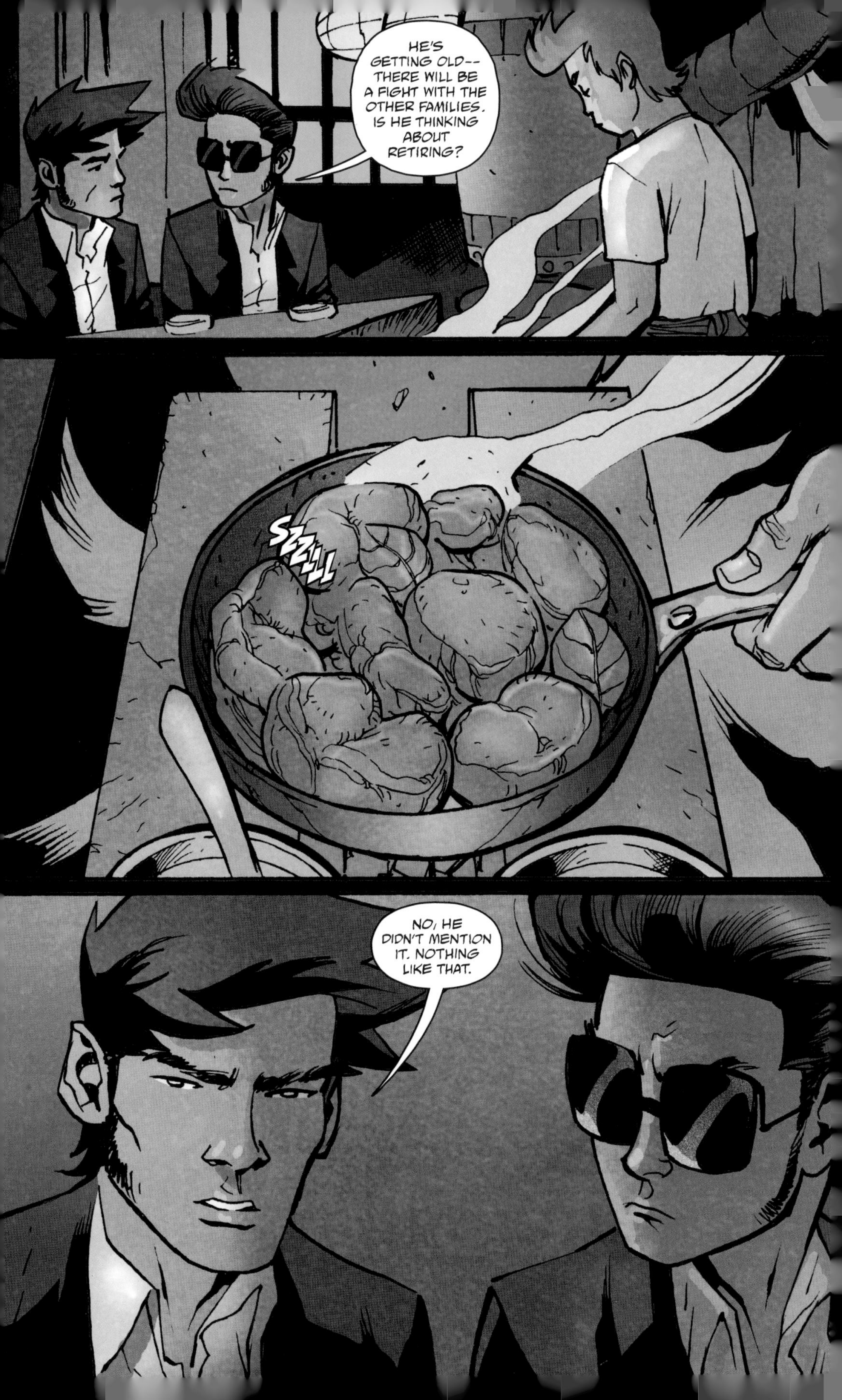
HE'S GETTING OLD-- THERE WILL BE A FIGHT WITH THE OTHER FAMILIES. IS HE THINKING ABOUT RETIRING?
SZZZZ
NO, HE DIDN'T MENTION IT. NOTHING LIKE THAT.

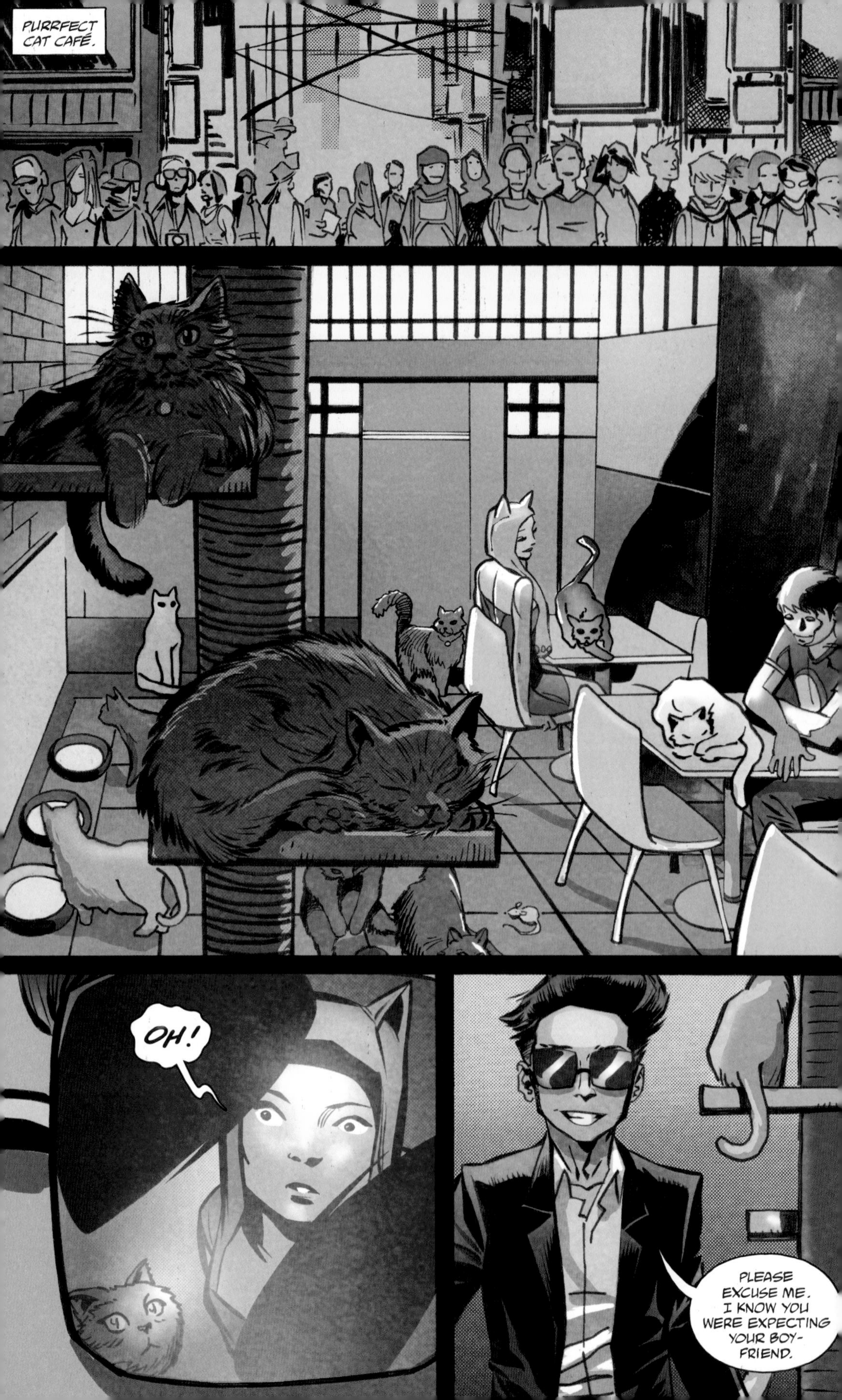
PURRFECT CAT CAFÉ.
OH!
PLEASE EXCUSE ME. I KNOW YOU WERE EXPECTING YOUR BOY-FRIEND.

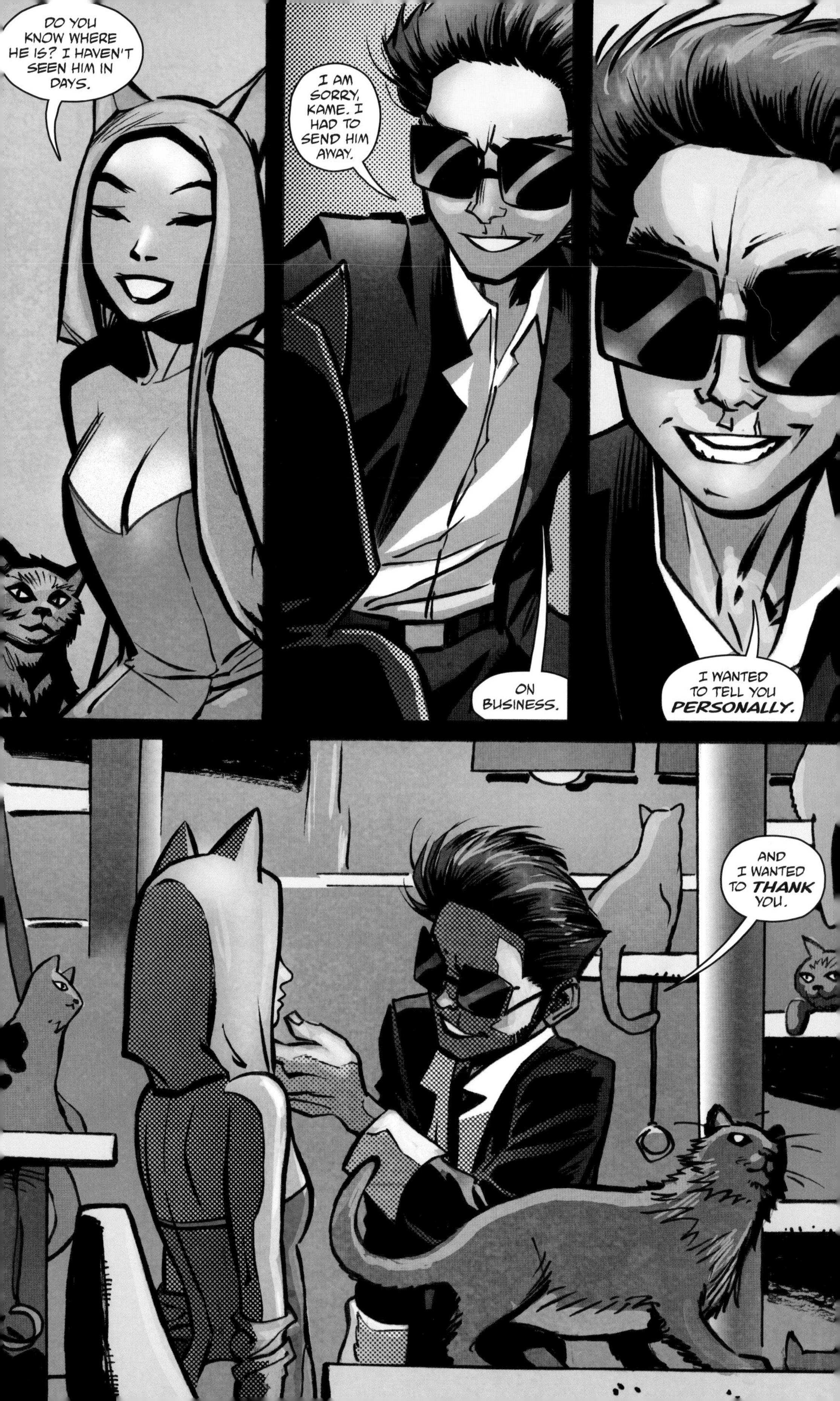
DO YOU KNOW WHERE HE IS? I HAVEN'T SEEN HIM IN DAYS.
I AM SORRY, KAME. I HAD TO SEND HIM AWAY.
ON BUSINESS.
I WANTED TO TELL YOU **PERSONALLY.**
AND I WANTED TO **THANK** YOU.

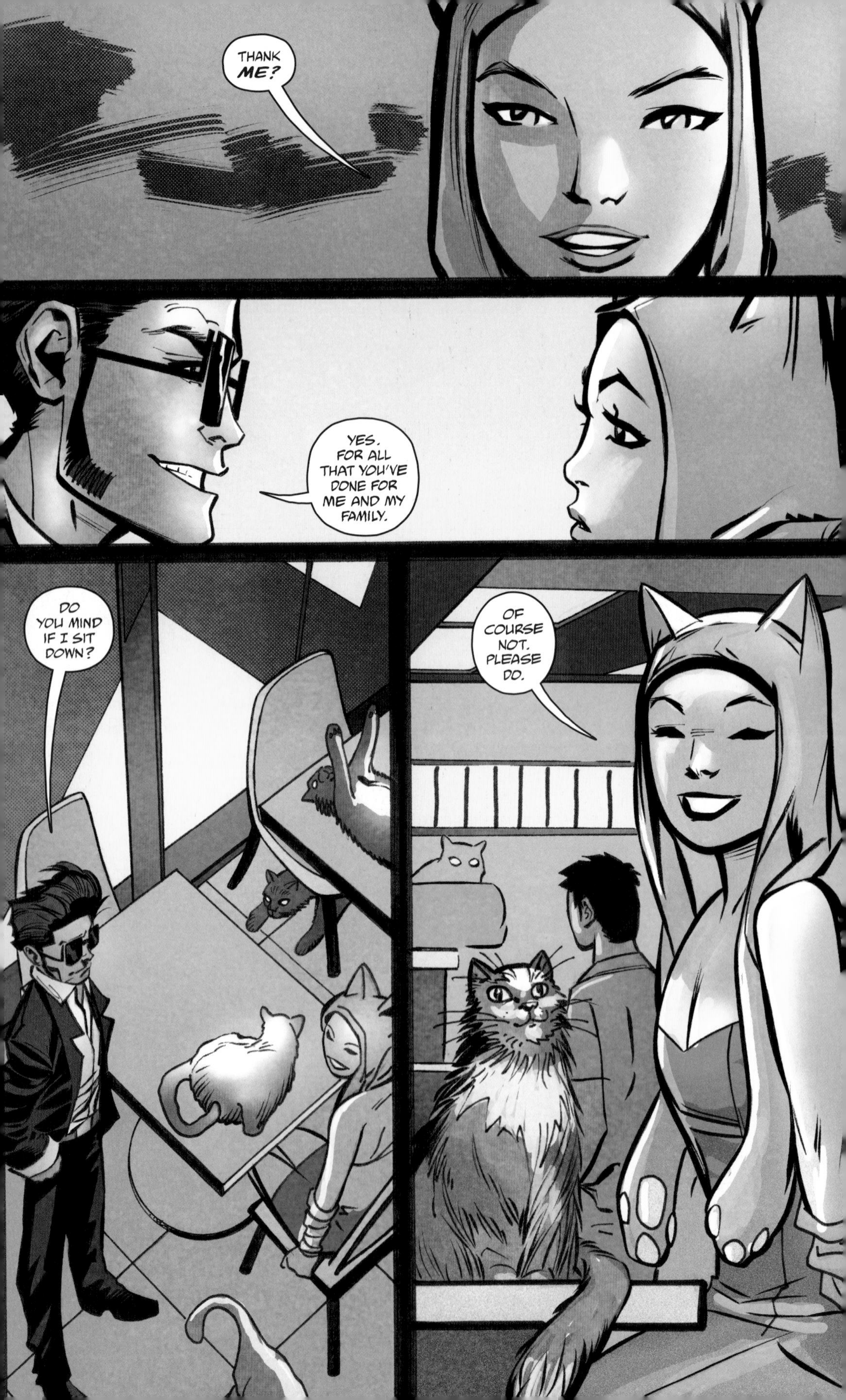
THANK ME?
YES. FOR ALL THAT YOU'VE DONE FOR ME AND MY FAMILY.
DO YOU MIND IF I SIT DOWN?
OF COURSE NOT. PLEASE DO.

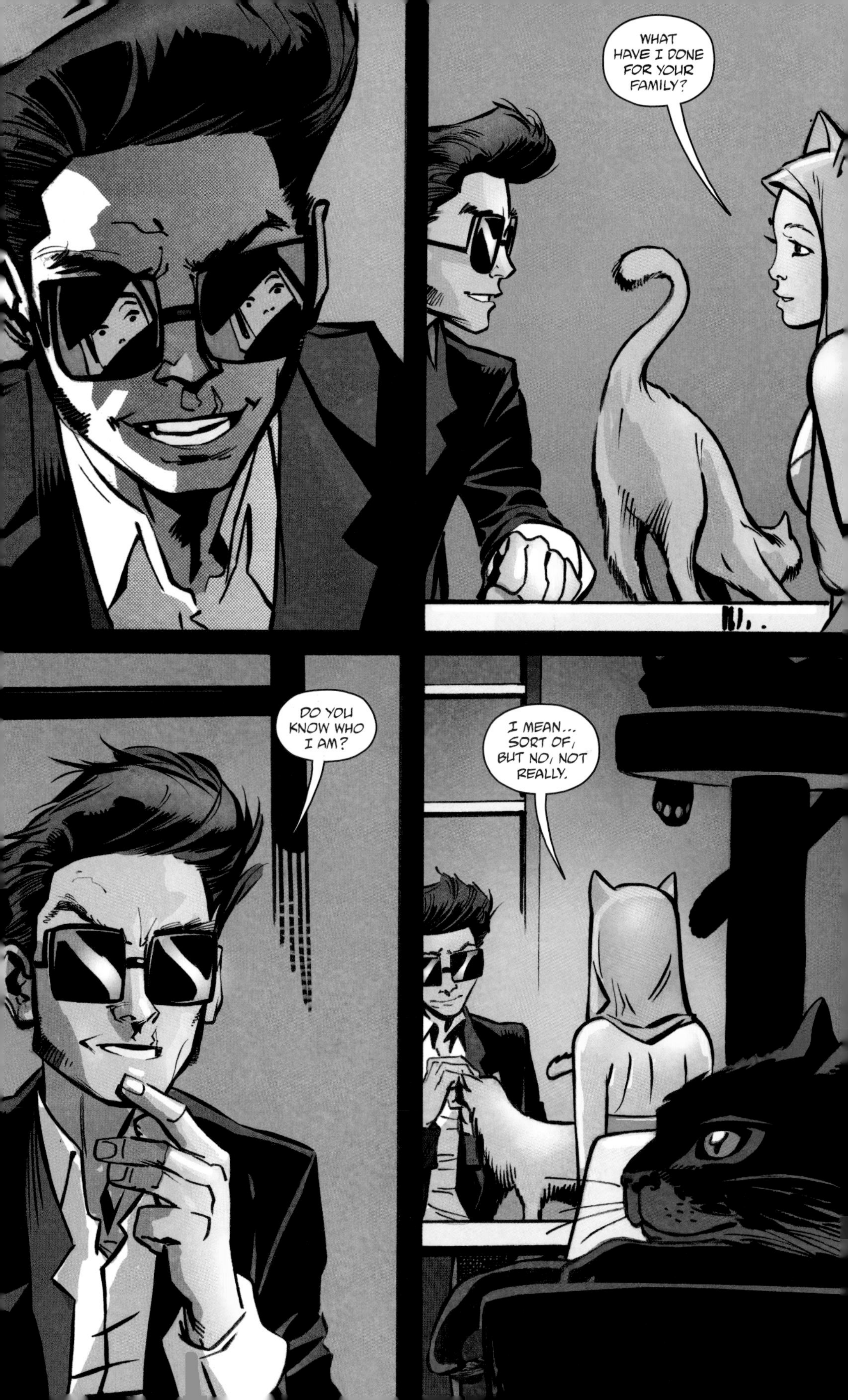
WHAT HAVE I DONE FOR YOUR FAMILY?
DO YOU KNOW WHO I AM?
I MEAN... SORT OF, BUT NO, NOT REALLY.

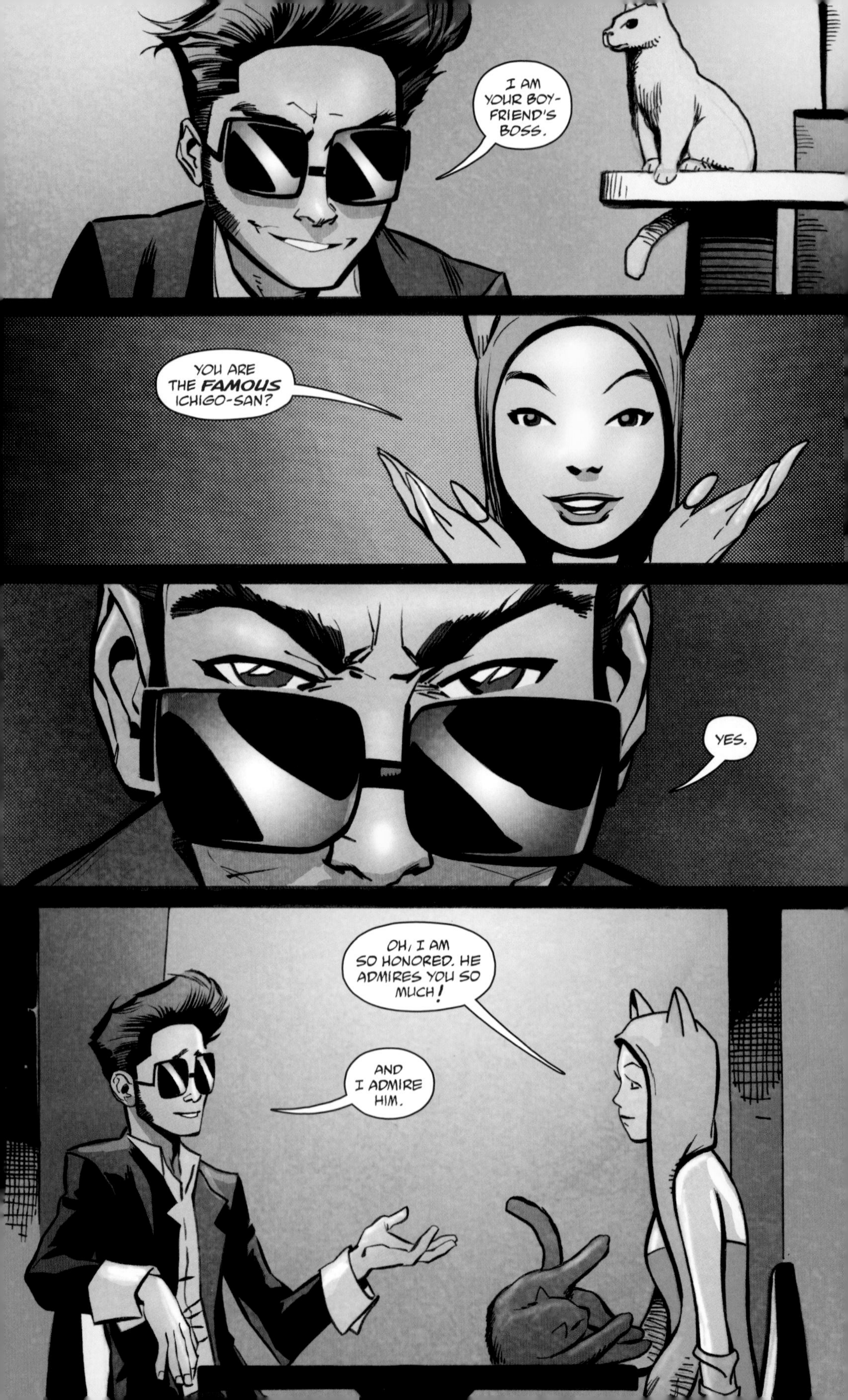
I AM YOUR BOY-FRIEND'S BOSS.
YOU ARE THE FAMOUS ICHIGO-SAN?
YES.
OH, I AM SO HONORED. HE ADMIRES YOU SO MUCH!
AND I ADMIRE HIM.

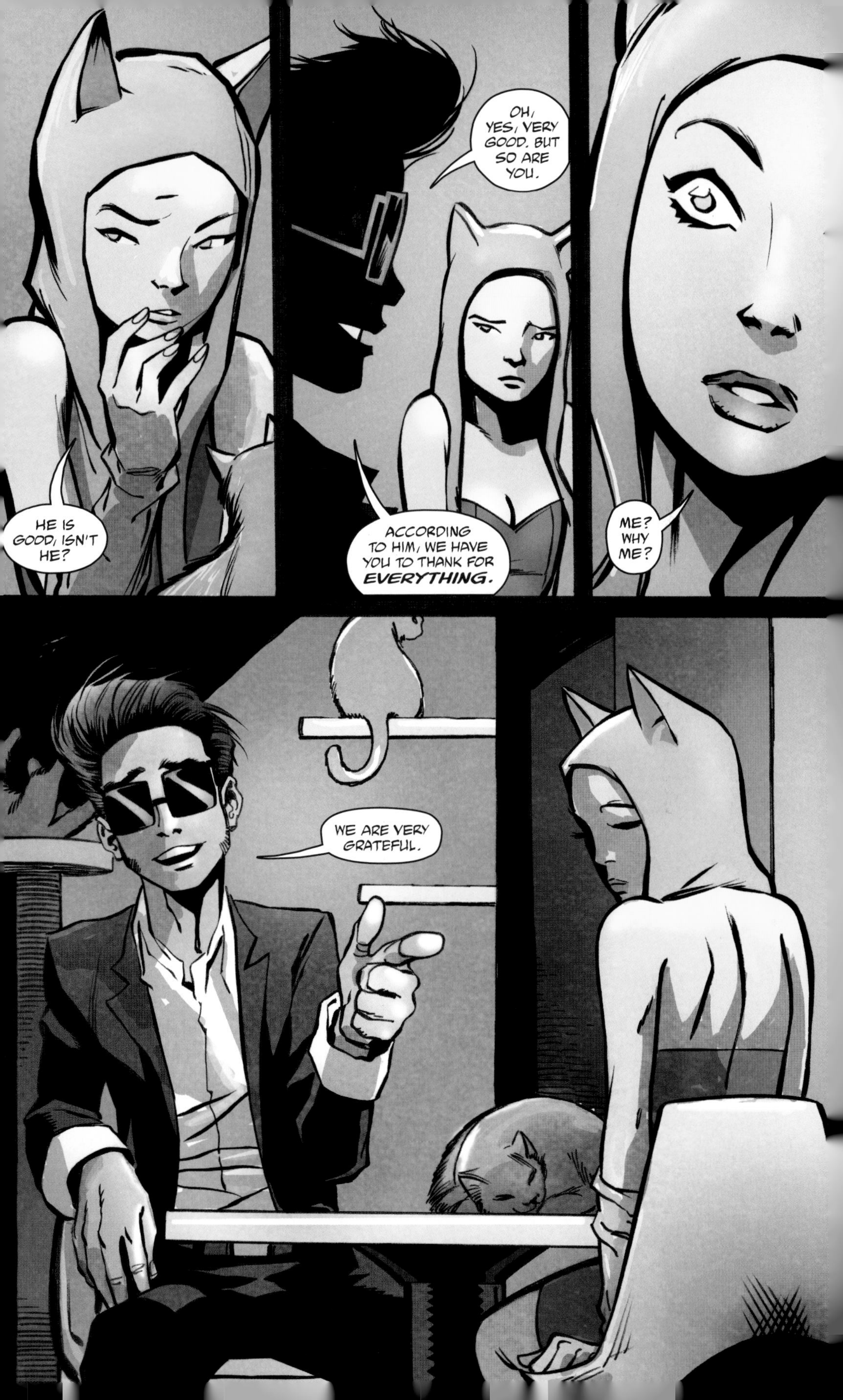
HE IS GOOD, ISN'T HE?
OH, YES, VERY GOOD. BUT SO ARE YOU.
ACCORDING TO HIM, WE HAVE YOU TO THANK FOR EVERYTHING.
ME? WHY ME?
WE ARE VERY GRATEFUL.

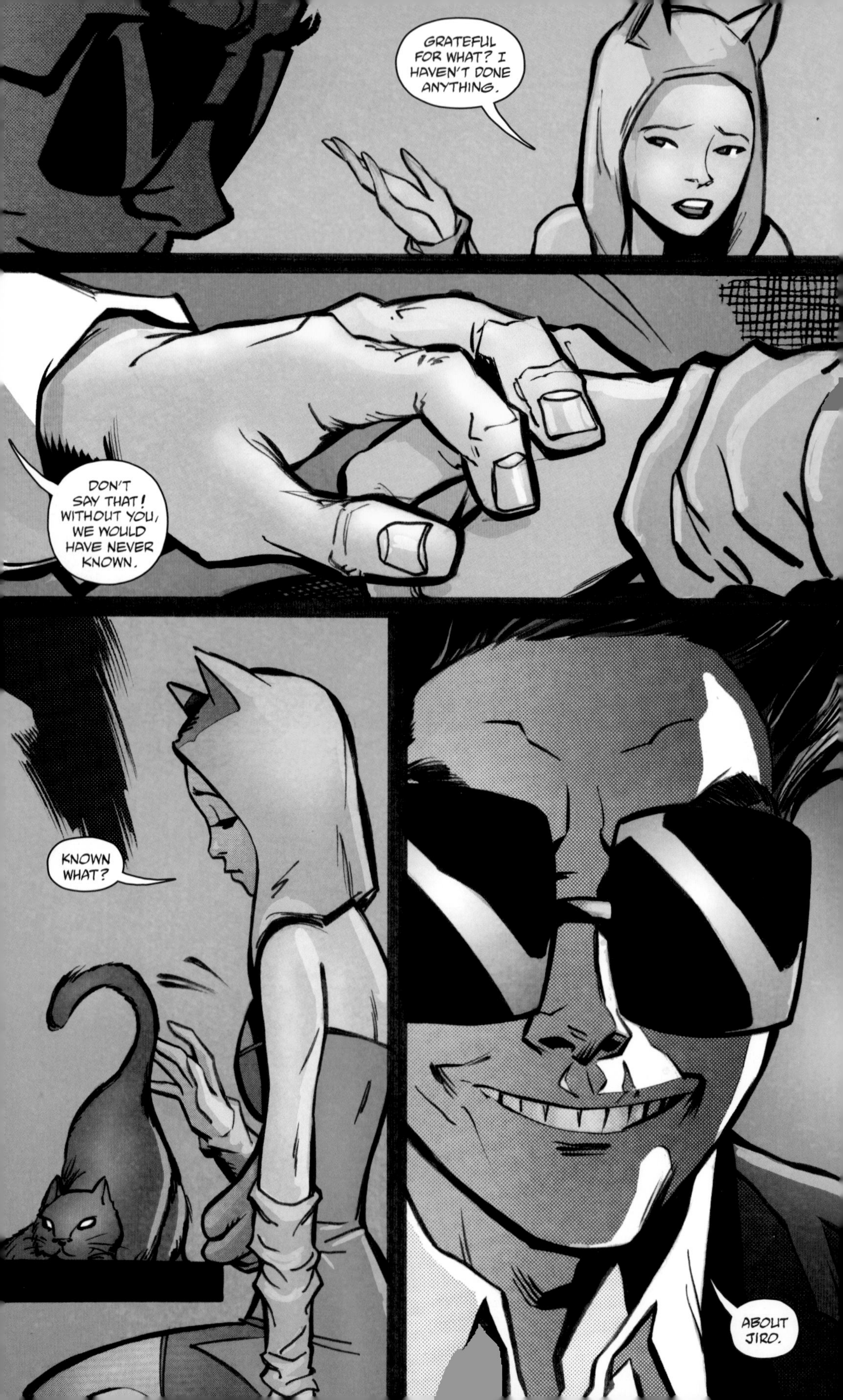
GRATEFUL FOR WHAT? I HAVEN'T DONE ANYTHING.
DON'T SAY THAT! WITHOUT YOU, WE WOULD HAVE NEVER KNOWN.
KNOWN WHAT?
ABOUT JIRO.

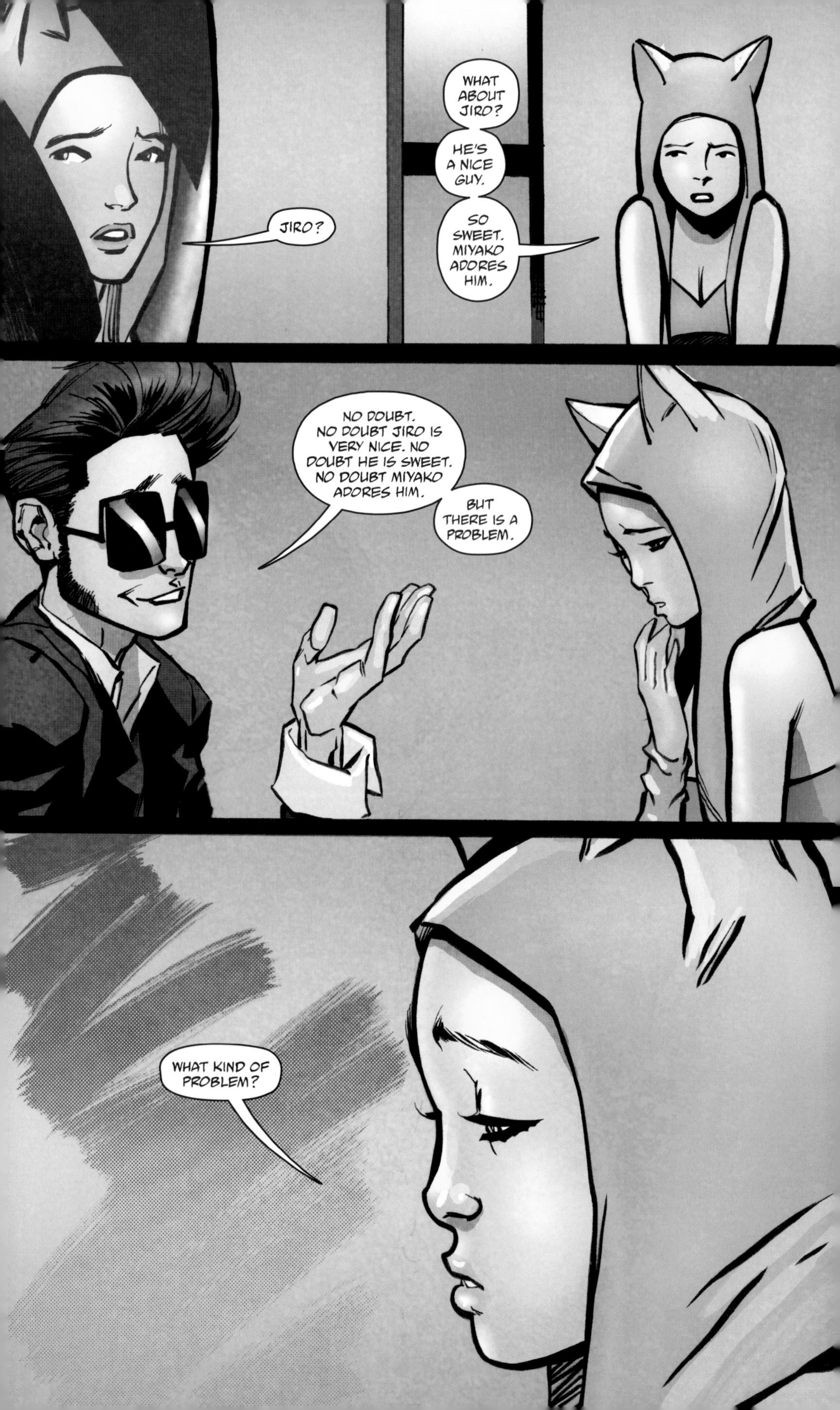
JIRO?
WHAT ABOUT JIRO?
HE'S A NICE GUY.
SO SWEET. MIYAKO ADORES HIM.
NO DOUBT. NO DOUBT JIRO IS VERY NICE. NO DOUBT HE IS SWEET. NO DOUBT MIYAKO ADORES HIM.
BUT THERE IS A PROBLEM.
WHAT KIND OF PROBLEM?

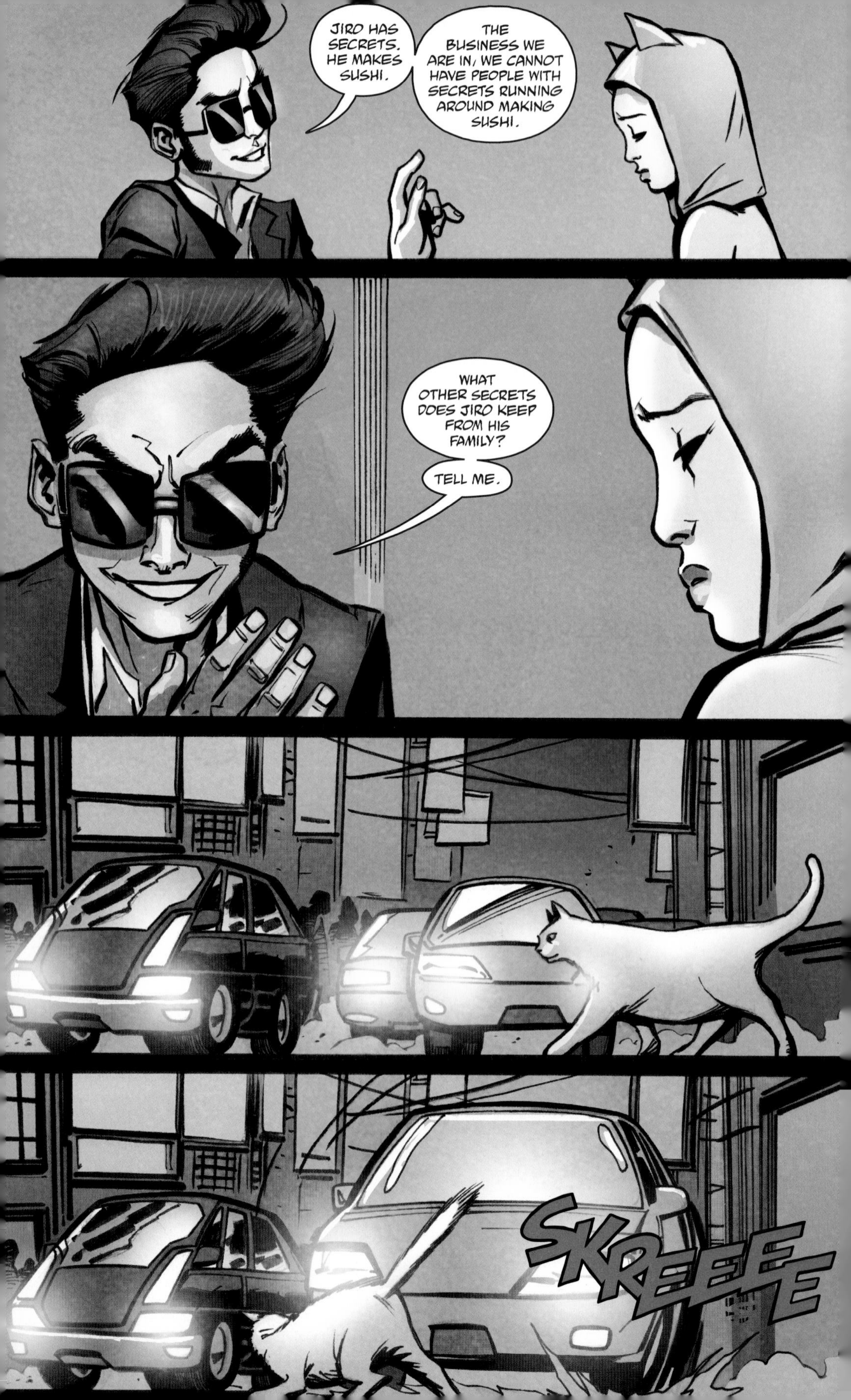

JIRO HAS SECRETS. HE MAKES SUSHI.
THE BUSINESS WE ARE IN, WE CANNOT HAVE PEOPLE WITH SECRETS RUNNING AROUND MAKING SUSHI.
WHAT OTHER SECRETS DOES JIRO KEEP FROM HIS FAMILY?
TELL ME.
SKREEEEE

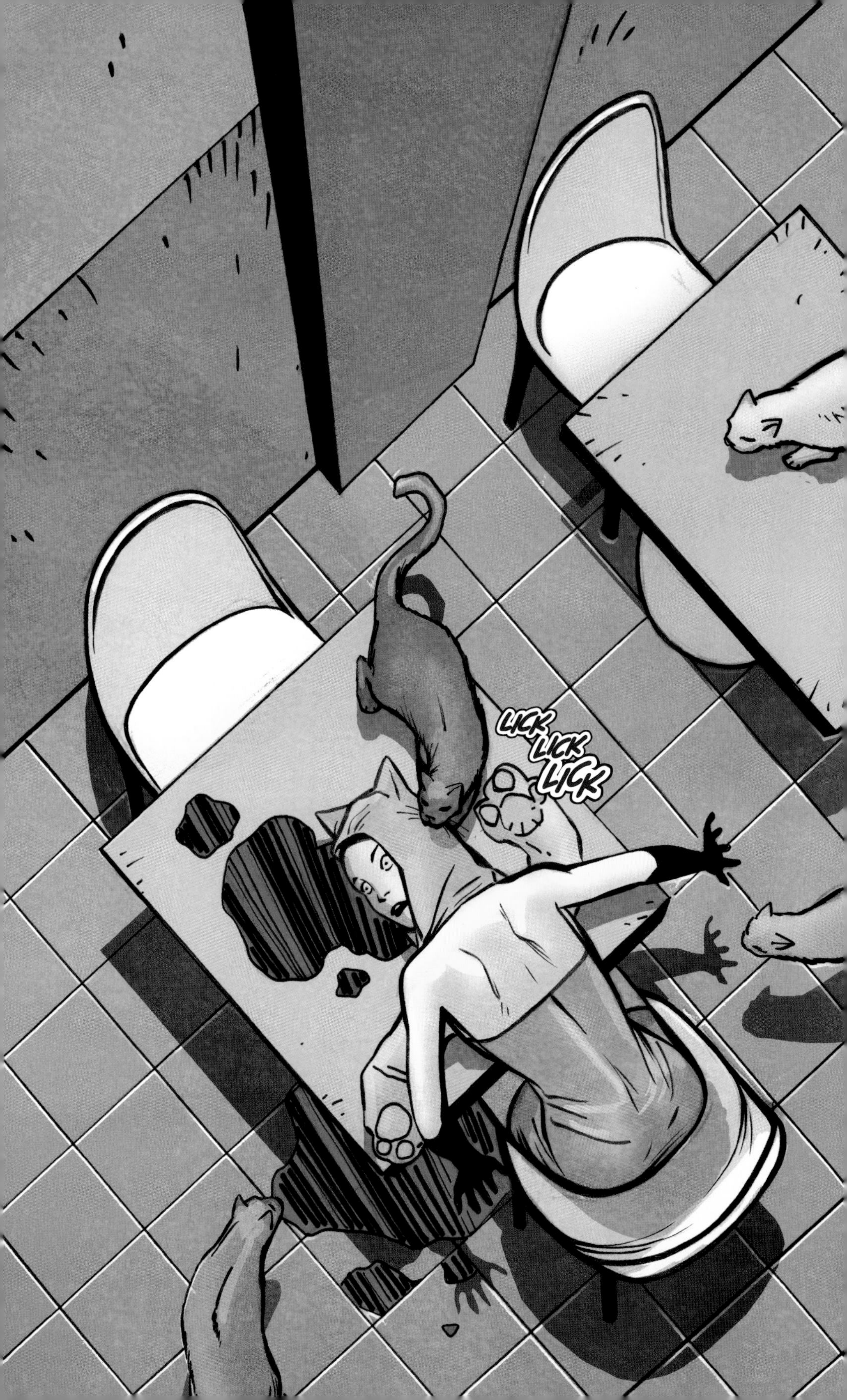
LICK
LICK
LICK

CHANKO NABE

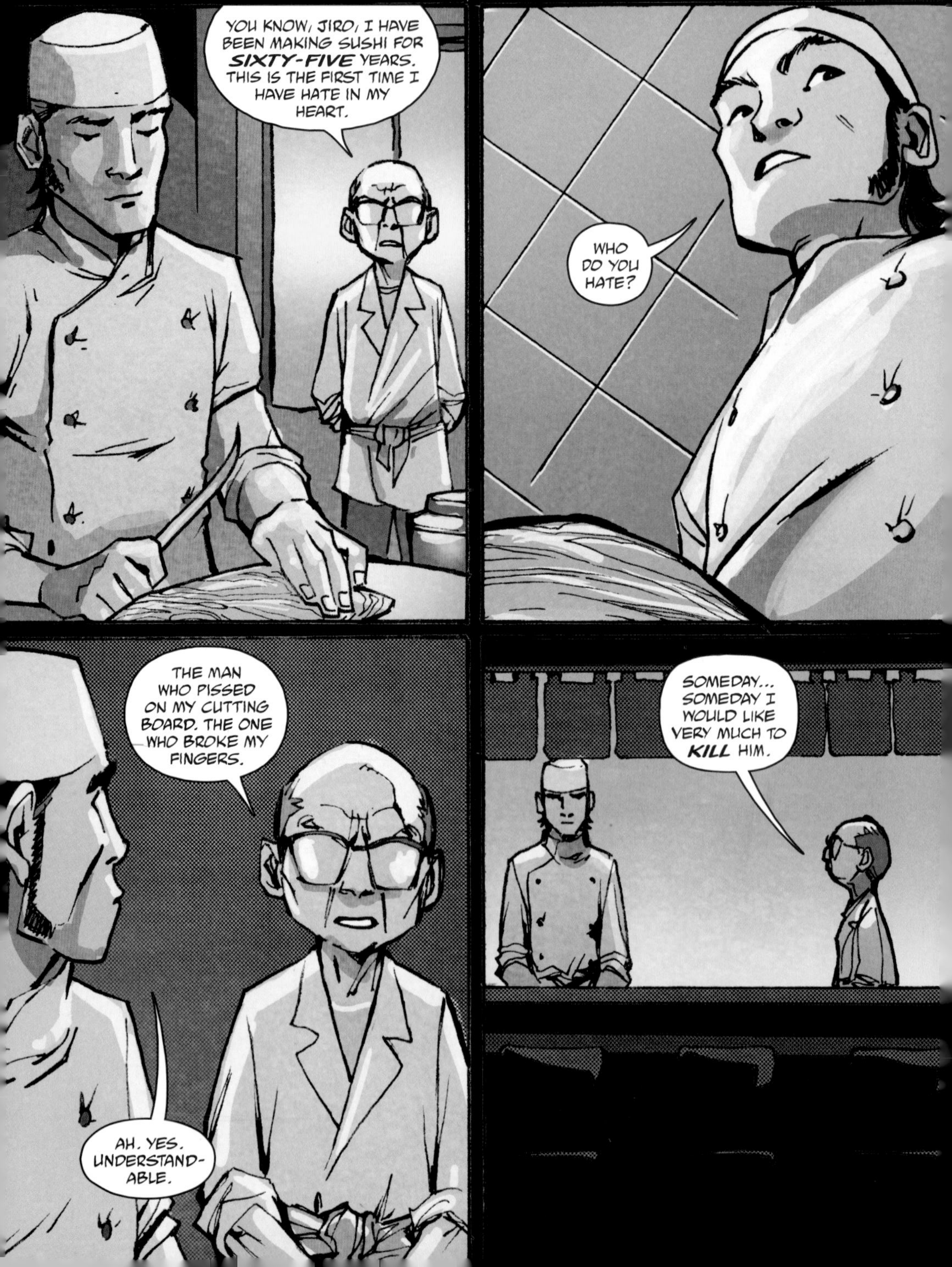
YOU KNOW, JIRO, I HAVE BEEN MAKING SUSHI FOR SIXTY-FIVE YEARS. THIS IS THE FIRST TIME I HAVE HATE IN MY HEART.
WHO DO YOU HATE?
THE MAN WHO PISSED ON MY CUTTING BOARD. THE ONE WHO BROKE MY FINGERS.
AH. YES. UNDERSTAND-ABLE.
SOMEDAY... SOMEDAY I WOULD LIKE VERY MUCH TO KILL HIM.

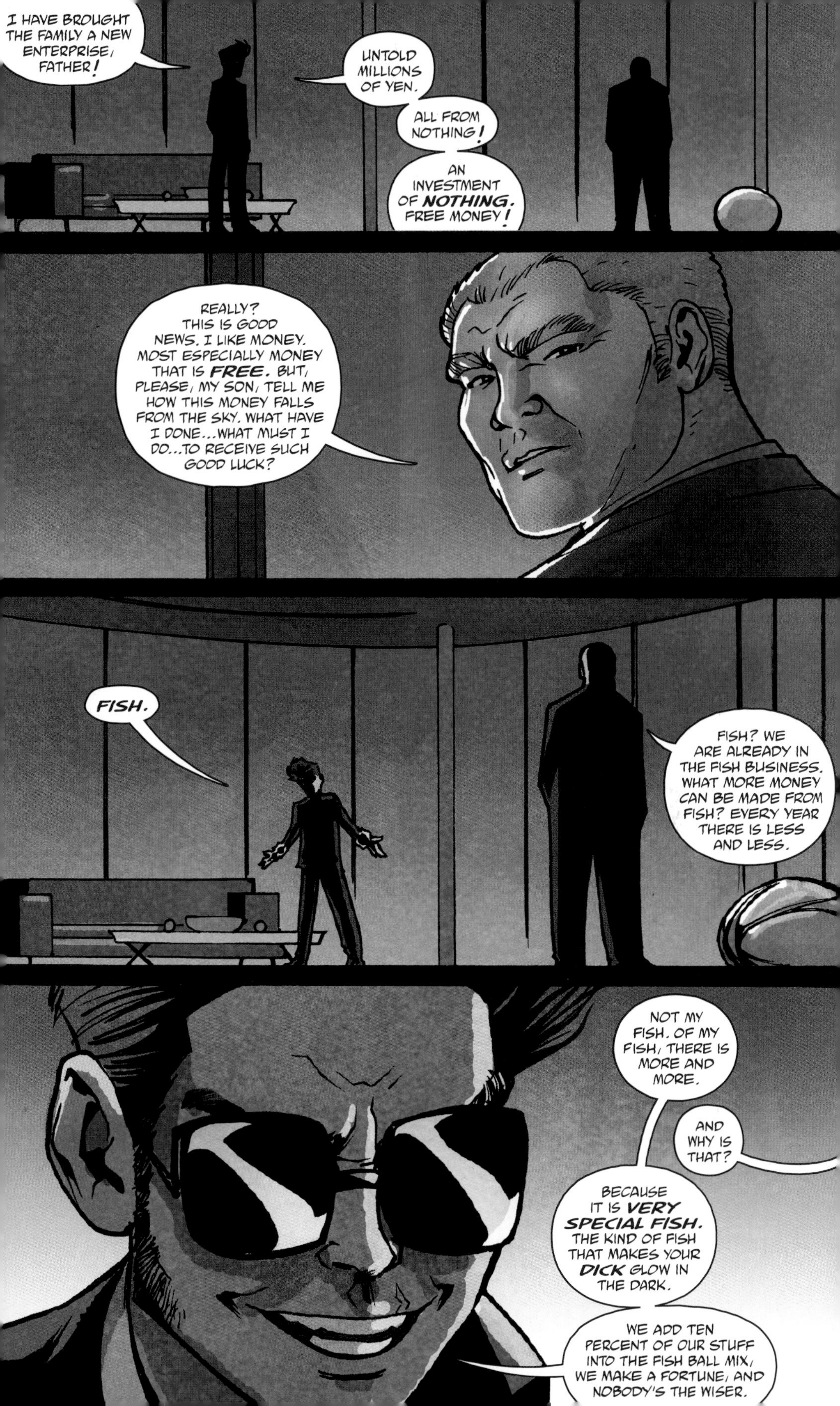
I HAVE BROUGHT THE FAMILY A NEW ENTERPRISE, FATHER!
UNTOLD MILLIONS OF YEN.
ALL FROM NOTHING!
AN INVESTMENT OF NOTHING. FREE MONEY!
REALLY? THIS IS GOOD NEWS. I LIKE MONEY. MOST ESPECIALLY MONEY THAT IS FREE. BUT, PLEASE, MY SON, TELL ME HOW THIS MONEY FALLS FROM THE SKY. WHAT HAVE I DONE...WHAT MUST I DO...TO RECEIVE SUCH GOOD LUCK?
FISH.
FISH? WE ARE ALREADY IN THE FISH BUSINESS. WHAT MORE MONEY CAN BE MADE FROM FISH? EVERY YEAR THERE IS LESS AND LESS.
NOT MY FISH. OF MY FISH, THERE IS MORE AND MORE.
AND WHY IS THAT?
BECAUSE IT IS VERY SPECIAL FISH. THE KIND OF FISH THAT MAKES YOUR DICK GLOW IN THE DARK.
WE ADD TEN PERCENT OF OUR STUFF INTO THE FISH BALL MIX, WE MAKE A FORTUNE, AND NOBODY'S THE WISER.

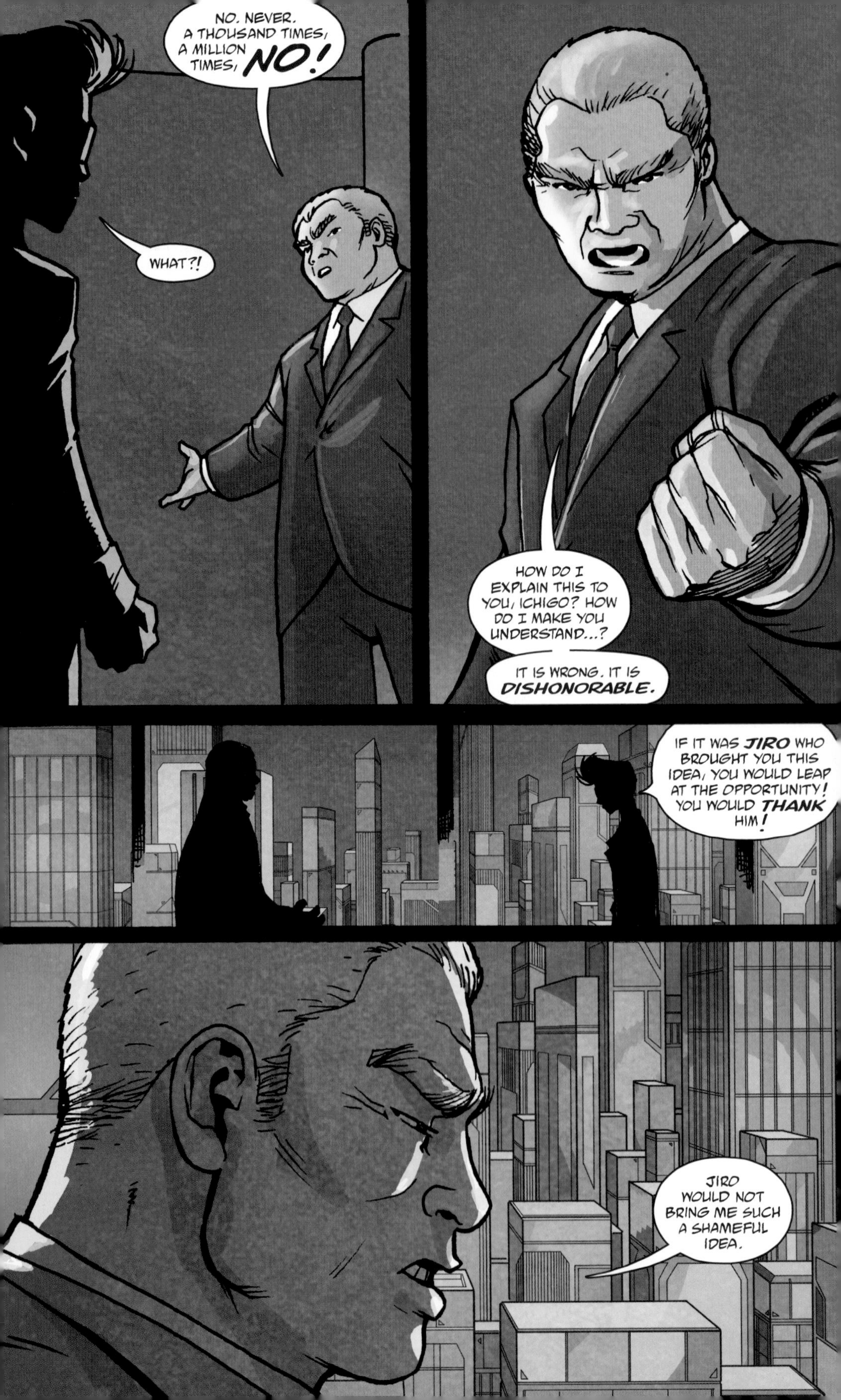
NO. NEVER. A THOUSAND TIMES, A MILLION TIMES, NO!
WHAT?!
HOW DO I EXPLAIN THIS TO YOU, ICHIGO? HOW DO I MAKE YOU UNDERSTAND...?
IT IS WRONG. IT IS DISHONORABLE.
IF IT WAS JIRO WHO BROUGHT YOU THIS IDEA, YOU WOULD LEAP AT THE OPPORTUNITY! YOU WOULD THANK HIM!
JIRO WOULD NOT BRING ME SUCH A SHAMEFUL IDEA.

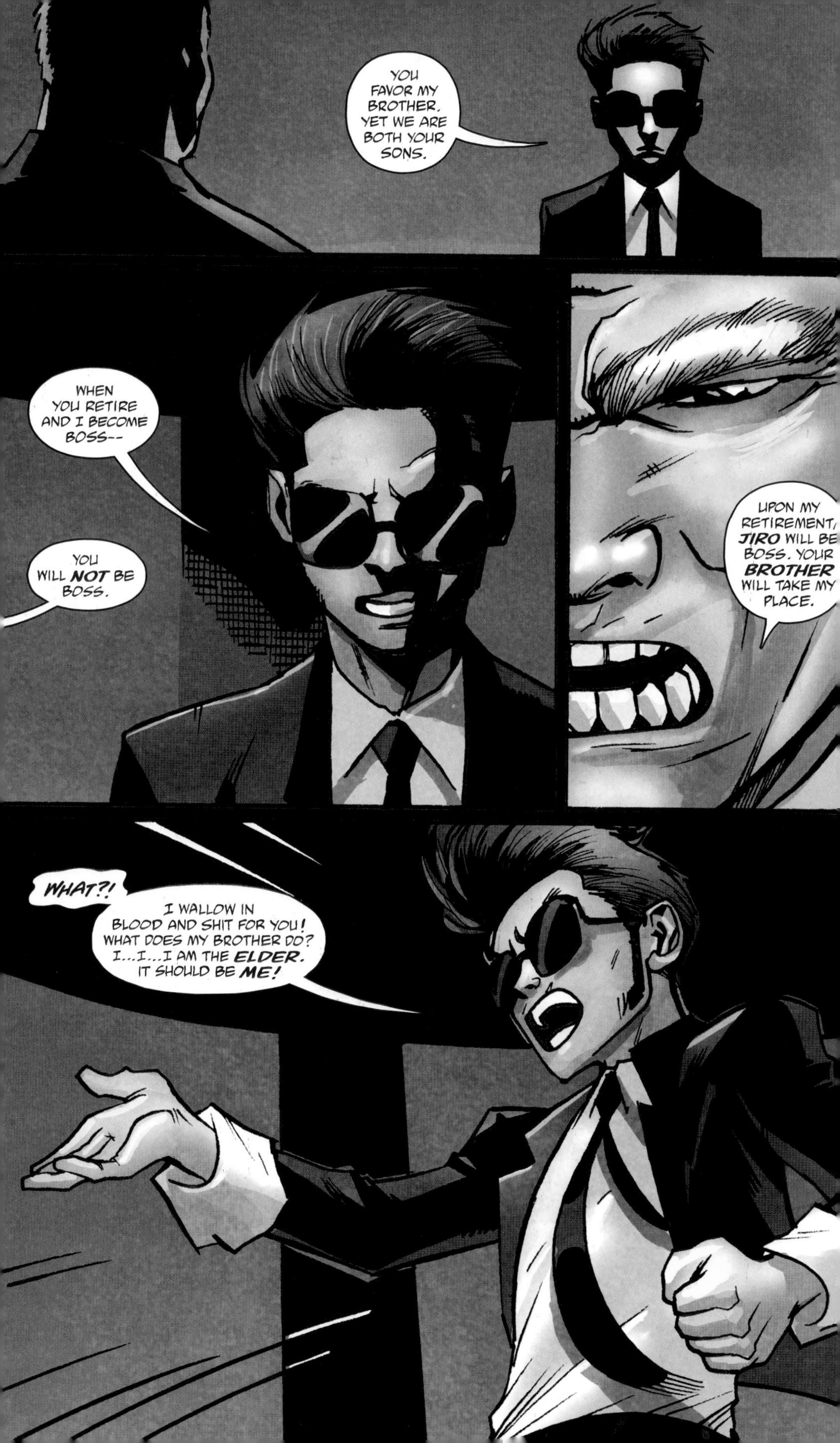
YOU FAVOR MY BROTHER. YET WE ARE BOTH YOUR SONS.
WHEN YOU RETIRE AND I BECOME BOSS--
YOU WILL **NOT** BE BOSS.
UPON MY RETIREMENT, **JIRO** WILL BE BOSS. YOUR **BROTHER** WILL TAKE MY PLACE.
WHAT?!
I WALLOW IN BLOOD AND SHIT FOR YOU! WHAT DOES MY BROTHER DO? I...I...I AM THE **ELDER.** IT SHOULD BE **ME!**

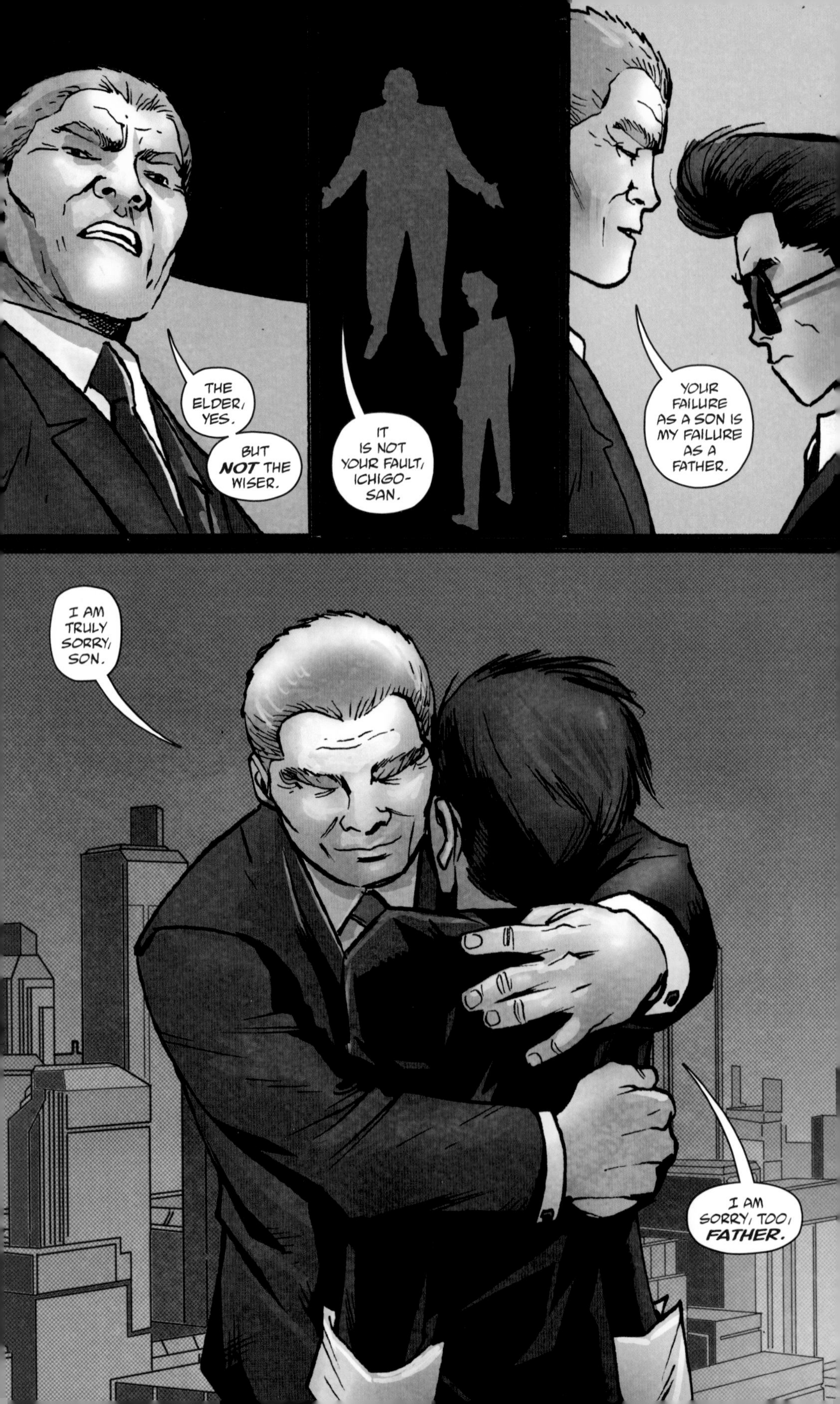
THE ELDER, YES.
BUT **NOT** THE WISER.
IT IS NOT YOUR FAULT, ICHIGO-SAN.
YOUR FAILURE AS A SON IS MY FAILURE AS A FATHER.
I AM TRULY SORRY, SON.
I AM SORRY, TOO, ***FATHER.***

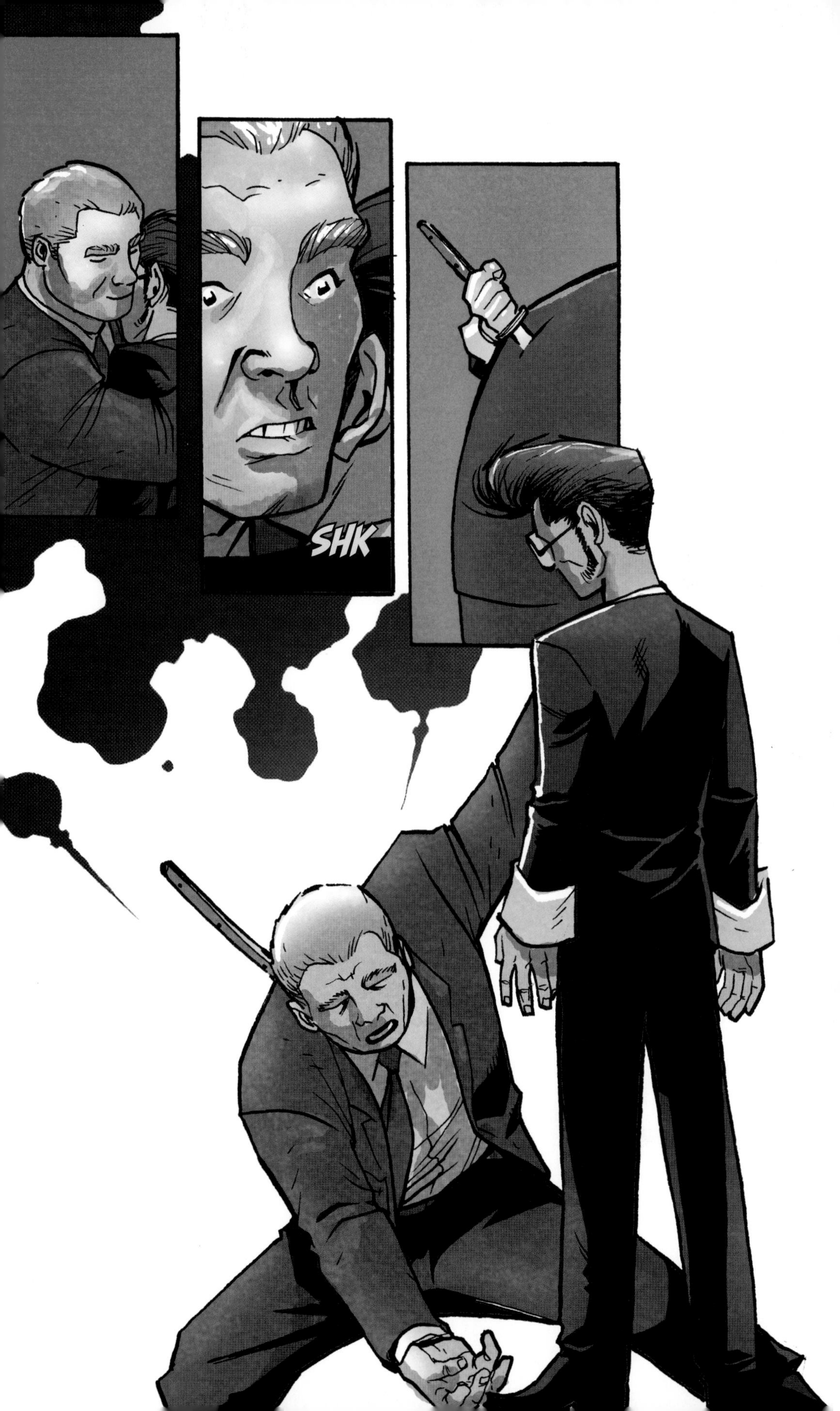
SHK

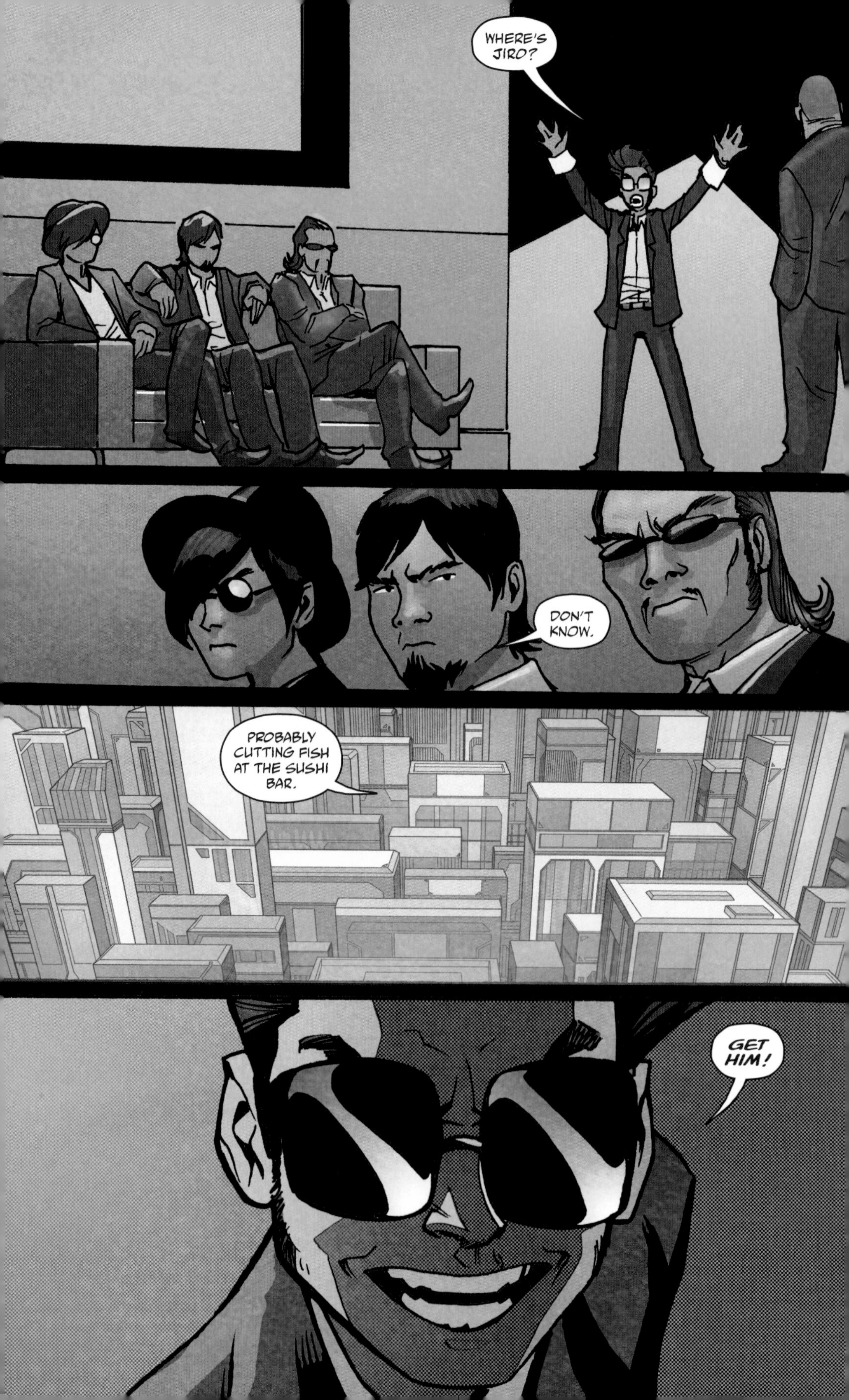
WHERE'S JIRO?
DON'T KNOW.
PROBABLY CUTTING FISH AT THE SUSHI BAR.
GET HIM!

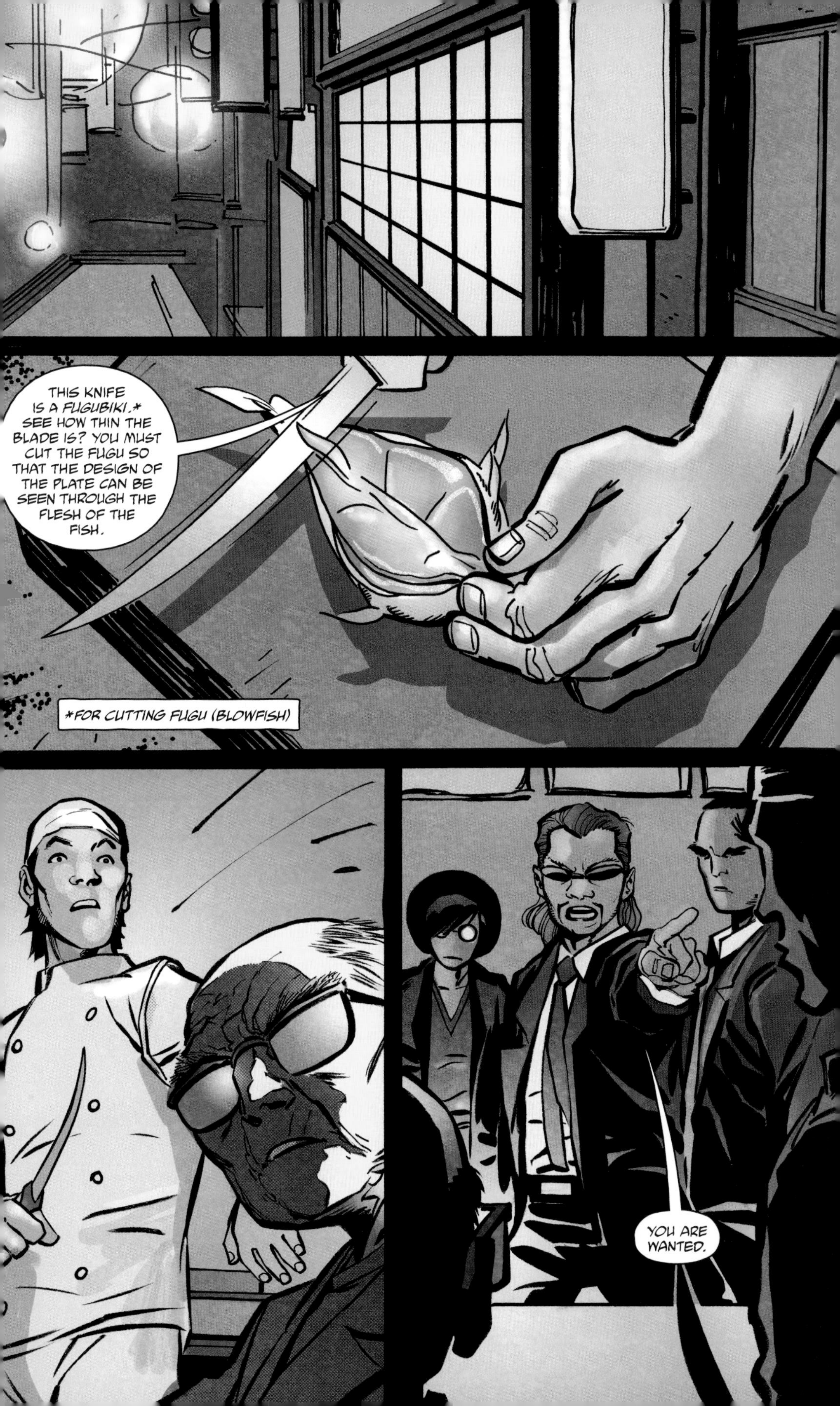
THIS KNIFE IS A FUGUBIKI.* SEE HOW THIN THE BLADE IS? YOU MUST CUT THE FUGU SO THAT THE DESIGN OF THE PLATE CAN BE SEEN THROUGH THE FLESH OF THE FISH.
*FOR CUTTING FUGU (BLOWFISH)
YOU ARE WANTED.

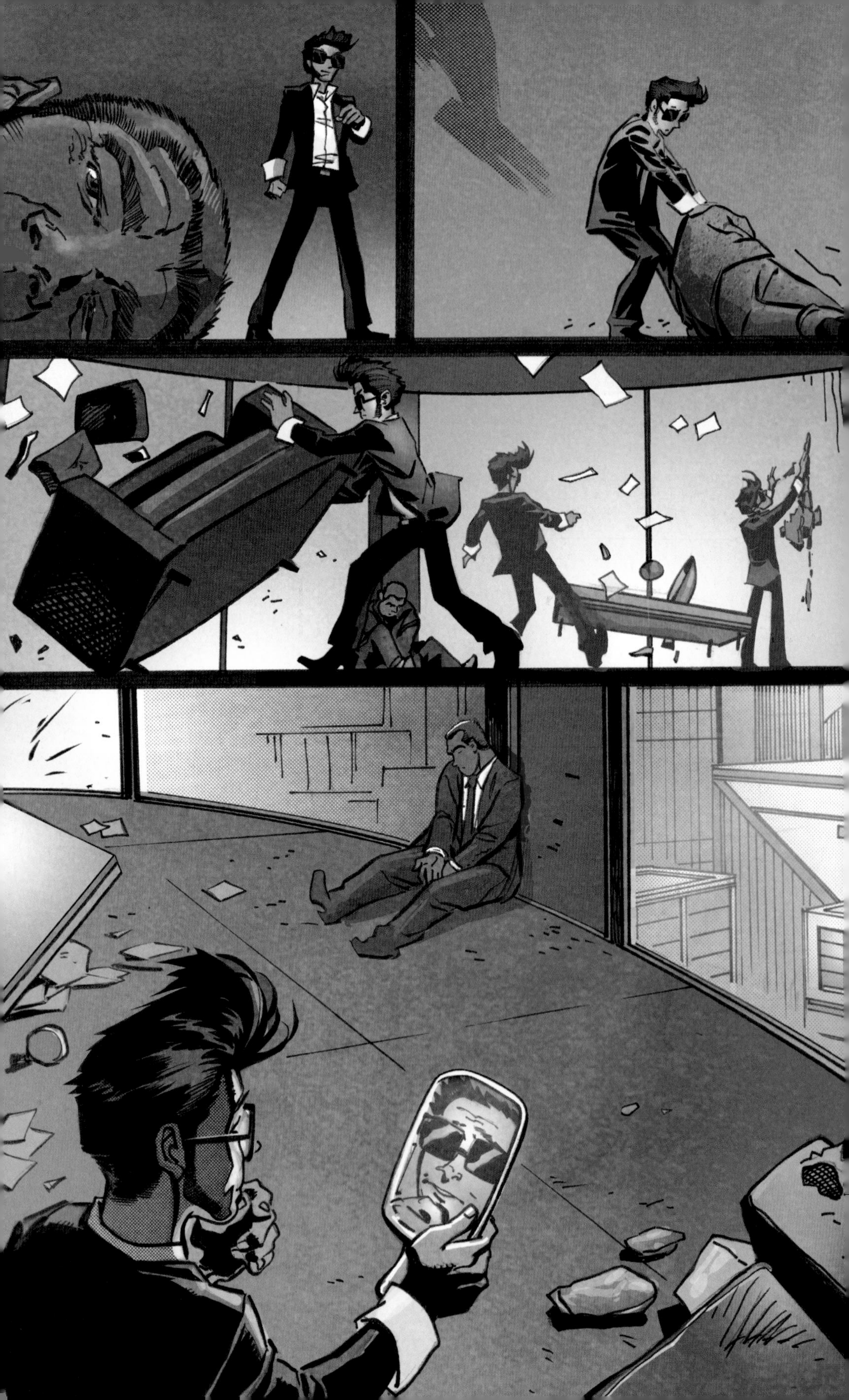

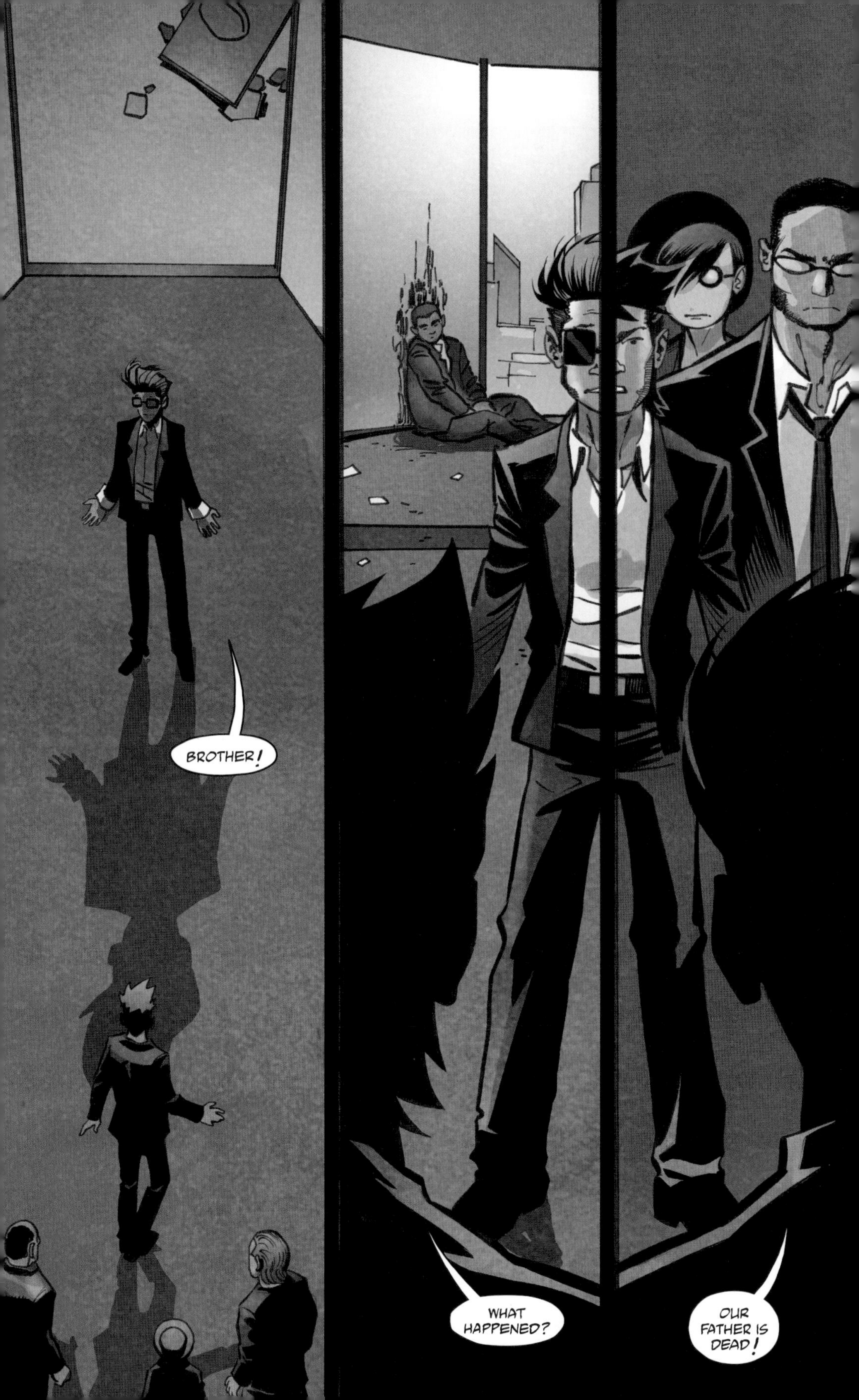
BROTHER!
WHAT HAPPENED?
OUR FATHER IS DEAD!

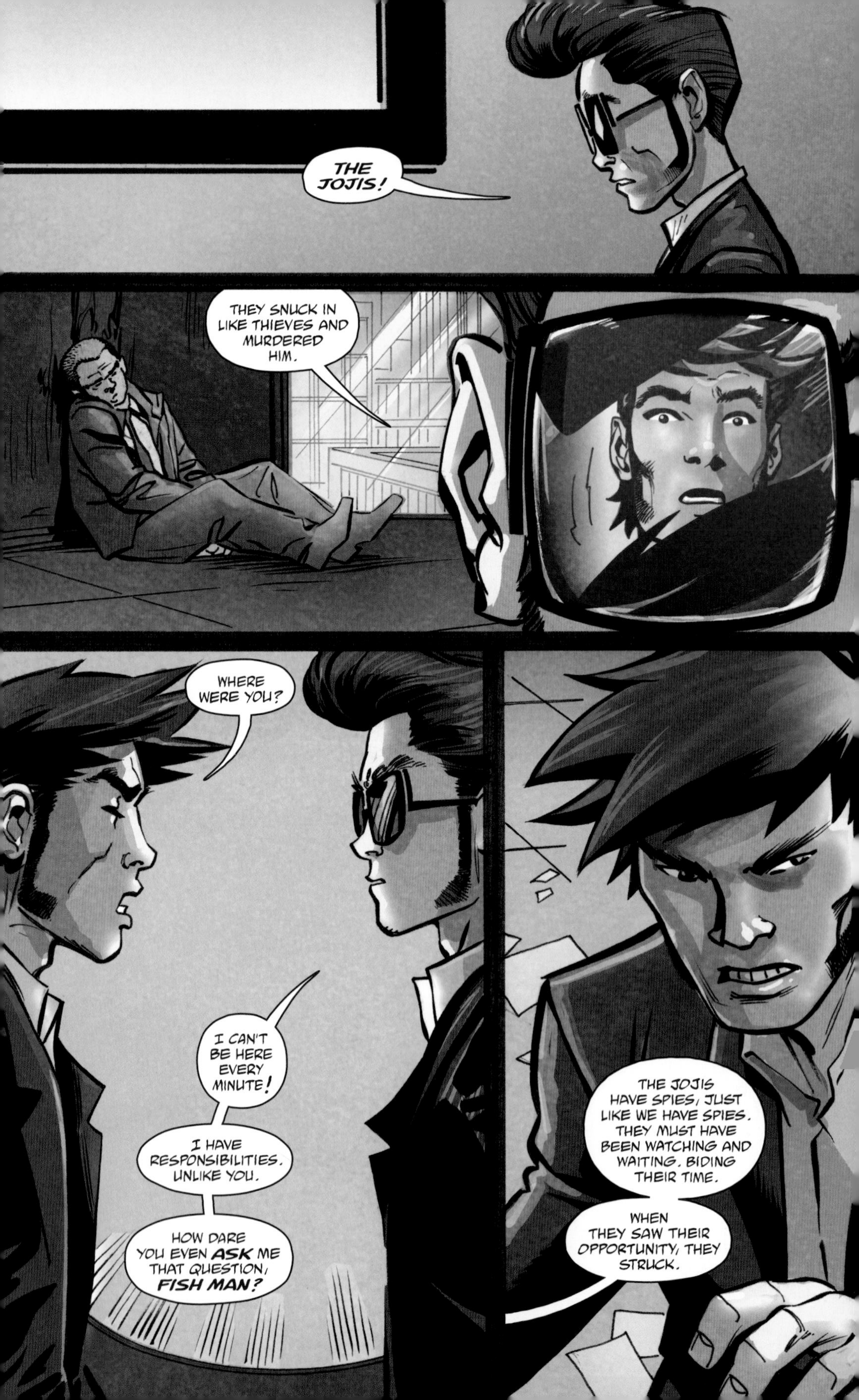
THE JOJIS!
THEY SNUCK IN LIKE THIEVES AND MURDERED HIM.
WHERE WERE YOU?
I CAN'T BE HERE EVERY MINUTE!
I HAVE RESPONSIBILITIES. UNLIKE YOU.
HOW DARE YOU EVEN ASK ME THAT QUESTION, FISH MAN?
THE JOJIS HAVE SPIES, JUST LIKE WE HAVE SPIES. THEY MUST HAVE BEEN WATCHING AND WAITING. BIDING THEIR TIME.
WHEN THEY SAW THEIR OPPORTUNITY, THEY STRUCK.

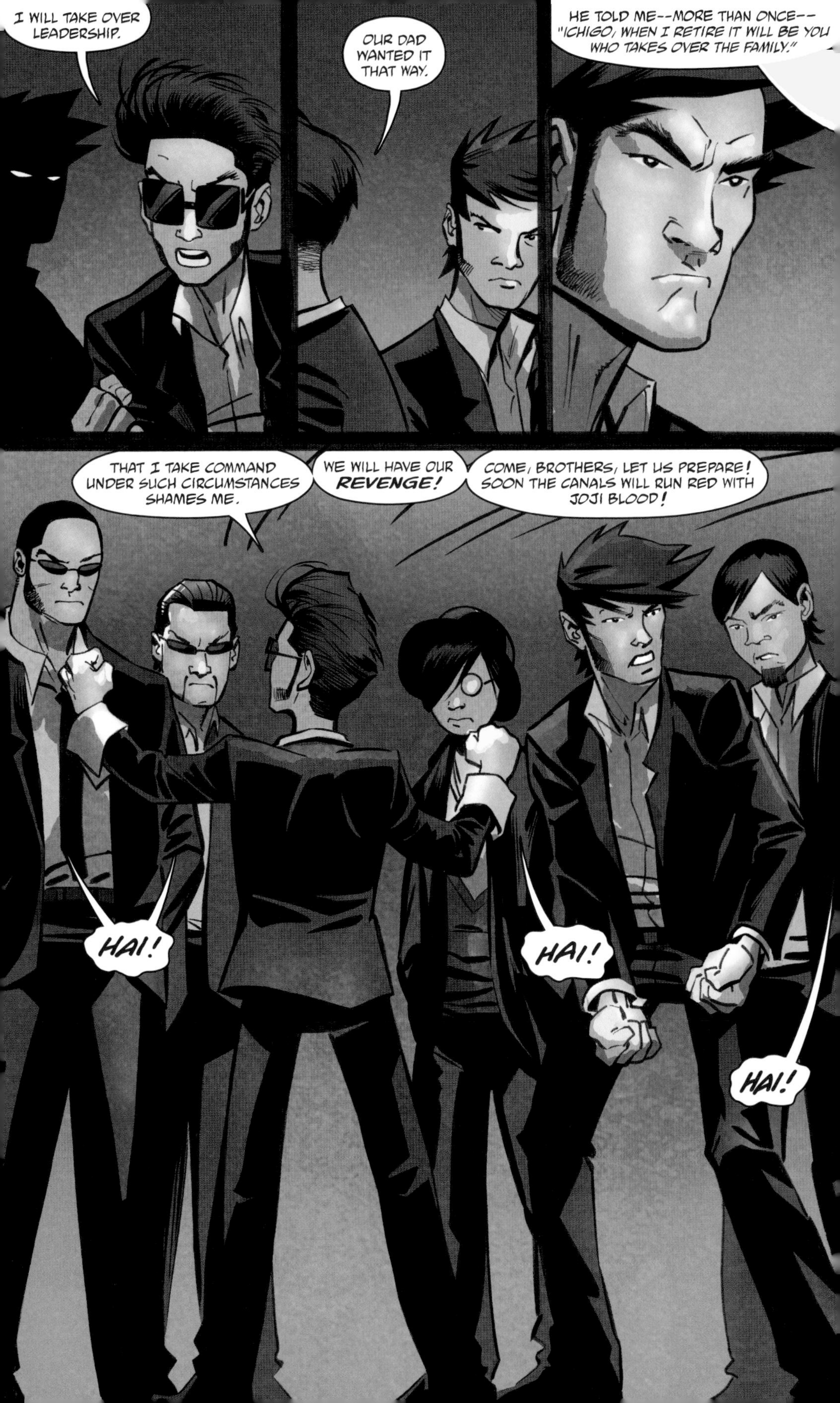

I WILL TAKE OVER LEADERSHIP.
OUR DAD WANTED IT THAT WAY.
HE TOLD ME--MORE THAN ONCE--"ICHIGO, WHEN I RETIRE IT WILL BE YOU WHO TAKES OVER THE FAMILY."
THAT I TAKE COMMAND UNDER SUCH CIRCUMSTANCES SHAMES ME.
WE WILL HAVE OUR REVENGE!
COME, BROTHERS, LET US PREPARE! SOON THE CANALS WILL RUN RED WITH JOJI BLOOD!
HAI!
HAI!
HAI!

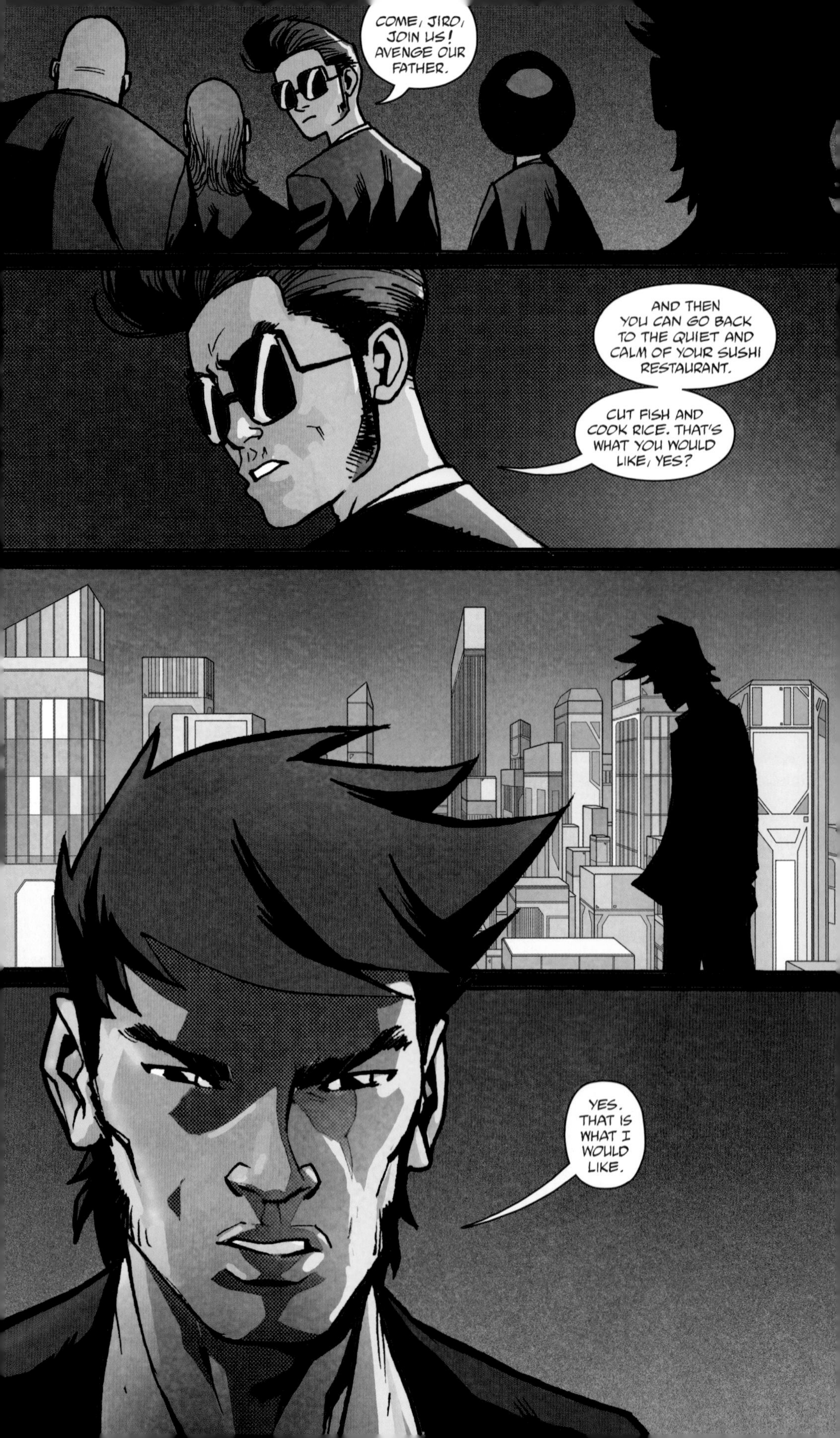
COME, JIRO, JOIN US! AVENGE OUR FATHER.
AND THEN YOU CAN GO BACK TO THE QUIET AND CALM OF YOUR SUSHI RESTAURANT.
CUT FISH AND COOK RICE. THAT'S WHAT YOU WOULD LIKE, YES?
YES. THAT IS WHAT I WOULD LIKE.

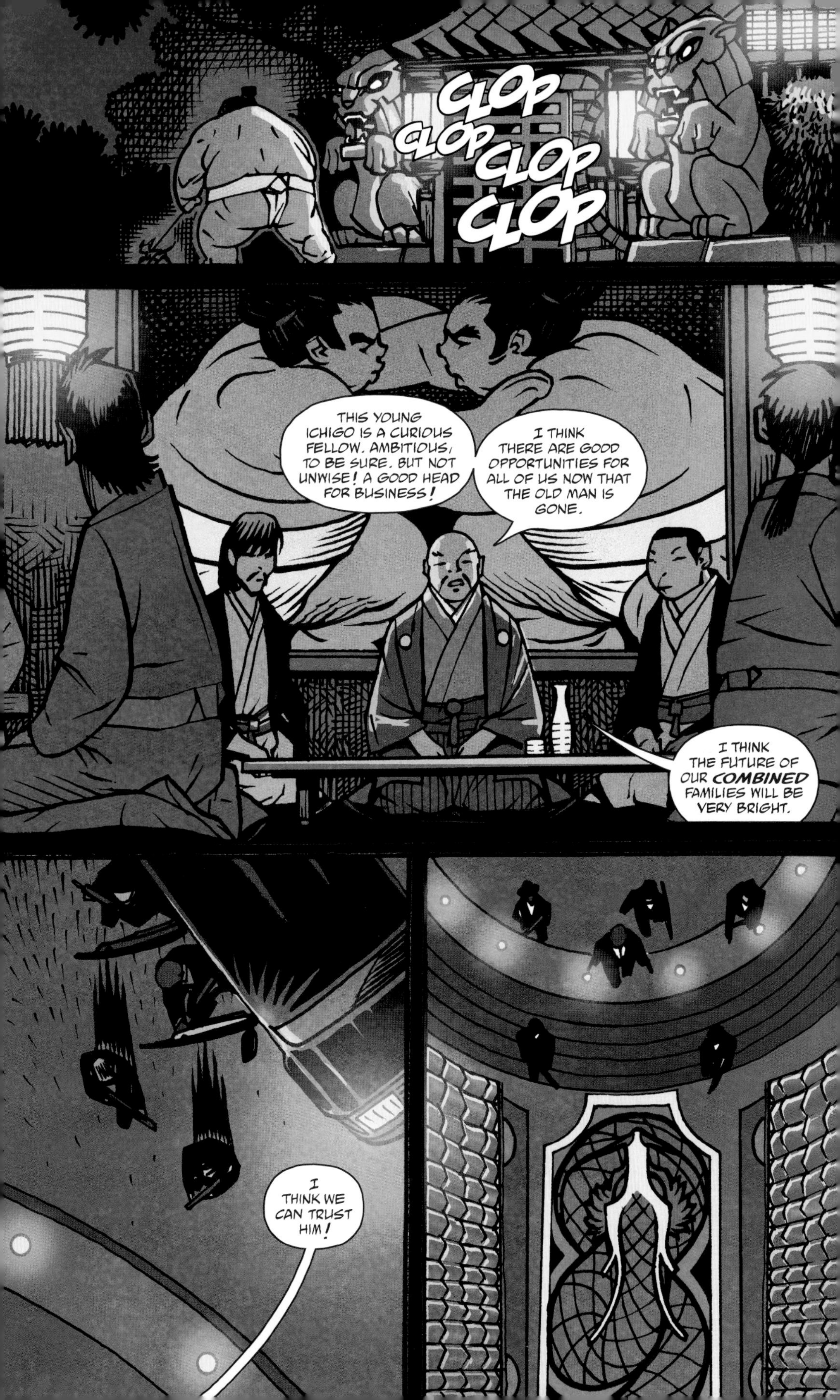
CLOP CLOP CLOP CLOP
THIS YOUNG ICHIGO IS A CURIOUS FELLOW. AMBITIOUS, TO BE SURE. BUT NOT UNWISE! A GOOD HEAD FOR BUSINESS!
I THINK THERE ARE GOOD OPPORTUNITIES FOR ALL OF US NOW THAT THE OLD MAN IS GONE.
I THINK THE FUTURE OF OUR *COMBINED* FAMILIES WILL BE VERY BRIGHT.
I THINK WE CAN TRUST HIM!

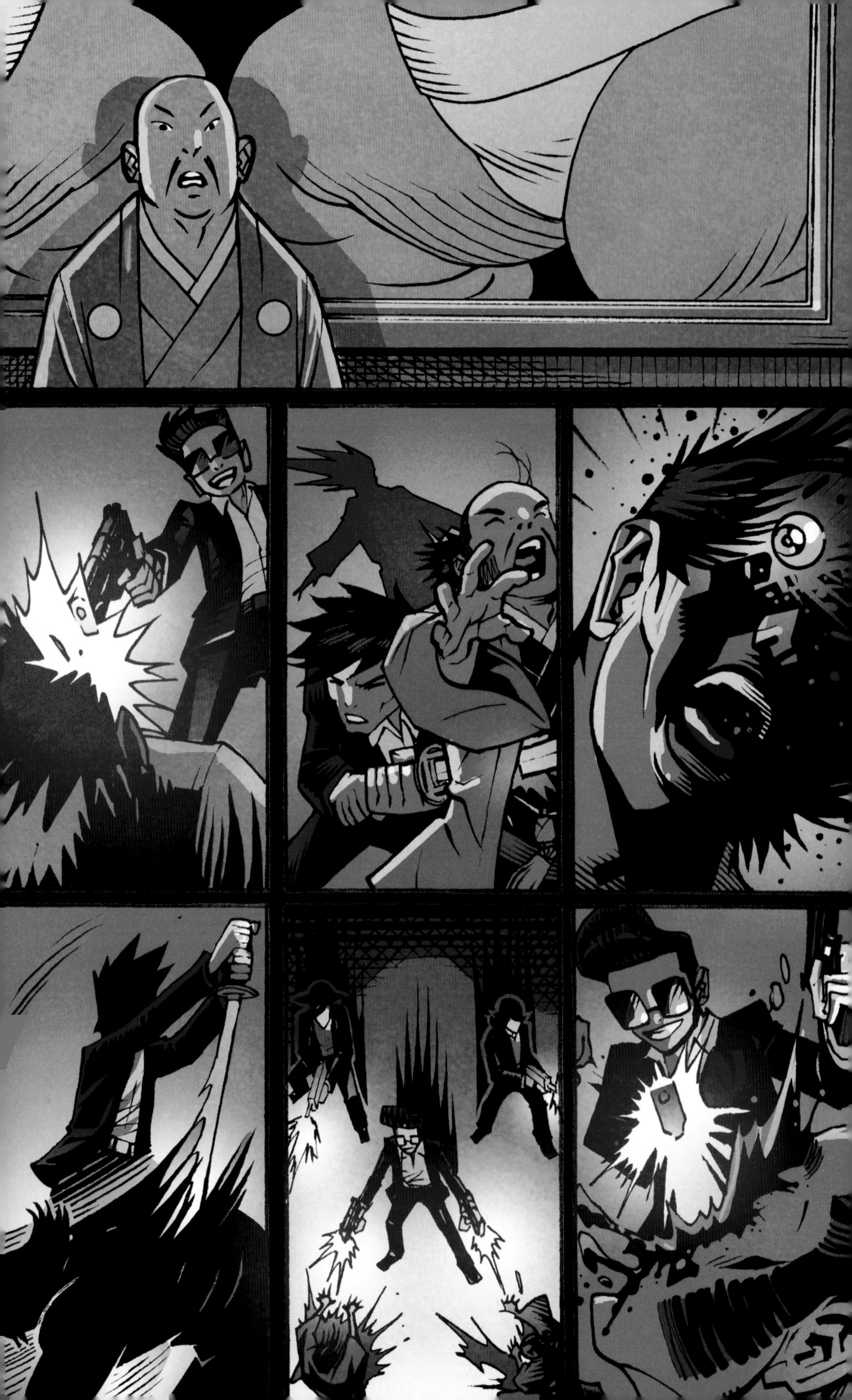

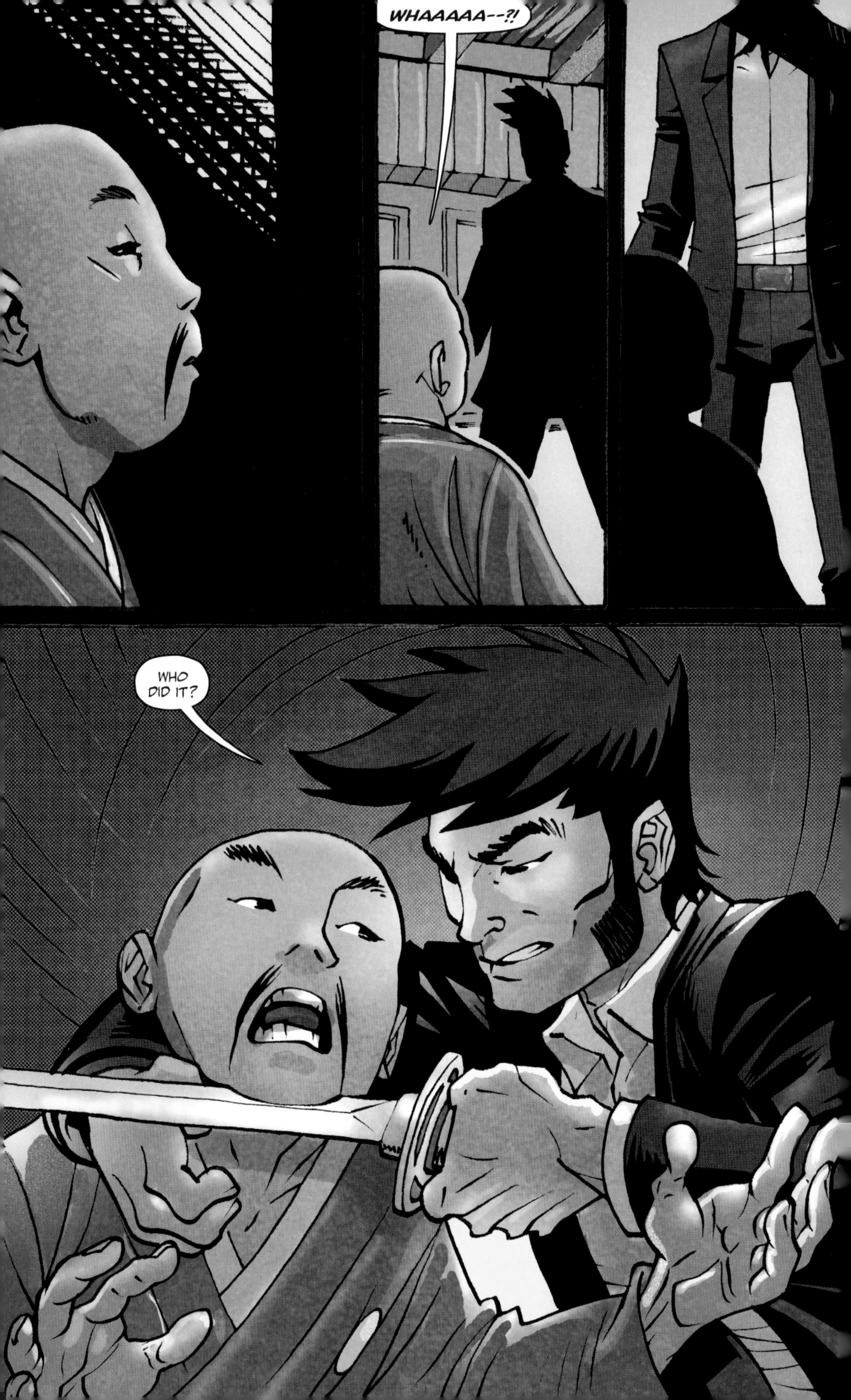
WHAAAAA--?!
WHO DID IT?

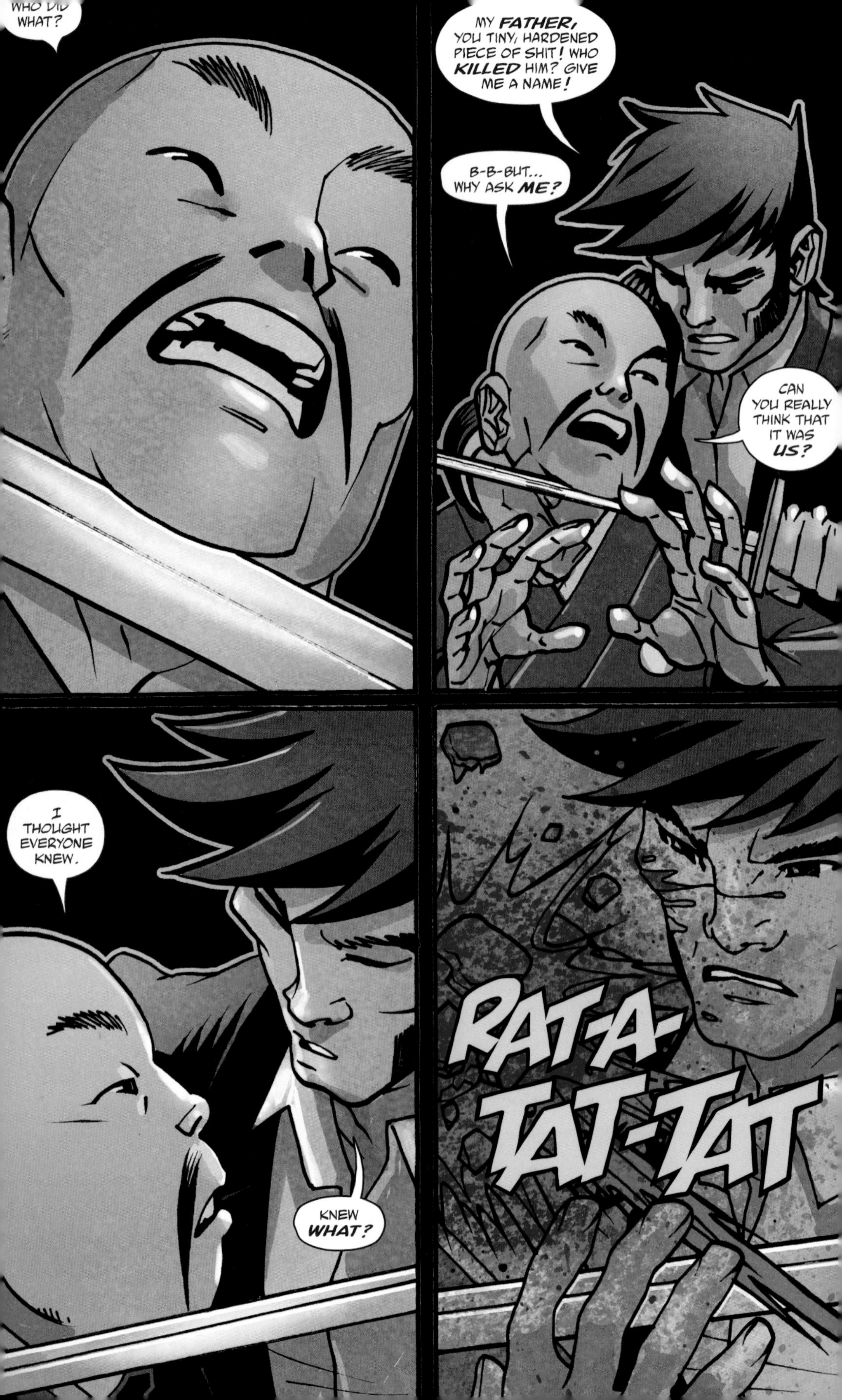
WHO DID WHAT?
MY FATHER, YOU TINY, HARDENED PIECE OF SHIT! WHO KILLED HIM? GIVE ME A NAME!
B-B-BUT... WHY ASK ME?
CAN YOU REALLY THINK THAT IT WAS US?
I THOUGHT EVERYONE KNEW.
KNEW WHAT?
RAT-A-TAT-TAT

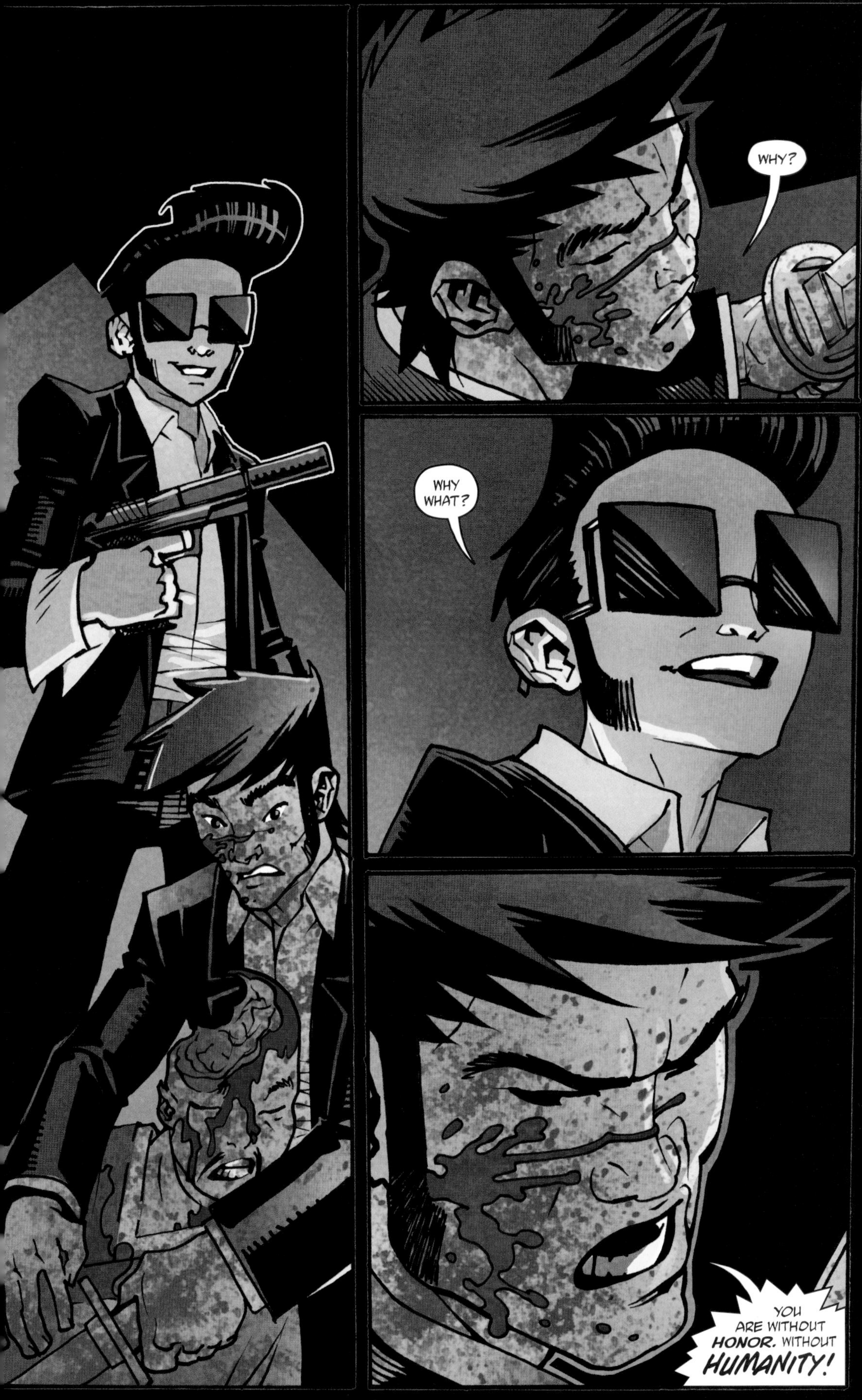
WHY?
WHY WHAT?
YOU ARE WITHOUT HONOR. WITHOUT HUMANITY!

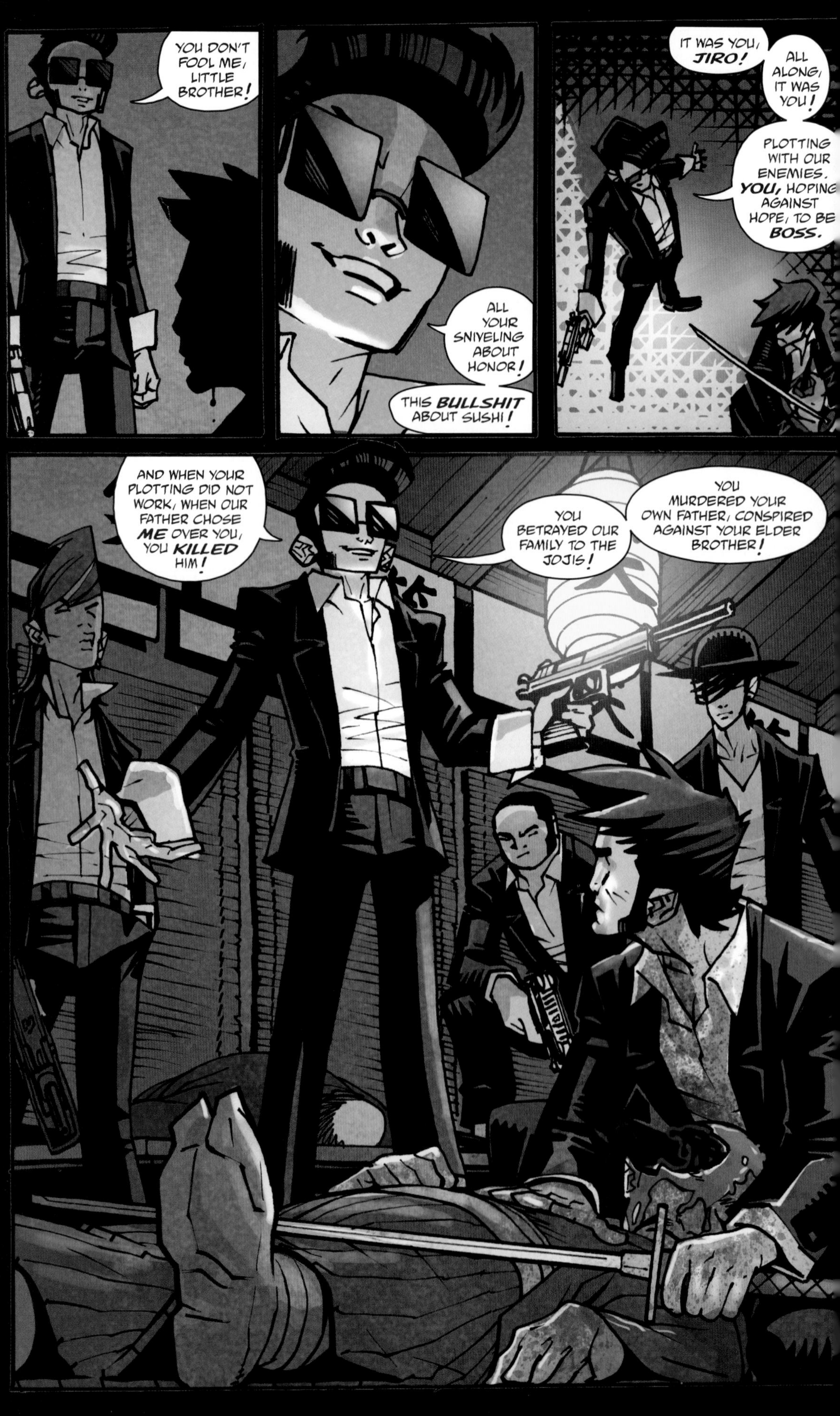
YOU DON'T FOOL ME, LITTLE BROTHER!
ALL YOUR SNIVELING ABOUT HONOR!
THIS **BULLSHIT** ABOUT SUSHI!
IT WAS YOU, **JIRO!**
ALL ALONG, IT WAS YOU!
PLOTTING WITH OUR ENEMIES. **YOU,** HOPING AGAINST HOPE, TO BE **BOSS.**
AND WHEN YOUR PLOTTING DID NOT WORK, WHEN OUR FATHER CHOSE **ME** OVER YOU, YOU **KILLED** HIM!
YOU BETRAYED OUR FAMILY TO THE JOJIS!
YOU MURDERED YOUR OWN FATHER, CONSPIRED AGAINST YOUR ELDER BROTHER!

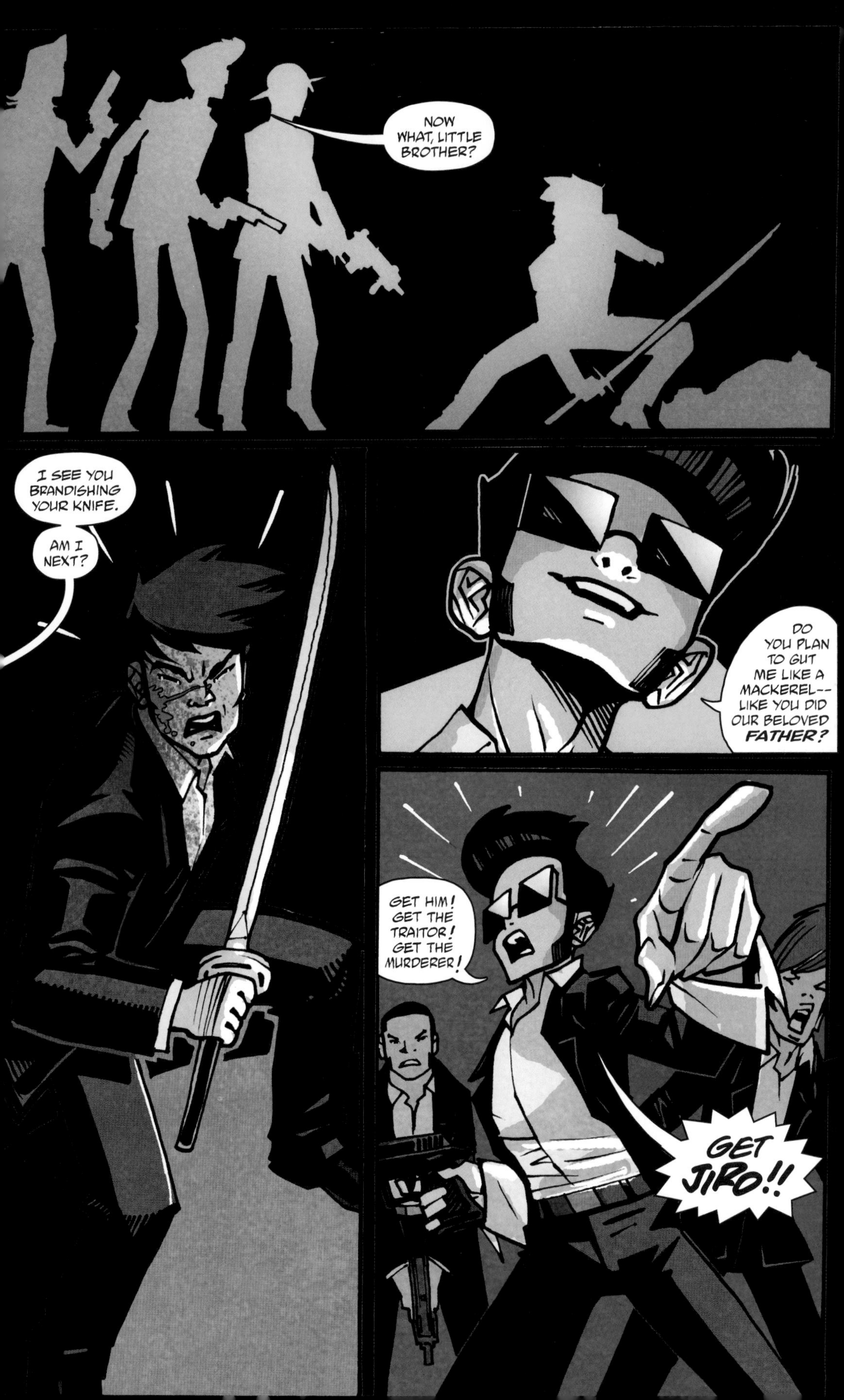
NOW WHAT, LITTLE BROTHER?
I SEE YOU BRANDISHING YOUR KNIFE.
AM I NEXT?
DO YOU PLAN TO GUT ME LIKE A MACKEREL-- LIKE YOU DID OUR BELOVED FATHER?
GET HIM! GET THE TRAITOR! GET THE MURDERER!
GET JIRO!!

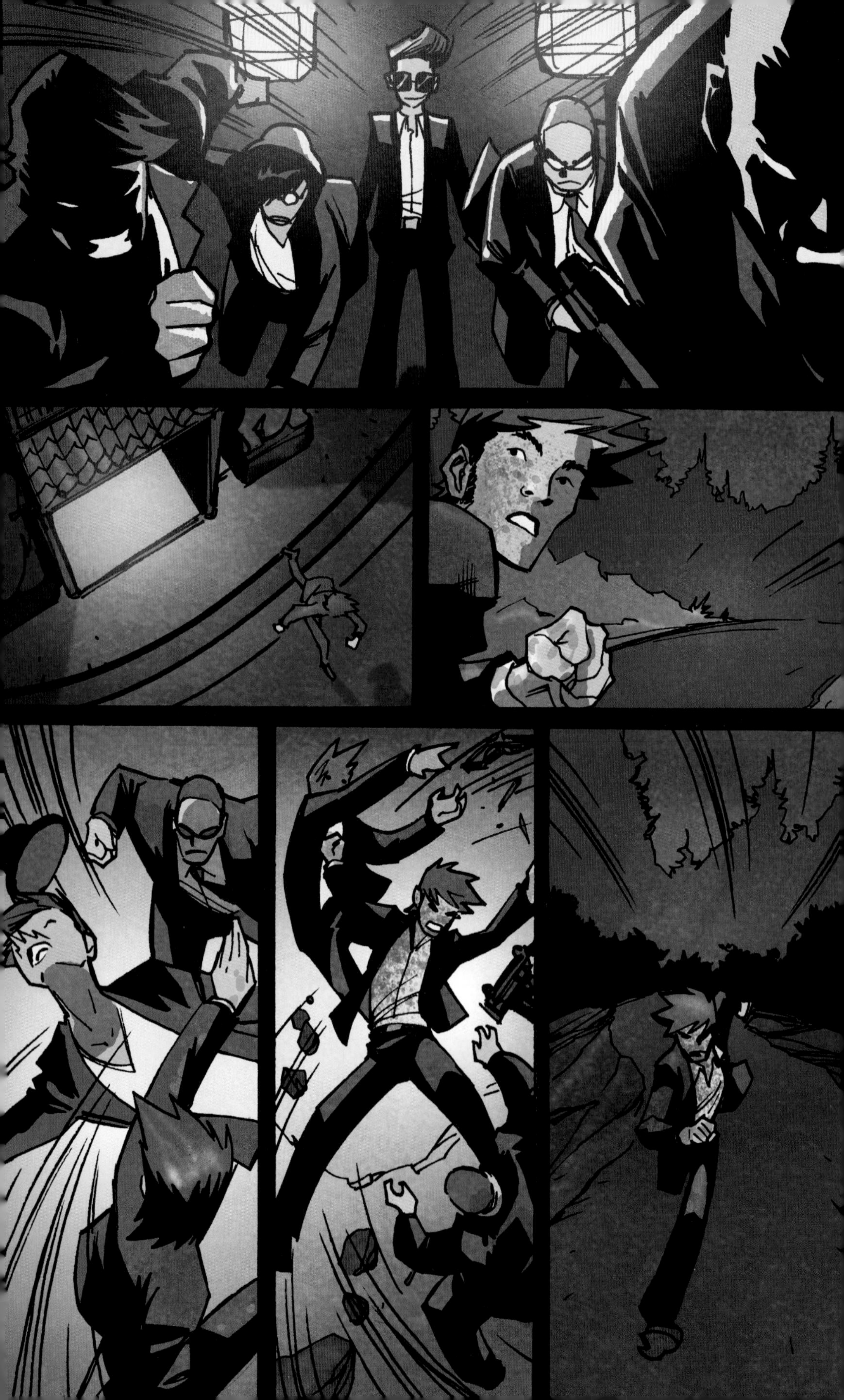

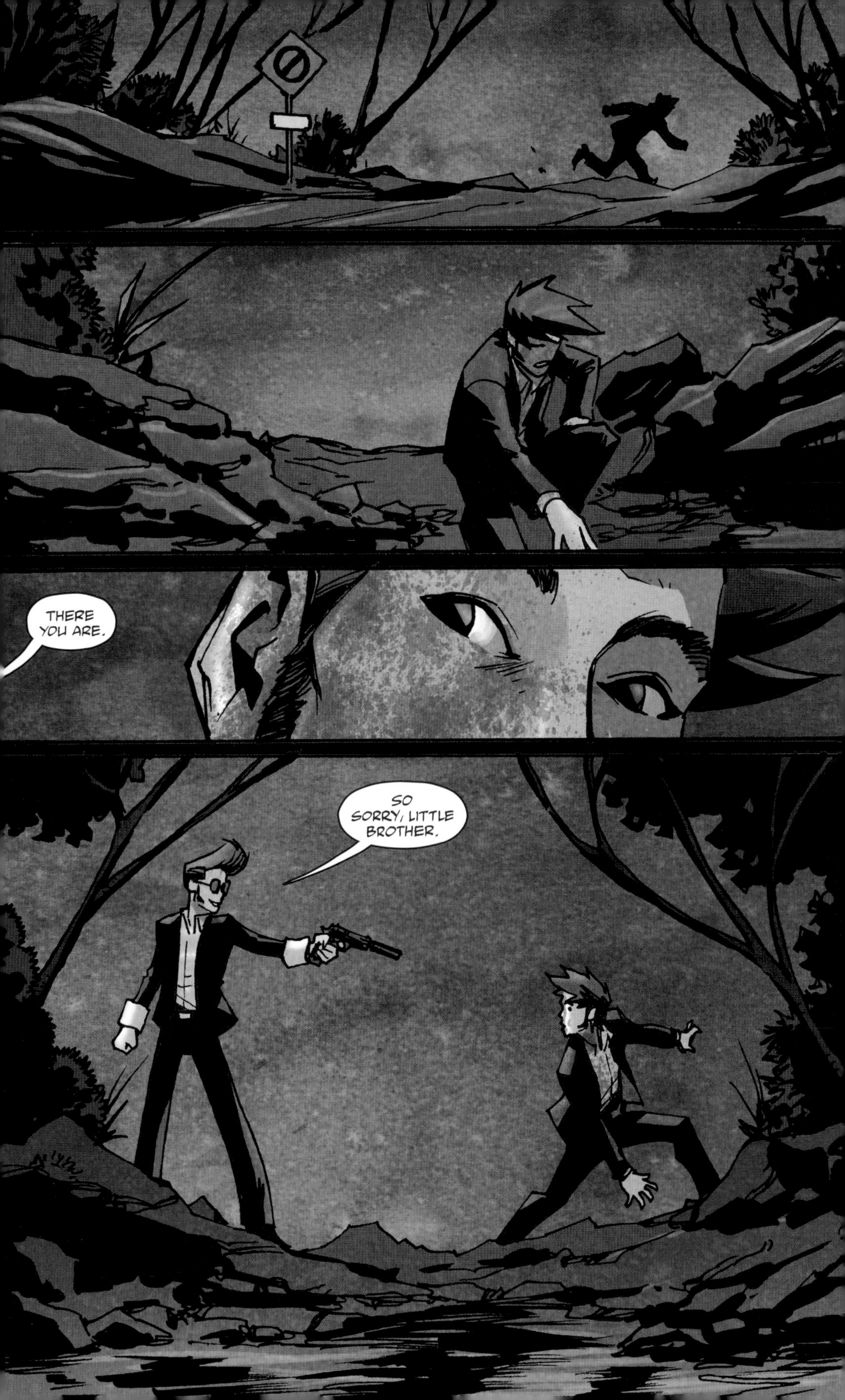
THERE YOU ARE.
SO SORRY, LITTLE BROTHER.

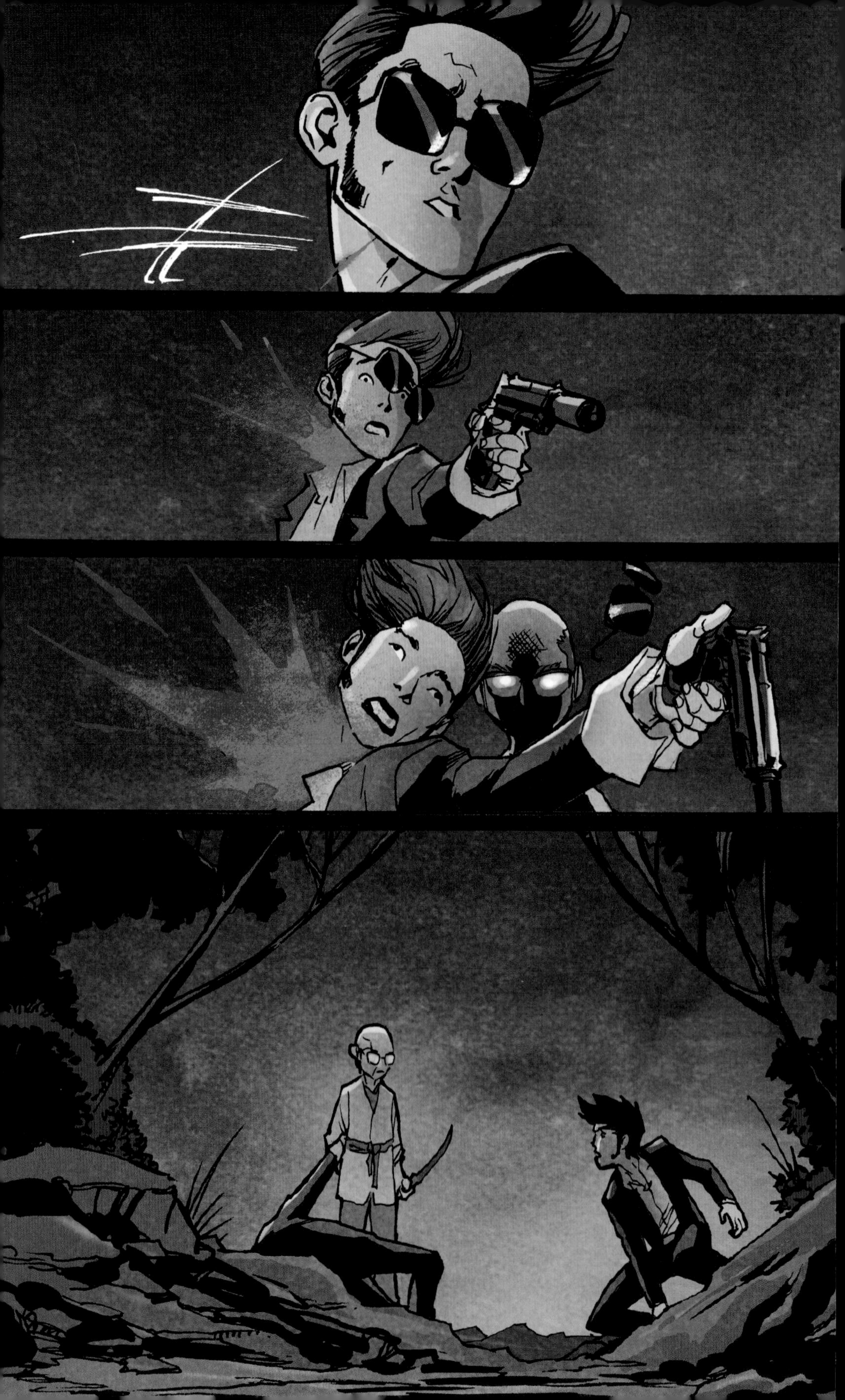

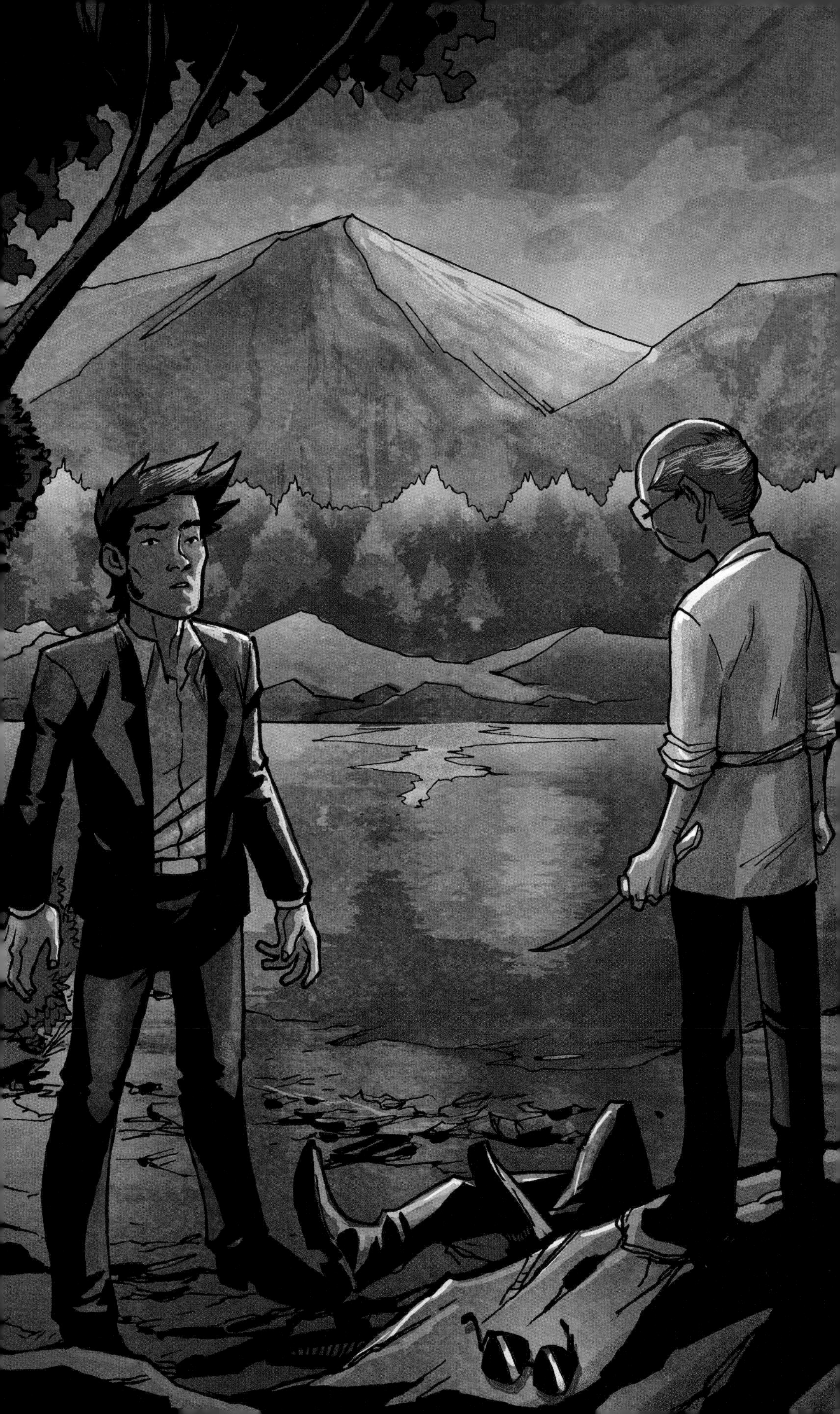

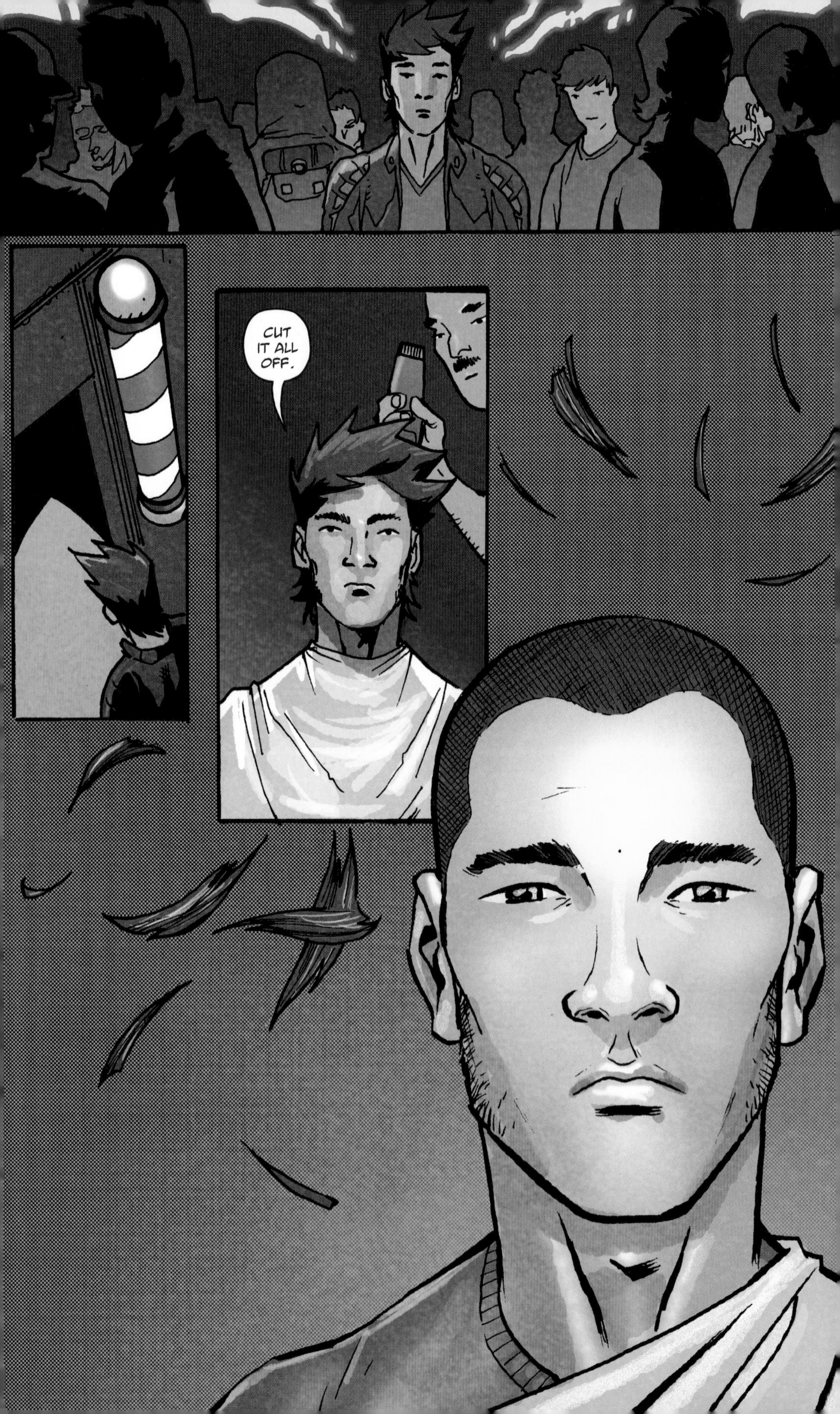
CUT IT ALL OFF.

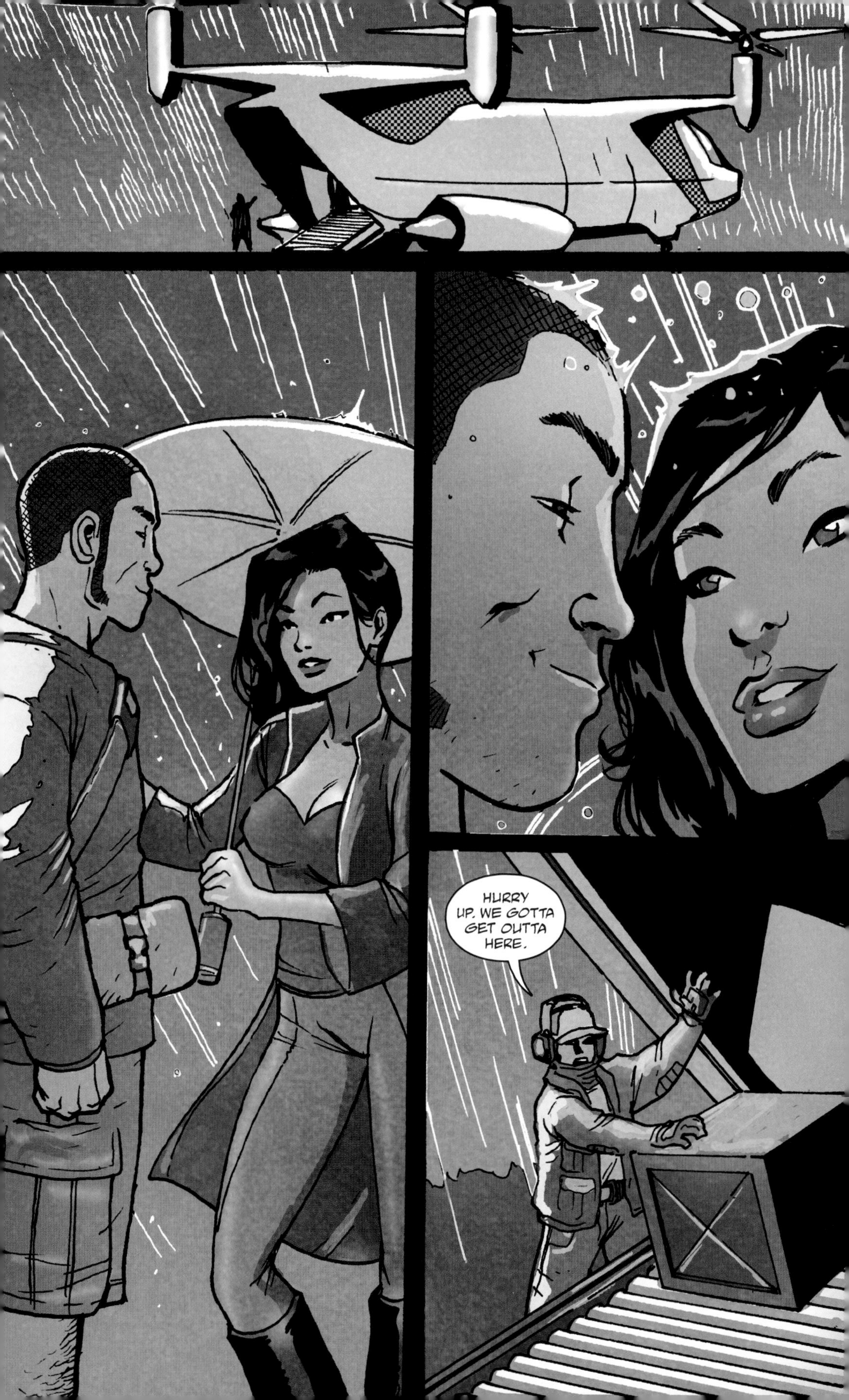
HURRY UP. WE GOTTA GET OUTTA HERE.

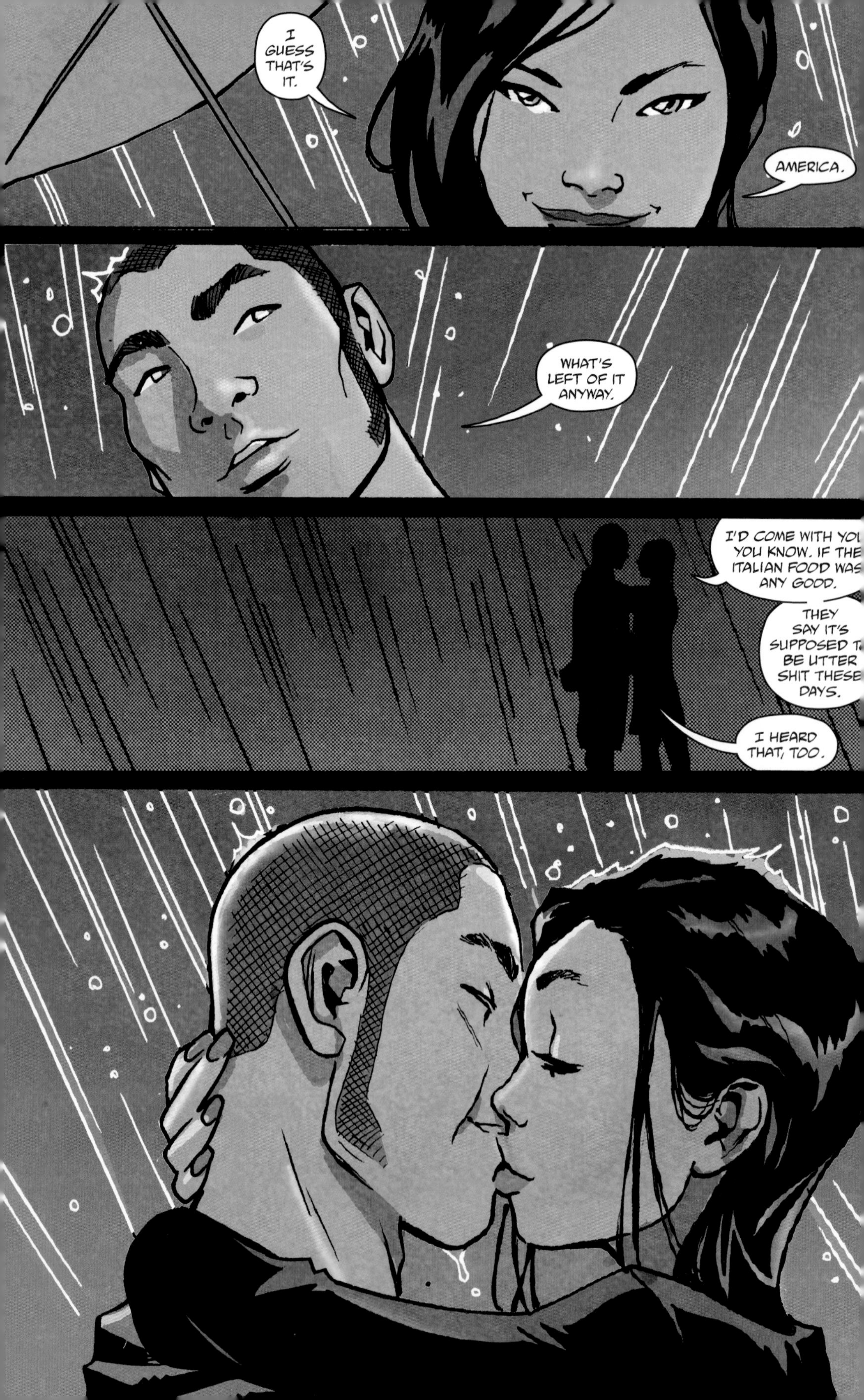
I GUESS THAT'S IT.
AMERICA.
WHAT'S LEFT OF IT ANYWAY.
I'D COME WITH YOU YOU KNOW. IF THE ITALIAN FOOD WAS ANY GOOD.
THEY SAY IT'S SUPPOSED TO BE UTTER SHIT THESE DAYS.
I HEARD THAT, TOO.

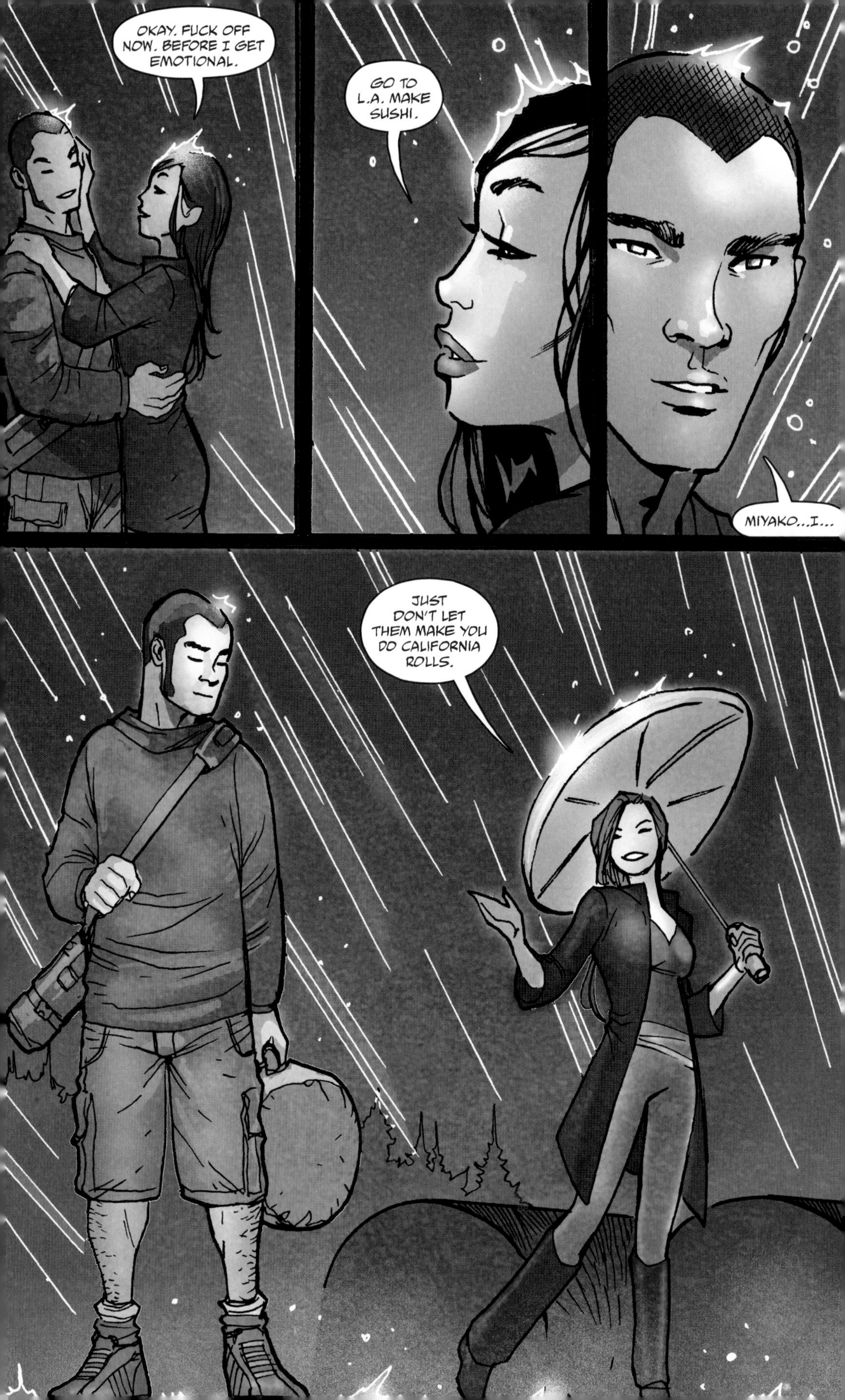
OKAY. FUCK OFF NOW. BEFORE I GET EMOTIONAL.
GO TO L.A. MAKE SUSHI.
MIYAKO...I...
JUST DON'T LET THEM MAKE YOU DO CALIFORNIA ROLLS.

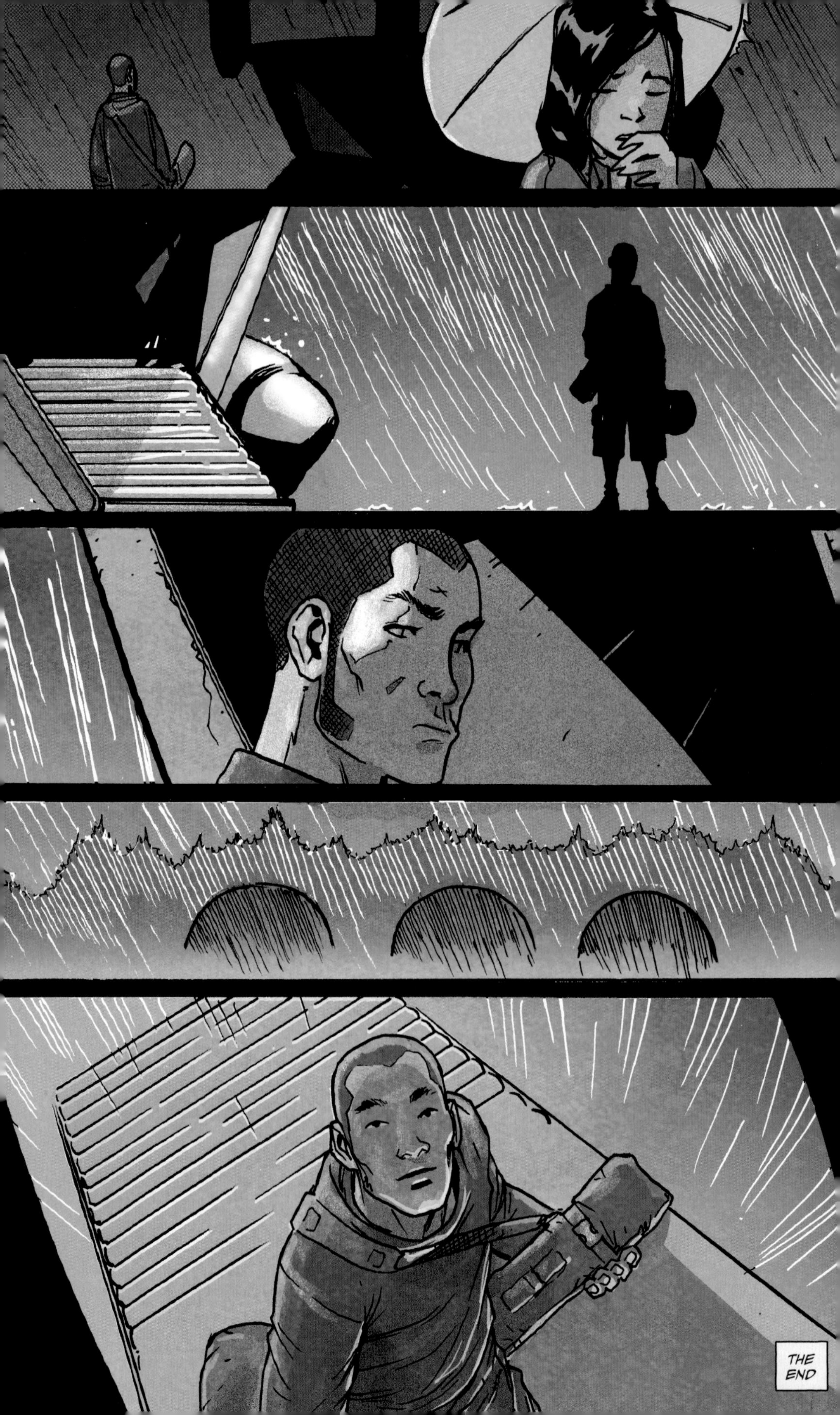
THE END

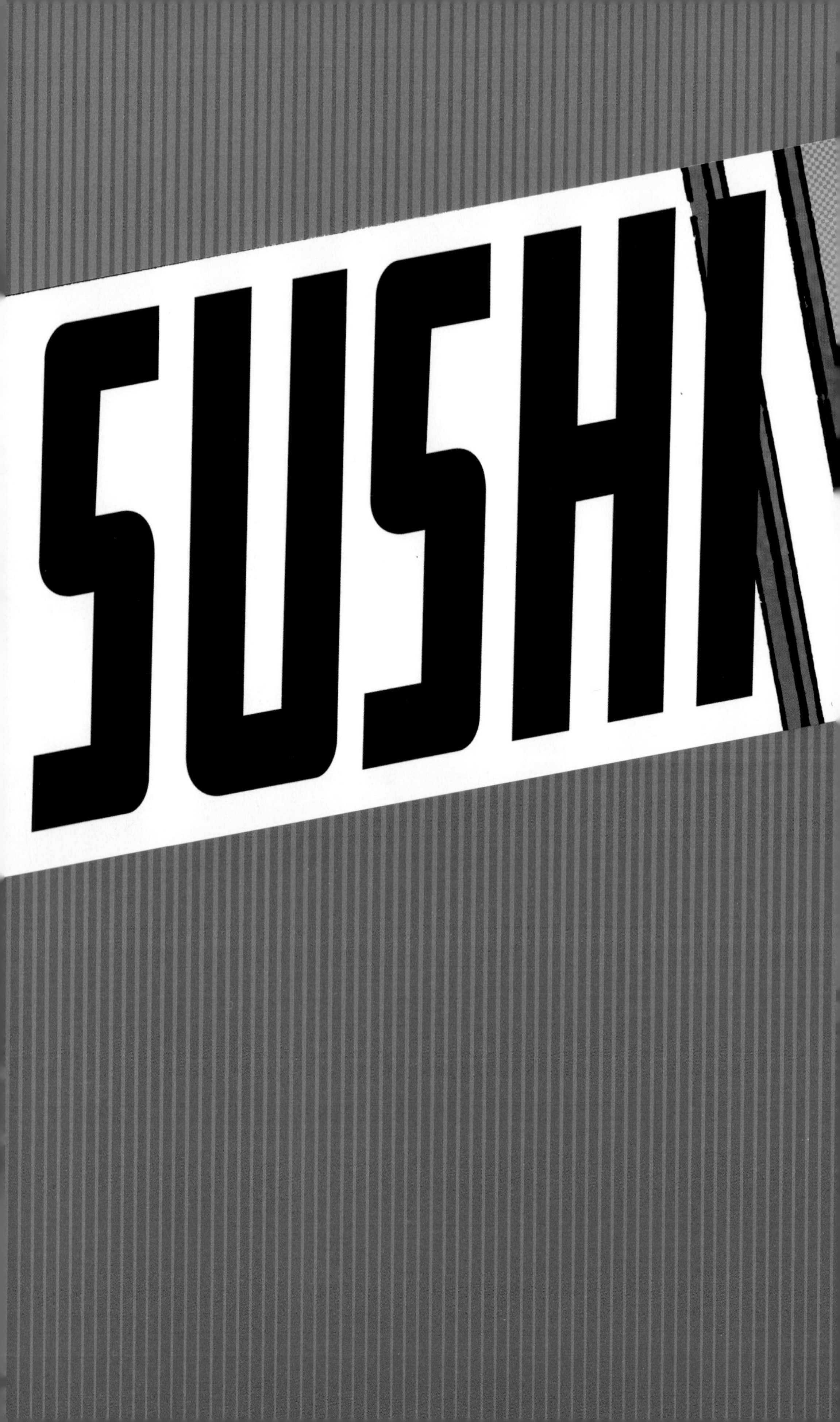
SUSHI

Anthony Bourdain is a renowned chef, New York Times best-selling writer of Kitchen Confidential and Medium Raw, and star of the Emmy-winning hit travel shows No Reservations, The Layover, and Parts Unknown. He is the chef-at-large at New York's famed bistro Les Halles and the author of the crime novels Bone in the Throat and The Bobby Gold Stories.

Joel Rose is the author of The Blackest Bird, Kill the Poor, Kill Kill Faster Faster, and the graphic novel La Pacifica. He lives in New York with his family.

Alé Garza began working in comics at age 18 as part of WildStorm, and quickly established himself as a fan favorite, contributing to titles like GEN 13, BATGIRL, TITANS/YOUNG JUSTICE: GRADUATION DAY, EVE: Protomecha, and Witchblade. He is also the creator of Ninja Boy. He currently resides in sunny San Diego with his lovely wife and inspiration, Elizabeth.

Harvey Award-winning artist **José Villarrubia** began his career as a painter, exhibited fine-art photographs for over a decade, and finally started working in comics as a colorist and photo-illustrator. He is best known for his colors for the Eisner Award-nominated series Fantastic Four 1234 and Desolation Jones, Eisner Award-winner BATMAN YEAR 100, and his collaborations with Alan Moore: Voice of the Fire, The Mirror of Love, and Promethea.

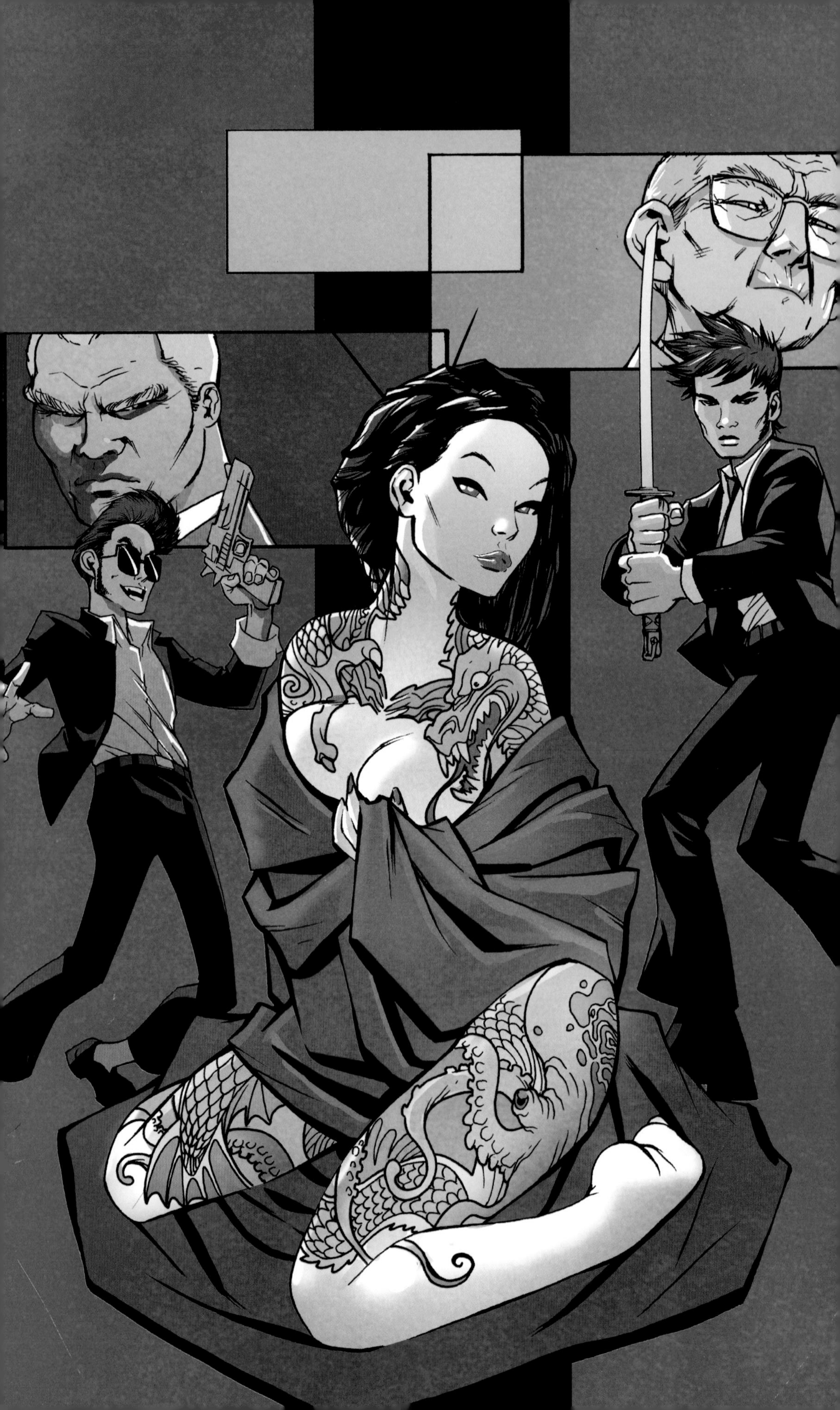

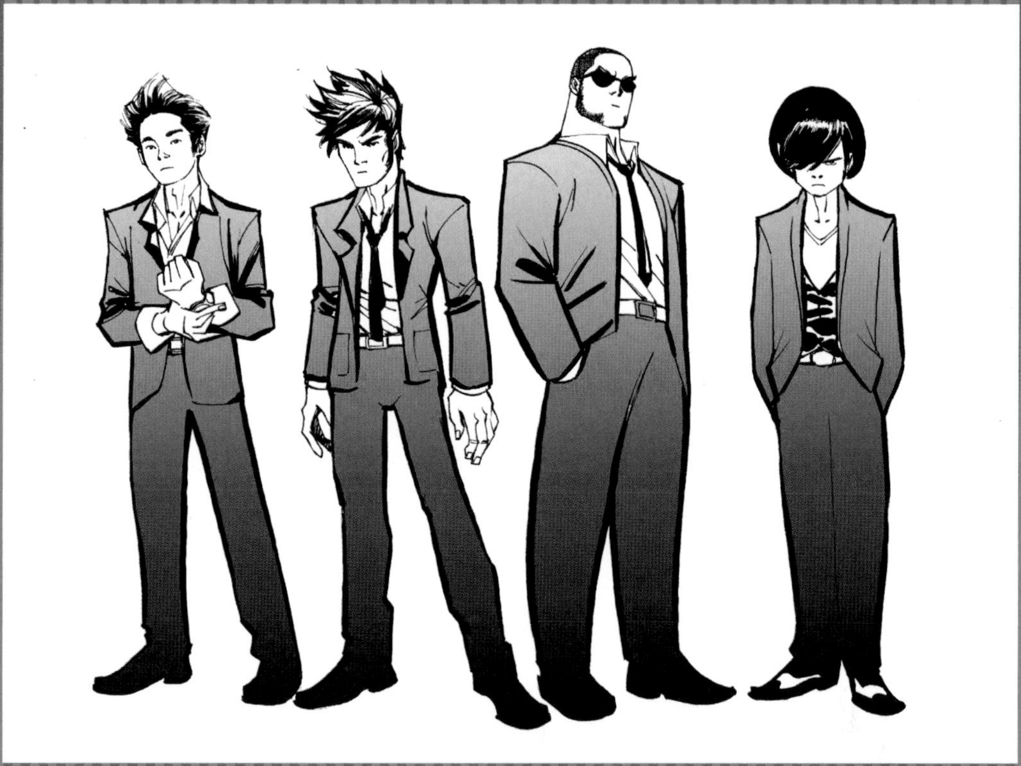

PREPPING THE INGREDIENTS

Character designs and sketches by Alé Garza

This page: Figuring out the look for Jiro and the other men. The group shot above is the only drawing of Ichigo without his glasses.

Previous page: A promo shot by Alé Garza and José Villarrubia.

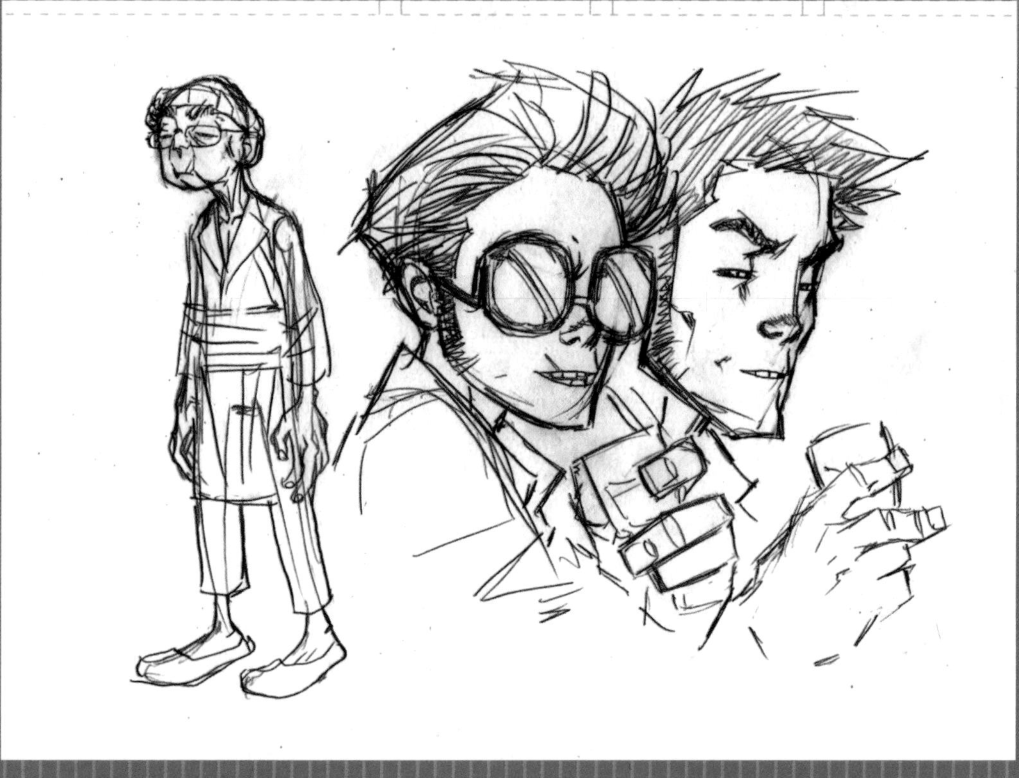

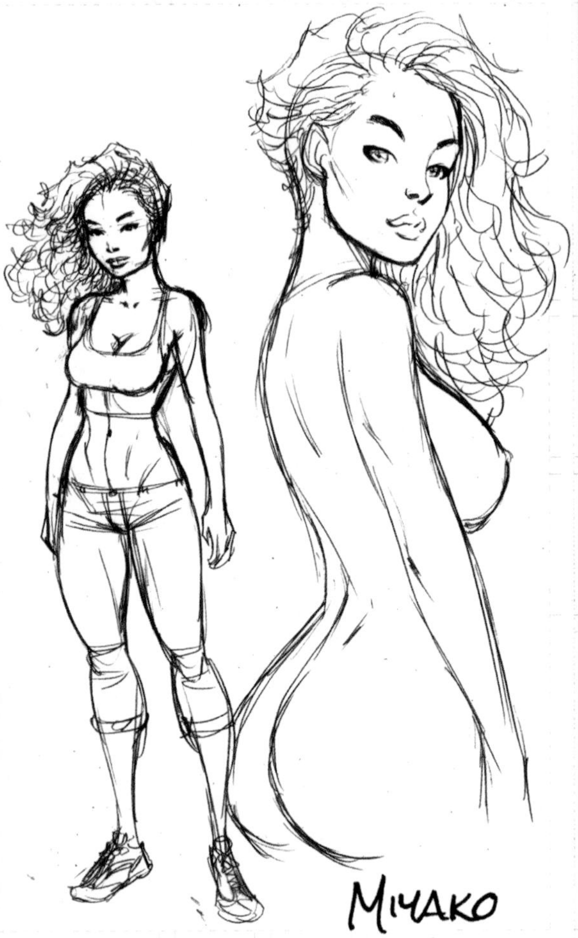
MIYAKO

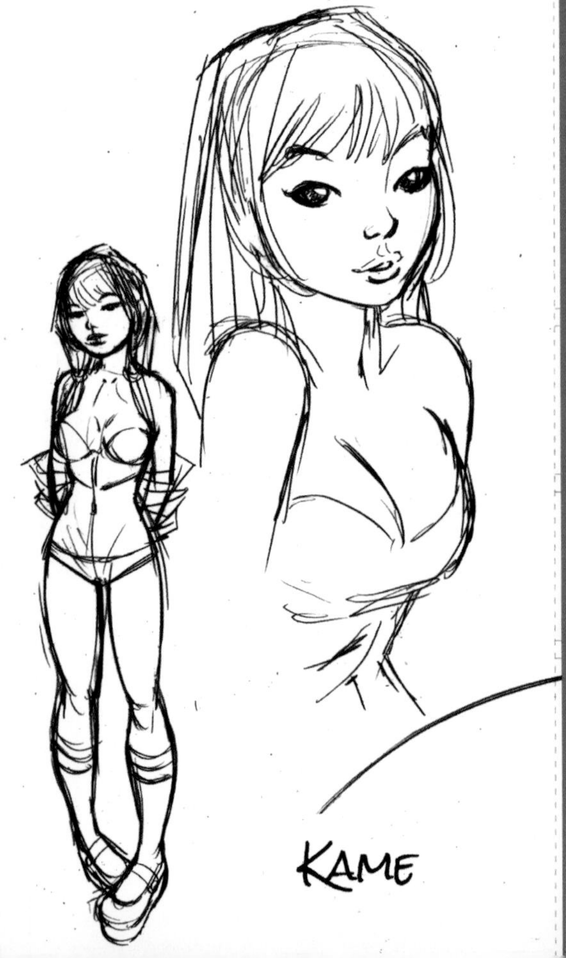
KAME

This page: Early sketches of the women of the story.

Next page: An example of Alé's page layouts.

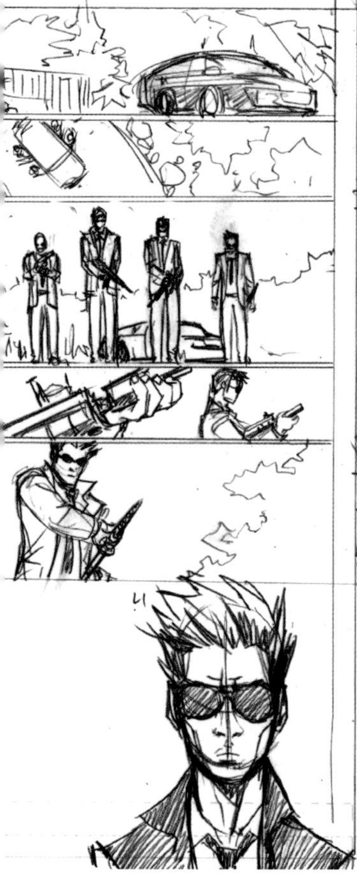
4

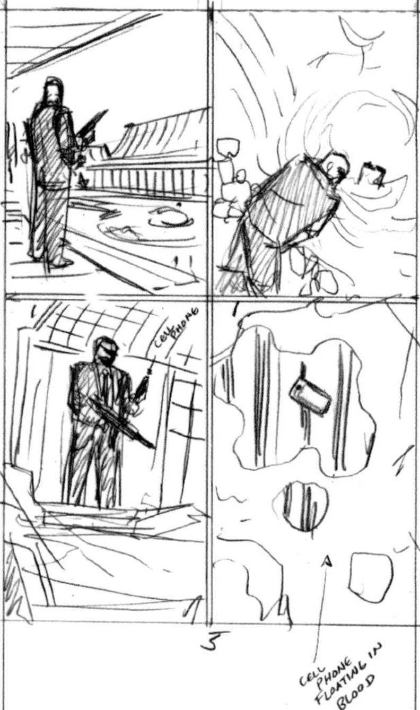
CELL PHONE
CELL PHONE FLOATING IN BLOOD
5

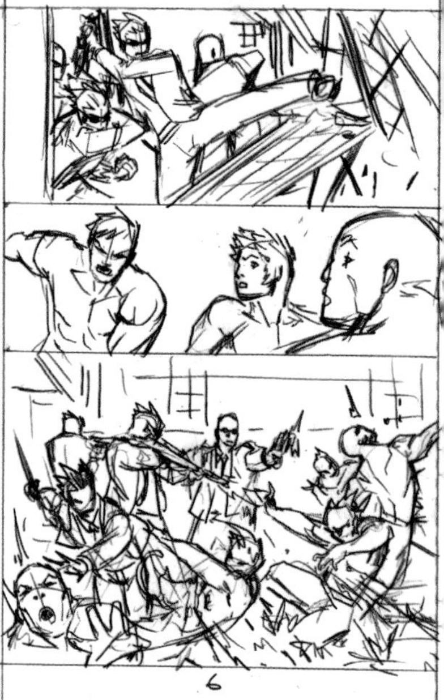
6

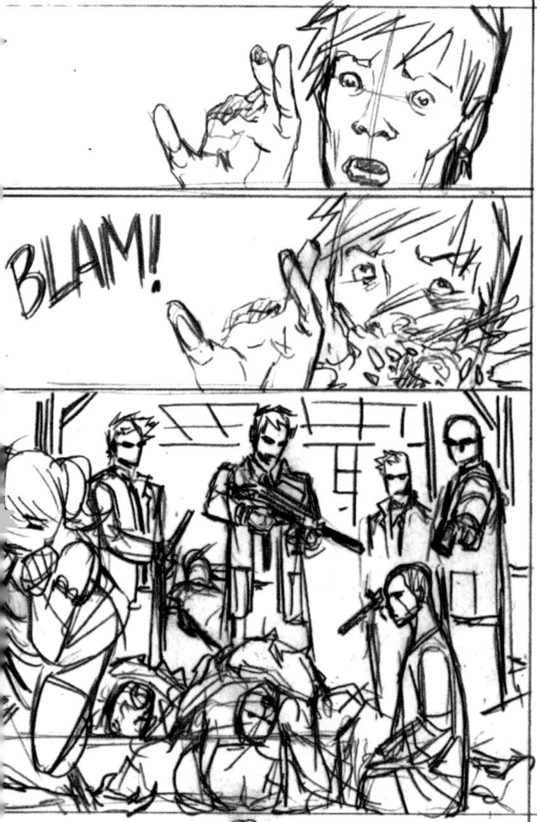
BLAM!
7

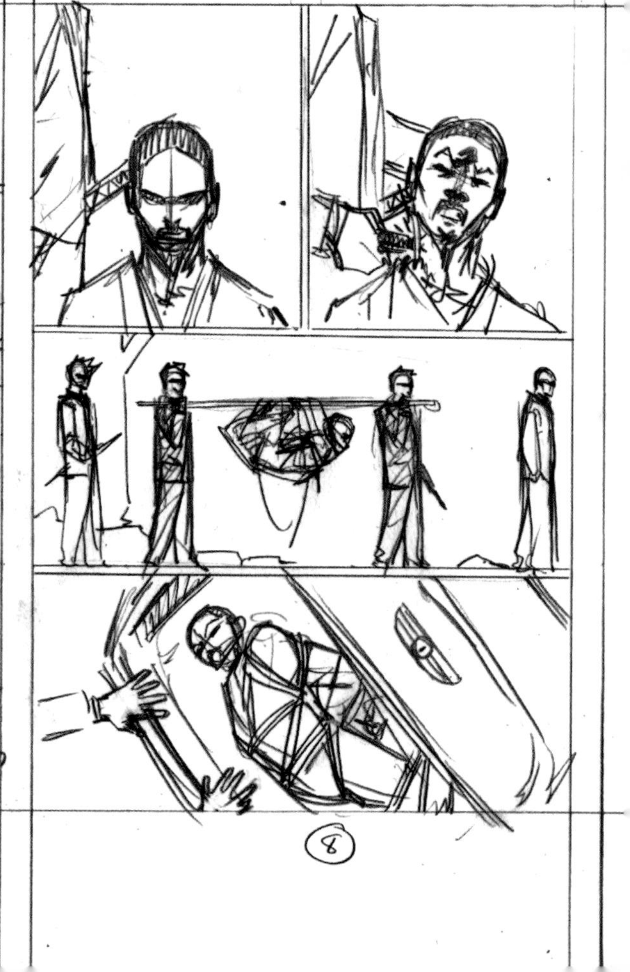
8

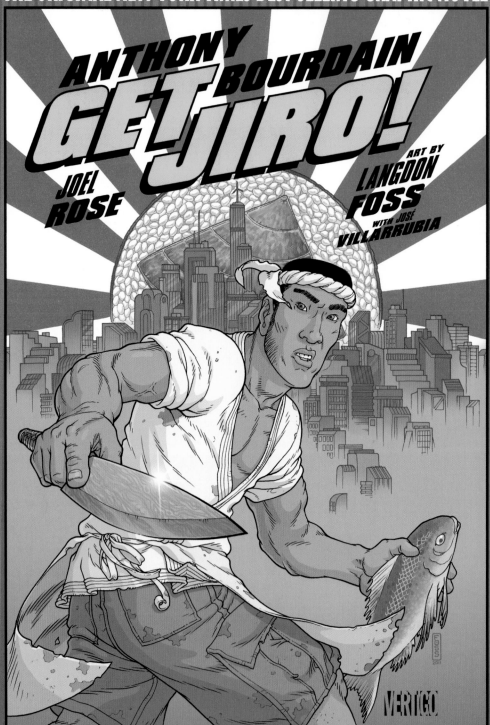

THE ORIGINAL NEW YORK TIMES BEST-SELLING GRAPHIC NOVEL

ANTHONY BOURDAIN
GET JIRO!
JOEL ROSE
ART BY LANGDON FOSS
WITH JOSÉ VILLARRUBIA

VERTIGO

ANTHONY BOURDAIN   JOEL ROSE   LANGDON FOSS

"GET JIRO! unfolds in a dystopian version of Los Angeles where today's (mostly) polite and academic discussions about food have evolved into grisly gastronomic feuds ... In some ways, GET JIRO! represents a coming-full-circle thing for Mr. Bourdain." – *THE NEW YORK TIMES*

AVAILABLE NOW